The Next Crisis

The Next Crisis

What We Think about the Future

Danny Dorling

VERSO
London • New York

First published by Verso 2025
© Danny Dorling 2025

The manufacturer's authorised representative in the EU for product safety (GPSR) is
LOGOS EUROPE, 9 rue Nicolas Poussin, 17000, La Rochelle, France
Contact@logoseurope.eu

All rights reserved
The moral rights of the author have been asserted

1 3 5 7 9 10 8 6 4 2

Verso
UK: 6 Meard Street, London W1F 0EG
US: 207 East 32nd Street, New York, NY 10016
versobooks.com

Verso is the imprint of New Left Books

ISBN-13: 978-1-80429-434-5
ISBN-13: 978-1-80429-436-9 (UK EBK)
ISBN-13: 978-1-80429-437-6 (US EBK)

British Library Cataloguing in Publication Data
A catalogue record for this book is available from the British Library

Library of Congress Cataloging-in-Publication Data
A catalog record for this book is available from the Library of Congress

Typeset in Sabon by Biblichor Ltd, Scotland
Printed and bound by CPI Group (UK) Ltd, Croydon CR0 4YY

For my students, who have taught me over many years.

Contents

List of Figures	ix
List of Tables	xi
Acknowledgements	xiii
1. Crisis	1
2. Those Costs of Living	25
3. Sharing the Work	57
4. War and a Home	91
5. Cradle to Grave	125
6. Climate Crisis	159
7. Biodiversity	197
Conclusion	235
Notes	271
Index	307

List of Figures

1.1: Frequency of use of the term 'crisis' in the English language, 1800–2019, p. 2
1.2: What the rest of the world is most concerned about, 2022–24, p. 14
2.1: How economists tend to report global trends in poverty over time, p. 30
2.2: The reported rise and fall in extreme poverty in the world: an economist's view, p. 32
3.1: 'Tick up to three issues' – what people care most about, UK, 2011–24, p. 74
3.2: How size of birth cohort influences immigration and emigration, p. 79
4.1: All deaths due to war in the world, by state, 1989–2022, p. 107
4.2: Share of wealth for richest 1% in four countries, 1895 onwards, p. 112
5.1: How much more likely people are to die in the US, by age, 2020s, p. 129
5.2: How the US compares in terms of life expectancy trends over time, p. 133
5.3: Life expectancy in US and England, by household income, in 2022, p. 134
5.4: Adults who believe a single secretive group rules the world, 2021 (%), p. 154
6.1: Global emissions of carbon dioxide by income group, in 2019 (tonnes), p. 163

6.2: Location of people who believe climate change is a hoax, 2020, p. 167
7.1: Cataclysmic scenarios for human population, 2020–2100, p. 217
7.2: More cataclysmic scenarios for human population, 2020–2100, p. 223
7.3: Going hungry is caused by poverty and inequality – not by droughts, p. 229
8.1: Frequency of mentions of inequality, *American Sociological Review*, 1936–2019, p. 238
8.2: World Bank's 2020 'nowcast' for global poverty rates, 2015–22, p. 263
8.3: Banner of East Bradford Socialist Sunday School, Fred Liles, 1914, p. 268

List of Tables

2.1: Claims made about extreme poverty in 1820 (less than $1.90 per day), p. 31

6.1: People dying due to climate-related disasters per year by decade, 1950–2022, p. 185

6.2: People affected by climate-related disasters per year, 1950–2022, p. 187

6.3: The ten deadliest natural disasters in the world, 2000–19, p. 188

6.4: Fifteen deadliest climate-associated disasters, 2000–22 (deaths), p. 189

6.5: Deaths attributed to the 2003 heatwave in Europe, by country, p. 190

Acknowledgements

I am grateful to Leo Hollis for his help in designing the concept for this book and his careful editing; to Natalie Hume for copy-editing the text; to Mark Martin and Nick Walther for shepherding the book through production; to Alice Burgeoned for her assistance in searching out sources, opinion and ideas not written in English; to Stacy Hewitt for her support, encouragement and advice over writing this book from when the pandemic began in 2020 through to the end of 2024; to Karen Shook for giving me her thoughts early in the writing of this book, including on whether I might be stumbling in the right direction, and for her work helping to improve the text in early 2024; to Ailsa Allen for so carefully drawing up all the figures; and to many others, but especially Alison Dorling, Bill Kerry, Katie Nudd, David Partridge, and Marcia Wheat, who commented on all these ideas in the summer of 2024. I am especially grateful to Qiujie Shi for helping me in 2023 to interpret the data from the Institute of Sociology of the Chinese Academy of Social Sciences, at the point when I was still writing and reorganising my thoughts and understanding. Those who love me have kindly given me the time, and space, and freedom to write. I am responsible for any errors and omissions and especially for the biases – but we are all responsible for each other; and our creations are never entirely of our own making. Neither are our crises. Thank you for reading.

1
Crisis

Welcome to the age of the polycrisis.
World Economic Forum, 2023[1]

It's not unusual to feel that we are living through a crisis, a time of intense difficulty or great danger. But this sentiment is a luxury. Only those of us who do not live by navigating a seemingly perpetual stream of daily adversities have the luxury of entertaining the idea of the wider crisis. To be able to afford the time to worry about what the next crisis might be is almost entirely an indulgence of those who, most of the time, are free from both great danger and substantial difficulty.

Consider how often the word *crisis* now appears in English-language publications. It was uncommon throughout the nineteenth century and up to the early 1930s, but in the mid-1930s its use began to surge (Figure 1.1). That surge appeared to abate in the late 1940s, but this lull was short-lived. Use of the term accelerated throughout the 1960s, and the word has become more and more common ever since. People may shout 'fire' more often, but it does not necessarily mean there are more fires than before. In the case of *crisis*, it might mean that a great number of us have more time to worry.

When considering Figure 1.1, the first thing to note is that while we clearly have mentioned crisis more often in recent times, this is not an indication that we have entered an age of cascading crises. Perhaps, counter-intuitively, we spoke of crisis, and often by

Figure 1.1: Frequency of the use of the term 'crisis' in the English language, 1800–2019

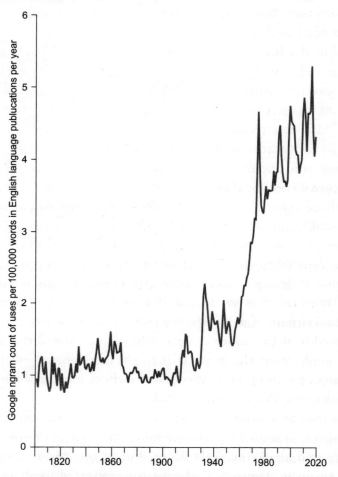

Source: Google Ngram – note that the last data point is 2019, so when Google update their viewer, mentions of the word 'crisis' will be seen to have risen again, because of the coronavirus pandemic which began then.

implication the next crisis, precisely because we were experiencing an increased capacity to sit back and think about the future. The period before the 1960s was one of almost constant wars, epidemics and pandemics occurring worldwide. Before the 1960s, there was so much infectious disease, so many famines and such frequent bad harvests, that we could have been forgiven for continually crying out, 'Crisis!' Yet we were restrained in our language.

The second fact worth noting from Figure 1.1 is that since the late 1960s there has been no let-up in our collective sense of crisis, at least not based on the frequency of use of that word in all the printed media surveyed. The word *crisis* was used twice as often in 1960, and four times as often since 1980, as it was in 1900.

So, was the rising frequency of the appearance of the word *crisis* just an increase in hyperbole, a tendency towards exaggeration? Did a new trend begin, led by some writers of the 1960s trying to gain readers' attention? Were more books being written by people who had the luxury to speculate on wider issues? There were more writers by then, and more people were able to read and to buy books than ever before. Perhaps it was just this social trend which stoked up the rhetoric? My point here is that, imagined or real, we have been living in an age of crisis for some time.[2]

Returning to the present, what are the major crises of our time and what do people, worldwide, concern their thoughts with? One way to try to answer this question is not to concentrate on what is written – since what writers are always at least partly motivated by is gaining attention. Instead, we can concentrate on what people themselves say most concerns them, and then look into each of those issues. You may be wondering why this matters, however. Why are other people's opinions of interest?

Why should anyone care what the rest of the world's population thinks, especially when they don't think the same way we do? I don't underestimate how difficult it is going to be to look at things this way – to try to take seriously distant others' collective worries. It is easier to dismiss the rest of the world than to admit that you might have a privileged view. You might question the surveys I draw on in this book. You might think that the masses are being led astray by pollsters and their weasel words. But before you decide that others' views on what matters most are less valid than your own, are you not curious to know more about them?

This book was originally going to be titled 'The Next Crisis: How We Think About the Future, and What We Get Wrong'. But my very thoughtful editor deleted the last five words and changed the 'how' to 'what'. The fourteen-word version was, admittedly, a little verbose. But I suspect he also worried that people are not that interested in hearing that they – we, all of us – might often be wrong. Of course, we *are* all wrong, often, about many things. But we do not necessarily want to pay to be told about it.

I have studied and written about crises before, but discretely, usually one at a time. In 1995, I published *A New Social Atlas of Britain*, about the various travails of my home country. Five years later, I wrote a book with my colleagues, *Inequalities in Life and Death: What If Britain Were More Equal?* It concerned the crisis of inequality, poverty, and unemployment, and how they and much else impacted on health. Not having work, not being needed, could be deadly too. Again, in 2005, I wrote with colleagues *The Great Divide: An Analysis of Housing Inequality*. By 2010, I thought I might have learned enough to make some more general suggestions, and I called the resulting book *Injustice: Why Social Inequality Persists*. That book was updated in 2015, and retitled *Injustice: Why Social Inequality Still Persists*. Crises can deepen and worsen. In 2020, I wrote a book with the longest title I have ever used: *Slowdown: The End of the Great Acceleration – and Why It's Good for the Planet, the Economy, and Our Lives*. I list these publications so you have a sense of my biases.

With help from many others, I wrote more books in between those listed above, as well as some academic papers, and an increasing number of commentaries written more for general readers than my university colleagues. I discovered that other academics are far more likely to read and debate their colleagues' ideas if they appear in a popular book. I learnt from being critiqued, from listening, and from new data. With colleagues, I wrote about other countries, mapped the continent of Europe, produced a world atlas, and became immersed in issues of health and demography, politics and voting, cartography and censuses.

I am a human geographer. We geographers are permitted to travel far and wide in our studies, to range across subjects and disciplinary approaches. A dozen years ago I moved back to the city where I spent my childhood and joined a large School of Geography and the Environment. I mixed with a great many climate change scientists in my new role, and began to understand much more about what most preoccupied them. This contributed to my decision that perhaps I could now – as much as ever – try to write something useful about what we often worry about most, when we are not just worrying about ourselves. I did this because I had begun to notice just how varied different people's greatest concerns were.

In my new academic home, in the university within Oxford (England), what clearly mattered most was climate change. Almost everything else seemed to be less important – after all, the folk I was working with were life's winners – climate change was the greatest threat to them. They had managed to secure a job in an elite institution and were able to afford a home nearby. There were no vacant shops in Oxford when I returned. The economy was booming. There was more work than there were people to work. During term time, the streets were full of beautiful people, often in ballgowns or dinner jackets. Having just arrived from Sheffield, I felt a little like Dorothy in the *Wizard of Oz* when she tells her dog, 'Toto, I have a feeling we're not in Kansas anymore.'

But it is important *not* to look at the very particular landscape around oneself and believe it is at all representative of the world. There is variability in the quality of information available across the globe, as well as in peoples' lives and fears. The University of Oxford has over one hundred separate libraries. As a boy growing up in the city, I was not allowed to use any of them; today, increasing numbers of Oxford students do not use them either, because most of what is in them that is of most use is also now available to almost everyone, anywhere, via the web. There are firewalls and paywalls, but none are as effective as the old stone walls used to be.

Different people receive different information depending on who they are and where they are placed. You will doubtless know that online advertisements target specific groups of people. But the older adverts in newspapers and on the sides of buildings were also targeted, if more crudely. People living and growing up in different counties always receive differing information, which also varies depending on their station in life, although in more equitable countries everyone is a little more likely to be told the same story.[3] So what is the aggregate story? What do most people fear the most, and why? And are they right or wrong? That is what I plan to try to answer here.

This book is structured in a simple way, but the outcome is counter-intuitive. Instead of ordering our fears by what we are *told* to worry about most, I have ordered them by what we *actually* worry about most. You might ask, as you ponder whether to read on: What do we learn as a result of this reordering? What can we do differently as a result of seeing the world in this way? I believe that considering the views of others can help reorder our own priorities. It could help make them fairer and more universal. When we realise we are not alone in our fears, they can seem more surmountable. And it points us towards what could indeed be the next crisis on a far surer footing than relying on our individual imaginations and our reading of a few opinion formers who have often been caught up in a group-thinking mind game.

Fearmongering

What are the biggest fears we have about the future? It is not a trivial question to try to answer. What are our greatest collective nightmares, and what dreams do we harbour about averting the worst of the next crisis?

The most fortunate of us, those who we might imagine have the most to lose, are often those who fear the unknowability of tomorrow more than the struggles of today.

Unsurprisingly, people in similar situations tend to share the same fears, which leads to a collective anxiety – visions of decline, or even despair – that can become powerful and sometimes overpowering. Those with the most resources of all usually have very different fears from the rest of us. Apart from anything else, they are often afraid of *us*. What if we wanted more of a slice of what they have?

Those with the least resources, who make up the large majority of humanity, almost always have very different fears than people who are comparatively or somewhat affluent. So, in truth, it is not just the worries of the elite that differ from our more mundane concerns. We who can afford to buy books are affluent too, even if we claim we are not. What of the people who have much less money than we might assume is normal? One person's impending crisis may already be the daily reality of countless others around the world.

So many different fears are possible, in an age when we are beginning to appreciate the finite resources of the world. One fear might be that those who already have the largest proportion of these resources will come after the rest of what we have collectively – the rare metals, the fossil fuels, the water in the aqueducts, our homes, our state health and education services – and they will try to privatise everything that is not already in their hands. Or they might behave in a way that will threaten us and our ability to thrive in an uncertain future. There are plenty of reasons to fear that the rich are out to get us. Ironically, these are fears mostly held by people only slightly less rich, who often see themselves as deprived in comparison: the kinds of people who gave us phrases such as 'the 99 per cent' and 'inequality and the 1 per cent'.[4]

In addition, while we may be good at diagnosing many of the maladies that afflict us, we are not so good at administering potential cures. We tend to seek short-term solutions: we try to be kind to the poor, but not to end poverty. We try to be aware of inequality and to curtail its worst effects, but not to ask what it is that we would have to do to lower it forever. We try to manage crises; but by doing so, we often perpetuate them. We frequently appear to have lost the ability to think about prevention, especially regarding war and greed. Meanwhile, the cures we prescribe appear to be becoming less and less effective.

It may seem that we are heading towards an age of compound crises: what might be called a polycrisis. And within this turbulence it becomes increasingly difficult to tell the difference between the flashing red rights, the alarm bells, the sirens, and that which is concerning but not immediately important. With so many crises preoccupying us, which emergency should the first responders attend next? To what should we be applying our energy?

In this book I cannot pretend to foretell the future, but I have some interesting data to show you, and here it is considered in ways I don't think have been prioritised enough before; and I share stories told by others that might help us get to the heart of this polycrisis. I'm inviting you to spend some time looking closely at what people around the world are most concerned about, rather than dismissing their fears as unfounded or misguided. Instead, I'm suggesting that you reassess your own assumptions, and question what they are based on. Taking seriously what we collectively think about our human future is one way to better understand the global present.

Risk management

How does one discover what people are thinking about? It's usually done by using prompts. We are so often told that certain things are a crisis – the climate crisis, the housing crisis, the financial crisis. However, using the word *crisis* in a survey question invariably steers people towards a particular answer and towards issues that others have already decided are crises.

In September 2022, the World Economic Forum's Global Risks Perception Survey asked over 1,200 experts across academia, business, government, the international community, and civil society what they considered to be the greatest potential crises of the coming year. The experts ranked the following as 'the top risks for 2023':

- the energy supply crisis;
- the cost-of-living crisis (rising inflation);
- the food supply crisis;
- cyberattacks on critical infrastructure.[5]

Looking back at 2023, energy was indeed very expensive and almost all other prices rose too, with food in particular costing more. But there was no great cyberattack to speak of that brought down critical infrastructure. Ironically, it was a bug in software designed to prevent cyberattack which caused the most harm to computers worldwide in 2024.[6] Absent from the list above were wars: unforeseen, ongoing, and long foreseen as likely, in the case of the Middle East. Unforeseen was the growing international outrage over the starvation of the people of Gaza, and the denial of their access to water. This was exacerbated by the apparent inability of the US to preclude, through better longer-term diplomacy and action, the ongoing killing of many tens of thousands of Palestinians in Gaza, many thousands in Lebanon, and the deaths of over a thousand people in Israel. The failure of international diplomacy in the continuing conflict in Ukraine has been staggering; as have the potential results of attacks within Russia, which were also unexpected. Other conflicts, often assumed to have no wider implications, were almost totally ignored, including those in Ethiopia, Sudan, Yemen, and across the Sahel.

We cannot know what is happening in the world, and what to worry about, simply by watching the news. Different news channels tell different stories. Most stories – even those concerning events that have led to many deaths and enormous suffering – never even make it onto the news agenda. Broadcasters' attention, and ours, moves quickly from item to item. Overall, the media we absorb steers our thinking.

One constant is that what we think is most likely to be the next crisis is typically what we are worrying about at the time we are asked. Our fears about future crises are usually extrapolations from what we are currently most concerned about. *Who* is asking and *how* they ask both have a great influence on the answers we give.

Looking again at the result of the World Economic Forum Global Risks Perception survey described above, it is important to note that the respondents were a very particular cohort. Where crisis interferes with the economy, it is often called 'risk', and in recent decades a whole risk-management industry has evolved, with a hierarchy of risk officers, directors, and even company vice-presidents, all of whom who have *risk* as part of their remit.

To judge from their professional online community group, the job of chief risk officers is to seek 'ways in which organizations can be better prepared to anticipate, manage and rebound faster from global shocks and their spillover effects, minimizing the impact of the next potential global shocks on markets and livelihoods'.[7] A crisis, especially the *next* crisis, is also an opportunity for them. Professional crisis managers have different priorities to most people. Their key concern is maximising the outcomes for their organisation, primarily their employers and shareholders, while minimising the threats to their business and themselves personally.

For those who responded to the World Economic Forum's Global Risks Perception Survey, the smooth operation of international markets was a top priority, and they apparently believe that most people's livelihoods and well-being depend on these markets. These experts are obliged to see market capitalism as the ultimate good in order to secure and keep their employment. But their blinkers need not limit our thinking.

Instead, let's look at a different survey, aimed at a different audience of respondents – aimed at you, and people like you, and many people very unlike you too. Because none of us are that similar to most people on this very unequal planet.

Which three of these alphabetically listed topics do you find most worrying?

Access to credit; climate change; coronavirus (COVID-19); crime and violence; education; financial/political corruption; health care; immigration control; inflation; maintaining social programmes; military conflict between nations; moral decline; poverty and social inequality; rise of extremism; taxes; terrorism; threats against the environment; unemployment.

Is your greatest worry a personal one? Or a general worry about what might affect just your family or those close to you? Is it a worry for the wider society you live in? Or for the whole world?

Once you've picked one, you may find the next choice is easier. What is your second greatest worry? What was the one you were dithering about possibly putting first? If you thought about it for long, it is probably one that should also be in your top three. Now all you have to do is pick a third and final one.

Figure 1.2 (shown a few pages ahead so as not to bias your answers) provides a snapshot of what most worried people around the world over the period from July 2022 to July 2024 (the average number of times people placed any one concern in their top three). It is ordered by the ranking in January of 2023 to give you an idea of how our concerns slowly change over time.

When we ask these questions has a great effect. Coronavirus was the tenth most concerning crisis in January 2023, but as you can see from the chart in Figure 1.2, it would rank lower in importance over this time period as a whole. It is not just timing that matters. You might be wondering about the effect of wording and how the question is framed. Perhaps more people might have put climate change among their top three concerns had the question ended 'for humanity as a whole', rather than 'for your country'. Perhaps if the word 'concerning', or 'frightening', had been used instead of 'worrying', the ordering might have been a little different too. It would have been, but probably not by much.

In the chapters that follow I'll try to persuade or at least argue with you that we are right to be worried about the future, and that we should learn to take more seriously the things that most other people around the world are most worried about, and I will try to demonstrate that it is possible to both enumerate and understand those wider concerns. I'll also offer reasons to worry less about some crises and more about others. In addition, I want to convince you that it would be better for us all if more of us believed that almost all these crises can diminish in the near future – in just a few human lifetimes. That so many of us rank the same few things so highly is a boon, not a problem. We come slowly to concentrate collectively on what matters most – too slowly for the liking of many, and not everyone will be in agreement on these priorities. But we get our concerns on the agenda collectively, and the only way we have ever solved crises in the past has been collectively.

Elite projection

What some people think of as being the most important issues in the future of the world are often of greatest concern to only a small minority of us. But if those people are affluent and powerful, the issues they care about are the ones that come to be called *the* crisis of the moment, and thus the subject of many high-profile books, news stories, and TV documentaries. A list of these could include cyberattacks, artificial intelligence, oil price hikes, and events preventing the shipment of goods; or, if you have an active imagination, artificial intelligence creating cyberattacks and digital viruses that infect our online life and take control – from diverting goods shipments to altering our desires and fears themselves. In contrast, the things that actually concern the majority of people worldwide are often dismissed as local issues of lesser importance, or even as simply how the world is. But if we came to see crises more clearly and how unevenly their impacts fall on people around the world, it might not have to be that way.

The concerns of the majority of people worldwide really are the most pressing issues we face, both now and in the near future. The risk-management professionals and other such experts do not know it all; they mostly work all too clearly in the interests of those whose views they reflect. They appear to come to incorporate those views in their own worldview, which they then impose upon the rest of us. This is what the public-transit (think buses) consultant Jarrett Walker calls 'elite projection'.[8]

Elite projection has profound consequences when it results in elites making decisions for the rest of the world, and it can be blamed for largely determining the fate of those with limited access to resources. But elite projection covers a wide spectrum, from the far-right zealotry of a few billionaire narcissists (the kind who dislike people who use buses), to well-meaning environmentalists working for international bodies with democratic funding, and of course university professors who write books such as this. Anyone can pick and choose which members of the elite to listen to, if any. I prefer those people who argue that, in a truly civilised society, the rich use public transport.[9] We all have our favoured sources, and we all present them as being the most reasonable.

The key report on how the world is really faring, especially for most poorer people, is the United Nations' (annual) Human Development Report. Achim Steiner, administrator of the United Nations Development Programme, who presented the Report for 2022, wrote:

> Climate and ecological disasters threaten the world daily. Layers of uncertainty are stacking up and interacting to unsettle our lives in unprecedented ways. People have faced diseases, wars and environmental disruptions before. But the confluence of destabilizing planetary pressures with growing inequalities, sweeping societal transformations to ease those pressures and widespread polarization present new, complex, interacting sources of uncertainty for the world and everyone in it. People around the world are now telling us that they feel ever more insecure. Is it any wonder, then, that many nations are creaking under the strain of polarization, political extremism and demagoguery—all supercharged by social media, artificial intelligence and other powerful technologies?[10]

It is worth questioning whether people around the world actually *are* telling us that they now feel ever more insecure. If you look at the measures of anxiety levels, that is not necessarily what you see. As one global polling company put it at the end of 2023: 'Unlike the previous few years, 2023 has been slightly less "unprecedented": there have been no pandemic restrictions, no record-breaking heatwaves, no energy supply shocks.'[11] So, belatedly (having prevented you from being influenced by the results by not showing them until now), here is Figure 1.2.

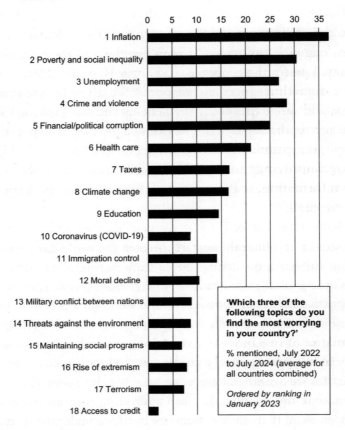

Figure 1.2: What the rest of the world is most concerned about, 2022–24

'Which three of the following topics do you find the most worrying in your country?'

% mentioned, July 2022 to July 2024 (average for all countries combined)

Ordered by ranking in January 2023

Source: What Worries the World, Ipsos, surveys of January and July in this time period, averaged.

Figure 1.2 shows what most people are currently anxious about. Over the relevant period, July 2022 to July 2024, anxieties shifted for many people. In July 2022, 14 per cent of people listed COVID-19 (coronavirus) as being among their top three concerns; by July 2024 that was just 4 per cent, a fall of ten percentage points. Of course, other fears were rising. Concerns about health in general (as opposed to COVID-19/coronavirus) rose by four percentage points, from being a top-three priority for 19 per cent in July 2022, to 23 per cent in July 2024. Immigration-control worries rose by a fraction more, from 12 per cent to

17 per cent. We are a very adaptable species when it comes to anxiety.

Could a rising sense of anxiety actually disguise a rarely acknowledged equilibrium? Things overall may not be getting any better, but nor are they getting much worse. Much is concerning, sometimes increasingly concerning; but for most people in the world, life expectancy is rising, infant mortality is falling, and hunger is abating by comparison with the experience of their parents' generation. Meanwhile, shelter, education, and health care are improving; and more people can read and write, and access information, than ever before in our history as a species – by a long chalk.[12]

We have never before been as connected as we are now. We can partly see this in our converging fears over the future, our relatively cohesive thinking on crises. Some newspaper columnists noted that, as the global population passed the eight-billion mark, our fears, particularly regarding human proliferation, were coalescing. We have only reached such huge numbers in very recent years, in just a matter of two or three generations. So much change came so quickly in our parents' and grandparents' lives that it is hardly surprising that we are still catching up on what it might mean.

Now that the world's human population growth is slowing almost as quickly as it was previously rising, this brings its own worries. How will we maintain our health services? How many immigrants will arrive? Will they be enough? In rich countries, the slowdown of population growth is feeding into a growing understanding that we will have to get better at sharing what we have with the rest of the world, which comprises far more people than in our parents' and grandparents' time. The geographical centre of the human world has shifted (south and eastwards), and it still has further to move. We now have a good idea of how our numbers are set to slow down in the very near future, and populations in many different places – almost everywhere worldwide – are now set to fall in the course of this century.

It is important that we get our futures in order: that we realise that much of what most concerns the rich, the elites of the West, are not the first priorities of the rest of the world. We must listen more and identify the data that will help bring these alternative perspectives into the light, so that we can all collectively make better decisions about what to do next. Perhaps the first thing to do is to return to that original list of eighteen crises above, the ones numbered in Figure 1.2, and group them in a way that actually reflects the views of the world as a whole, and then work out our route from there. This book aims not to stop you thinking about the future as concerning, but instead to consider how to turn crises into shared challenges – even opportunities. Because too much fear and despair can result in apathy and fatalism.

What worries?

Many high-profile pundits' preoccupations about the future are not covered in detail or at all here, because those subjects simply do not feature in most people's greatest concerns and are unlikely to do so any time soon. A space race and worries over whether it will be governed by the anarchy of the commons, or the collusion of China and the US in establishing their leaders' rule-based duopoly of power over other planets, are not at the forefront of anyone's thoughts, other than a few very atypical men. Similarly, the concerns that far-right pundits keep trying to force up the agenda are largely ignored in this book because they are not the overriding concerns of any significant majority of people. These include issues such as multiculturalism, liberal universities, and political correctness. Instead, this book focuses on what most people worry about when they think about the future. Current concerns are all, in fact, concerns about the future. Unless the aim is to try to distract, we have enough to worry about in the world without inventing new fears.

The chapters that follow are organised thematically by the issues identified in 'What Worries the World', a large, ongoing global survey of people's greatest concerns and the source of Figure 1.2.[13] The polling organisation, Ipsos, began its monthly survey in 2011, and by 2022 over 30,000 adults were being interviewed each month. The survey includes India but not China. A very similar survey has been taken in China every two years since 2006 by the Institute of Sociology of the Chinese Academy of Social Sciences and its findings (up to 2021) have been used here to inform the order of the content that follows, and the emphasis given to each subject. These series of polls are combined in Figure 1.2 to ensure that the issues covered are each given a weight that does not reflect only one particular recent month and year.[14] In the pages that follow, we will consider which issues are slowly rising and falling in importance, and why. Our concerns change, and I would suggest that perhaps it is these changes that can offer us the most useful hints about what is likely to be the largest crisis in the coming years.

The concerns highlighted are those of the majority of people surveyed worldwide and are highly influenced by views from India and China, the world's two most populous nations. It should be noted, however, that a middle-income, middle-class bias persists because not all of the poorest countries of the world are included in the Ipsos surveys used to structure this book, although South Africa, Malaysia, and Brazil are included, and the coverage is as widespread as it is currently possible to be. It is also significant that the poorest people in the countries covered by the surveys are much less likely to have taken part (including in the survey by the Chinese Academy of Social Sciences).

Many of the global concerns covered in the following pages are themes that our recent ancestors had little reason to worry about, or even to be aware of. The newest in terms of our awareness include climate change and biodiversity loss. Others are ancient, such as the questions of who it's OK to exploit, who is currently being most exploited, who you should defend, and what happens when exploitation is normalised. Many remedies are old; but some are very new and only just emerging.

Each chapter that follows focuses on a different current crisis. Although these are sometimes described as worries or preoccupations, to those suffering from them most, they are all crises. Chapters are arranged according to what people around the world were most worried about from July 2022 through to July 2024. This was when we were emerging from the worst of the pandemic. What preoccupies us personally, at any one time, tends to fade as we age, and occasionally fades very quickly. The greatest fears caused by the emergence of COVID-19 are now mostly memories, but a general concern about our health remains. At the same time, we were beginning to worry more about inflation, about a new war in Ukraine, and then a much deadlier war on Gaza and in that wider region.

Although certain events may feel unique and some dominate temporarily, the average ranking of issues in this twenty-four-month period is very close to that of similar surveys for the longer time period of 2017 to 2022. I have chosen the year 2017 as a start date because by then most climate scepticism had abated, and so climate issues were not underrepresented as they might have been if surveys from a longer time period were used. Nevertheless, as is revealed by the order of the chapters in this book, which reflects what these surveys show, when it comes to the things that concern us most, climate is far from the top of our collective current and likely immediate future fears.

The organising principle here is thematic because the greatest misconception in what we think about the future is about the relative importance of each of these issues. Furthermore, the aggregate concerns of most people – those with the luxury of having wider concerns beyond simply food and shelter – produce an order that we should take seriously. This ranking forces us to consider our priorities in relation to what is currently affecting people badly and what is most likely to continue harming more people, unless these issues are better addressed.

Many of these top concerns have tended to be seen as ones of only local importance: as second-order issues that each country's government should attempt to address internally; or they are seen as inevitable, as an everyday reality rather than a crisis. But they are in fact far nearer to universal worries than others often suggested, to such an extent that we should recognise them as key global issues.

The thematic arrangement of the material also opens up a space to discuss the way that demography affects attitudes: how our changing numbers and projected population changes are likely to affect each of our current more serious concerns. Half a century ago, well over a third of all people on the planet were children, and now they comprise less than a quarter. Soon fewer than a billion people will be older than me, born in 1968, and seven in eight will be younger, despite the great slowdown in births. A great baby boom – almost certainly the final great baby boom – lies just beneath my cohort.

Each chapter that follows tells the story of who says a particular issue matters the most and, tellingly, why many better-off people are oblivious to it. This encourages us to think about what people do *not* think about, as much as what they do. For example, some issues are little addressed (or even little discussed) because most of the political class believes that other issues are more significant.

The pages that follow suggest that many of those in power around the world today are hampered by a highly skewed set of views about which issues are most important, and perspectives that are increasingly partisan and unimaginative. Perhaps the findings revealed here can help in a small way to counter the inaccurate reports and distorted attitudes on poverty, war, crime, climate change, and inflation that are driving the current consensus among those whose views carry the most weight.

If you do not think we are currently on the wrong track, then why do the Ipsos surveys indicate that nearly two-thirds of the world's people think we are heading in the wrong direction? What is the connection between sharing resources, uncertainty, and work? Why is it the young and wealthy who are most concerned about climate change? Why has the population of China been most worried about health care for many years, despite having one of the best health-improvement records of any large country?

Everything can appear to be, and is, connected. The subjects of every chapter in this book are all far from unrelated, even if they may appear to be separate issues. The cost-of-living crisis is connected to our ability (and inability) to share the planet with each other and other species. This in turn influences the extent of crime and war, the cost and difficulty of affording a home, issues of health care and the adaptations we must make to being an ageing society, and wider concerns over both education and politics. So, too, we can see the intimate connections between concerns about climate crisis, future access to food and water, energy, travel, human effects on biodiversity and how we in turn might be affected by that.

Perhaps surprisingly, when you look at them together, most of our greatest concerns are day-to-day ones. In the spring of 2022, the primary concern in the world was inflation, with 32 per cent of people in Ipsos's 'What Worries the World' (as the pool of data is sometimes called) suggesting it was the biggest worry facing them and their country. By the summer of 2023, inflation and the rising cost of living was the highest concern of 27 per cent of all people surveyed, but was falling slightly as other worries began to rise.[15] By then it had been the top global concern for seventeen months running, peaking in June 2023, when it appeared in the top three concerns of 40 per cent of all people worldwide. Whether that will be the highest peak it reaches in our lifetimes, we do not know. Runaway prices caused by global hyperinflation could become the next crisis if certain goods and resources are soon much scarcer. By June 2024, inflation was up again as a great global concern, included in 33 per cent of people's top three, and pessimism was again on the rise in most countries.[16]

The second-largest issue in the spring of 2022, at just a single percentage point lower, was poverty and social inequality, a key concern of 31 per cent of people worldwide. It was at exactly the same level of concern in the summer of 2023, and had dropped by only two percentage points, to 29 per cent, by June 2024. The next three significant concerns, according to people around the world averaged over a few years, were not far behind: unemployment (29 per cent, dropping to 27 per cent by 2023, where it remained in 2024); crime and violence (25 per cent, rising to 30 per cent by 2023 and staying there in 2024); and financial and political corruption (24 per cent, up to 27 per cent in 2023 and down to 25 per cent in 2024).[17] The sequence of Chapters 3–5, as you can see from the percentages given in parentheses, is therefore in some ways a little arbitrary. Each of these three sets of issues are of near equal importance when averaged over time. However, as we shall see, their importance across space is highly variable.

Inflation is a worry, both regarding prices now and what will happen if they continue to rise higher than wages; it is a concern about something that has recently changed and about a change to come. Concerns about poverty and inequality also reflect disquiet about what the world is becoming, as much as what it is. The idea of unfairness increasing is far more abhorrent to us than the inequality that we have become used to.

We worry about what our children will inherit and what chances they will have as much as we worry about ourselves, and much more than we worry about ourselves in very old age. Fear over unemployment is mostly about what might happen, rather than what is happening now: most people who worry about unemployment are employed. Similarly, the majority of people do *not* often personally experience crime or violence in any one year, but they worry about what might happen to them in the future. Concerns about financial and political corruption are arguably as much about the future and what might happen as about the present. If our politicians became less corrupt, we think, our future would be more certain and less precarious.

In that same 2022 survey, a large majority of people worldwide (63 per cent) thought that the country they lived in was headed in the wrong direction in terms of the issues that most concerned them. By 2023 that majority had risen to 64 per cent, a change that was probably not statistically significant; neither was the fall to 62 per cent by early 2024. What really matters, however, is not the fluctuation, but how high those numbers are. In the UK, the proportion rose to 65 per cent in early 2024, and to 72 per cent by July 2024. This was despite people in the UK being offered a general election that month so that in theory they would get to choose the direction!

Worldwide, by April 2022, the coronavirus pandemic had dropped out of the top five greatest global concerns for the second month running (to the eighth greatest, with 18 per cent of all those surveyed putting it in their top three worries). By June 2024 only 4 per cent of people worldwide put the pandemic in their top three concerns. There were other issues that worried people less than the coronavirus, but which were nevertheless of great importance. Military conflict between nations was a major concern for only 14 per cent of people worldwide, despite the war in Ukraine that began in 2022. As an issue, war ranked eleventh out of the top eighteen, between climate change and immigration control – subjects that were similarly not at the top of most people's minds. It was still in eleventh place by June 2024. In December 2023, concern about terrorism and military conflict fell across most of the world, having risen abruptly the month before as Israel's armed forces killed thousands of women and children, and a smaller group of men, in Gaza. People can very quickly become used to the most terrible of events – although of course the Ipsos survey did not ask the views of people living in what was left of Palestine.

The six key themes based upon the January 2023 data inform the way that I have structured the six main chapters in this book:

2. Those Costs of Living: inflation, and poverty and inequality, all combined (worries 1 and 2);
3. Sharing the Work: unemployment and issues of immigration control (worries 3 and 11);
4. War and a Home: crime and violence, corruption, and conflict[18] (worries 4, 5, 12, 13, 16, and 17);
5. Cradle to Grave: health care, taxes, education, and social costs[19] (worries 6, 7, 9, 10, 15, and 18);
6. Climate Crisis: climate change (worry 8);
7. Biodiversity: threats against the environment (worry 14).

These worries could be combined in different ways, but over the last decade that the Ipsos survey has been run, the groupings above tend, in combination, to rank in this order. You may wonder at this point why I have not combined climate change with threats against the environment, instead of presenting them as two separate chapters: Climate Crisis and Biodiversity. That is one of my indulgences, and a concession to those who are likely to be my most sceptical of readers, because they believe these issues should be tackled first. I would reply that at least I have given them a chapter each, rather than just one; but that is a bias of mine. For most people worldwide, they are issues of less importance.

People appear to consider crises as being of different orders of importance depending on their distance from them in time or space. The cost of living is near to an everyday crisis for the majority of people. Poverty, inequality and their repercussions may feel a little further away, for most. Often further away again is the imminent threat of unemployment. War is usually an even more distant crisis. But crime is frequently felt to be nearer to home. Confusingly, our cradle-to-grave crises are immediate for some, memories for others, or purely hypothetical for a privileged few. Distant injustices are things to worry about only when the family are fed and safe.

2

Those Costs of Living

The rising cost of living is the top concern for 93% of Europeans, followed by the threat of poverty and social exclusion (82%).

Albena Azmanova,
professor of political and social science, June 2024[1]

Those costs of living are the most basic of costs. They include paying for food, for shelter, for clothing, for travel to work, and for health care or education where it is not provided free at the point of need. When these costs rise due to inflation, when people become too poor to pay for what is normal in the society in which they live, and when economic inequality rises or is high, there is crisis. Rising costs of living – through inflation, poverty, and inequality – have come to represent the greatest crisis of our times. Which of those three factors seems to be the most important changes from time to time, but they are all intimately connected. The fact that a decade ago this was not the highest priority for the majority of people surveyed worldwide helps illustrate how a new dominant crisis can emerge, while others subside.

If we are interested in what the next greatest crisis might be, we need to be aware of how crises rise and fall in importance over time. Unemployment (not being able to find work) is now not as great a concern for most people worldwide as it was recently, and so it is the main focus of the next chapter of this book. Had this book been written ten years ago, this present chapter would have principally been about unemployment. Roughly a decade ago, the summary of all the Ipsos surveys taken in 2016 reported:

> Unemployment remains the biggest concern globally – as it has been since the start of our survey series in 2010. What's worth noting, though, is that its lead on other issues has slowly but surely reduced over this time. In European countries, unemployment is clearly the chief worry. Crime and violence is the core issue for Latin American countries, whilst in North America healthcare is the leading concern (33%). Concerns about terrorism are also rising.[2]

Seven years later, by December 2023, inflation had been the greatest concern worldwide for twenty-one months. Only in Peru, Brazil, the Netherlands, Indonesia, and Israel did it not appear in the top three concerns of at least a quarter of all people. But over a third of survey respondents in Peru and Brazil ranked poverty and social inequality as a top concern, as did 44 per cent of respondents in Indonesia.[3]

There is always great geographical variation in our greatest fears. In the Netherlands the same survey showed climate change (27 per cent) ranking higher that month. But that does not mean that the Dutch are more inclined to focus on global concerns because they are perfectly happy with their own country; in fact, far-right parties in the Netherlands have been working for years to stoke up hatred of immigrants. As a result, in the winter of 2023 it was not the Dutch Greens but the far right that gained a record high (for a far-right party) number of votes and seats in the Dutch national election. Conversely, in Israel the war on the population of Gaza trumped every other concern: 64 per cent of those surveyed listed terrorism as their greatest concern, almost four times as many people as in the next most fearful country and seven times more than the global norm. In Israel the previous year, violence had been the greatest concern of the majority of those surveyed (59 per cent). Note also that better-off people are typically overrepresented among the respondents in these surveys, and sometimes entire populations are excluded. Those in Palestine – the Gaza Strip and the West Bank – were almost certainly not surveyed by Ipsos; they are very rarely ever asked their views in surveys of this kind. Since October 2023 it has been impossible to survey people in Gaza.

Our worries depend on our immediate circumstances. Most people do not live in or near a war zone. For the vast majority of people worldwide, even the best-off half, it is the reality of everyday life (and the fear that things will not get better) that dominates people's thoughts. Nonetheless, it is worth asking how inflation, poverty, and inequality rose so rapidly to the top of the global agenda after 2016, because this shift shows that it is not inevitable that they should dominate. And how did this constellation of concerns about money become the top concern almost everywhere in the autumn of 2023, apart from for those in a very few places (such as the Netherlands) who were distracted by internal politics, and those surveyed in Israel, distracted by the immediate fear of violence?

In 2016, poverty and social inequality were only the third most important concern of all those surveyed around the world, and exactly a third of all people cited those two issues among their greatest three concerns. Back in 2016, 11 per cent mentioned inflation, making it only the eleventh-greatest concern at that time. Even by 2017, unemployment remained the largest concern overall, but the researchers producing these figures noted that 'its lead over poverty/inequality and corruption diminished over the year. This fall in concern about unemployment has been driven by big drops in worry about job security in established nations including Canada and the US.'

By January 2022, poverty and inequality combined had become the second-greatest concern, three points above unemployment, and four below the pandemic. However, by April 2022, just four months later, the pandemic had plummeted to the eighth-greatest concern (18 per cent listed it in their top three). Inflation was first, at 32 per cent, and poverty and social inequality was second, at 31 per cent. These changes were driven partly by what people were being told by news media, and partly by their own experiences. They were told that the COVID-19 pandemic had essentially ended, even though it had not. The mass unemployment that many feared the pandemic might bring had not occurred, owing largely to state intervention via furlough schemes in those countries rich enough for unemployment to be a possibility.[4] And so, with those two great concerns abating, and the cost of living rising, the April 2022 Ipsos report noted: 'Poverty, inequality and inflation rose to the fore.'

Those cost-of-living issues remain at the fore as I write, in the summer of 2024, and check the statistics in early 2025.

Inflation becomes a problem when wages, salaries, and benefits do not rise in line with prices. It is just as much about material living standards as are concerns over poverty and inequality. When inflation takes place without commensurate rises in wages and welfare benefits, it affects a great number of people very quickly. The poor suffer most when prices rise, but inflation also eats up the wealth of the rich. In November 2023, faced with claims that poverty was rising in Britain, the government responded that in the UK there were 'about 1.7 million fewer people living in absolute poverty as compared to 12 years earlier'. This was a deceitful answer, built on sophistry – and revealed how little that government cared.[5]

A particular form of deception often occurs when worldwide trends are considered by those in places of plenty. Our World in Data is a website built by researchers employed by the University of Oxford. It presents a message of apparent constant improvement in the face of huge need and concern, and in many cases a very obvious lack of social and economic progress. Based on Figure 2.1, you might ask: how can the cost of living, poverty, and inequality be the greatest worries in the world if the situation is getting so much better so very quickly? This is what the Our World in Data (OWID) graph shown here in Figure 2.1 implies, but its apparent simplicity is misleading.

By presenting data in a particular way, it is possible to convey a particular message. For example, in the US, the UK, and a few other similarly acquisitive countries, we do not teach economics as we should. Instead, we teach a form of economics that tells the story that very rich people prefer you to hear.[6] According to this mythical version of economics, as the likes of Elon Musk have prospered, so has almost everyone else. This is the usual way in which Figure 2.1 is interpreted. One line represents everyone who has between two dollars a day and two billion dollars a day to get by. Elon Musk had a wealth estimated in excess of US$241 billion in late 2023, so even if he spent only 1 per cent of that each week in a year, he would be spending a little over two billion each week: US$334 million dollars a day, or £4,000 a second. But he could spend much more than that, for as long as he lived. Does it make sense to put him in this group?

The money of the rich, if unchecked, grows so quickly that someone like Musk might never run out of money to spend as long as he was not utterly foolish with his investments. For the very wealthy, capitalism is a Midas machine that turns the objects they touch into more wealth for them; and it does so to the detriment of almost everyone else. Because at the same time as the wealthy are turning everything they touch to gold, the tiny bit of savings most of us hold grow dull, and turn to stone. The profit of the wealthiest is derived from immiserating billions of others and taking endless (and growing) small slices of money from them.[7]

The view that wealth has trickled down to give almost everyone an ever greater income, if not showering them in abundance, is visualised by Figure 2.1. That graph very clearly suggests that extreme poverty became less and less of a problem around the year 1968. But this is only the case if you measure poverty in one particular way, by an absolute amount. You are only poor by this definition if you are surviving, or not surviving, on a fixed sum of money – on what US$1.90 a day bought you just a few years ago. With inflation, that paltry sum of money is worth less now: to make it equivalent, a higher actual amount will be needed.

If the story really were as simple as 'poverty has never been lower', as many conventional (conservative) economists argue

Figure 2.1: How economists tend to report global trends in poverty over time

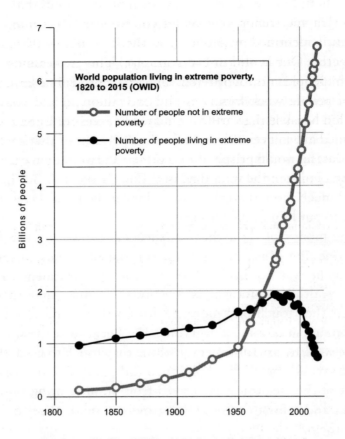

Source: Our World in Data (OWID), which relies on what some might call questionable data and assumptions. OWID, World population living in extreme poverty, 1820 to 2015. (Extreme poverty is defined as living on less than 1.90 international-$ per day. International-$ are adjusted for price differences between countries and for price changes over time). Last accessed 7 August 2024, ourworldindata.org/grapher/world-population-in-extreme-poverty-absolute.

and as the above graph suggests, then why are concerns over the cost of living now so widespread and pronounced? Furthermore, why are poverty and inequality being seen as the leading issues of concern around the world, along with the rising cost of basic goods and services in comparison to wages? Despite this conundrum, Figure 2.1 is not entirely useless: it points to one thing that is very telling – the year 1968, when the lines cross.

Demography

Demographic trends are connected to each of the major crises currently identified by people around the world. In 1820, according to the 'Our World in Data' graph (Figure 2.1), almost 90 per cent of people in the world were extremely poor. The large majority of people worldwide were living in villages and were often well fed because they grew food, but the food they grew was not included in what economists calculated, because it was not traded. The dataset is comprised of two groups that add up to just over a billion people in the year 1820 (see Table 2.1).

Table 2.1: Claims made about extreme poverty in 1820 (less than $1.90 per day)

117,436,202	Number of people not in extreme poverty
964,925,108	Number of people living in extreme poverty

Source: OWID based on World Bank (2016) and Bourguignon and Morrisson (2002). OWID, 'World Population Living in Extreme Poverty', Our World in Data, last accessed 7 August 2024.

Note: International-$ (dollars) are adjusted for price differences between countries and for price changes over time (inflation).

Let's take the 'Our World in Data' information at face value and not question the methods used in the original source, published in the *American Economic Review* in 2002, and let's not – for now – question the thinking behind the subsequent updating that was required.[8] What does that table really show, and why? Figure 2.2 takes exactly the same data as that shown in Figure 2.1 above, but now shows the annual reduction in the numbers of people said to be living in extreme poverty which the data series implies.

What we are being asked to believe is that for the whole 160-year-long period from 1820 to 1980, the numbers of people living in extreme poverty grew each decade by between 0.2 per cent and 0.8 per cent a year on average; and then suddenly – apparently due to some economic miracle, perhaps as a result of

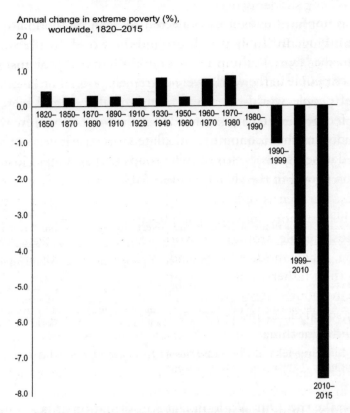

Figure 2.2: The reported rise and fall in extreme poverty in the world: an economist's view

Source: Our World In Data (OWID). Data used to construct Figure 2.1, but now showing the change as an annualised rate by nearest decade.

the wonders of neoliberalism, with more things being traded more freely – extreme poverty plummeted.

If it is true that everything changed after 1968, what happened then? And why did this then accelerate into the 1980s and beyond, to create this great transformation? Was it associated with Ronald Reagan becoming governor of California in 1967, thirteen years before he went on to become president of the US? Or does it fit with the rise in popularity of Margaret Thatcher in the UK in the late 1970s? Both politicians, Reagan and Thatcher, were certainly closely associated with a particular brand of economic thinking, neoliberalism. More importantly, neoliberalism has ushered in a wider application of economics that paints a false picture of poverty having suddenly been vanquished after 1968.

It is not hard to ridicule a great deal of these economists' way of thinking. In Table 2.1, for example, what exactly does the number 964,925,108 imply? Does it really mean that the economists of today can produce estimates to the nearest individual for periods over 200 years ago – precise estimates of how many people were extremely poor and how many were not? There is often an implication in this work that you, the reader, should not worry your (by implication, little) head over what exactly went on then or now, but merely be thankful that you live in a time of such riches. But that is only one way of telling the story, and there is another far more convincing explanation.

Most people around the world today who are poor are also young. Their mothers also tend to be poor, slightly more often than their fathers. But what matters more for someone's chances of being poor – above all else – is where they are born, then into what social class, and lastly when they were born (age and cohort are different things). It is only after all that, that concerns such as the old being less likely to be poor than the young matter. Because the rich generally live longer than the poor, older people often appear to be richer, but poverty often rises again in very old age. You might think that it is the economic rise of China that made all the difference, but that came later. Instead I would suggest that we should look at birth rates to begin to understand why 1968 was the turning point in the two graphs just described (Figures 2.1 and 2.2); and we should realise that although there were suddenly fewer very young people, not everyone was suddenly better off. That is only the case if your measure of income is as crude as gross domestic product (GDP) divided by population.

The peak birth year of humans in global history was 1968, when 122 million babies were born worldwide: 4 per cent more than the year before. In absolute numbers, there were more conceptions in the 1967 summer of love, worldwide, than had ever occurred before. In relative terms this was the highest ever year for new births as a proportion of the whole population. After that year, however, the number of births began to fall in most years and never again rose as quickly in any single subsequent year. The next absolute peak in global births was in 1990, when there were 142 million births. These were the children of those children of '68; they had become parents at a modal age of twenty-two.

The overall growth in births was much smaller, however, in the years up to around 1990, than had been the case in the 1960s. This can be measured by the average *change in the rate* per decade. What this shows is that just before, but almost synchronous with, an abrupt fall in extreme poverty, far fewer children were suddenly being born worldwide.[9] So in the late 1960s and throughout the 1970s, it was in the poorest countries, and to the poorest families, that the fall in extreme poverty was greatest.

Chinese women went from having six children each, on average, to their daughters having two, in just a single generation. This was before China introduced any policies limiting the size of families. Conceptions also fell in India, and all of South Asia, with the decline accelerating most quickly between 1962 and 1972.[10]

Poverty, as measured crudely by the economists, fell in these years largely because fewer children were born poor; it had nothing to do with the claims for trickle-down wealth that dominated the Reagan-Thatcher era and beyond. Women, especially poorer women, were increasingly able to refuse sex, and access to contraceptives and abortions improved.

If births matter that much, then what is currently projected by the United Nations to happen next is very good news. As I write in 2024, births for the first half of the 2020s are still falling rapidly, in fact by more than 1 per cent in many individual years. A graph can be drawn using the global data that shows the UN population projections for changes in future births globally, smoothed over five years. Only three of those five-year periods projected *after* 2024 see small increases in annual rates. These are when most of the children born around and shortly before the year 1990 will have all of their own grandchildren. Before then, and after then, these graphs would show a decline. The projected rise in the human population of our planet between 2025 and 2040 is not really a rise, then: for a short time there will be more people who can be parents, but they will not have anything like the number of children their parents had.

I have written elsewhere that I think that the UN continuously overestimates how many children people will have.[11] I would be surprised if we see even the tiny increases in total births currently projected occur at the rates published prior to 11 July 2024. That was the date when the UN figures were last updated, and when we discovered that we were yet again having fewer and fewer children than we thought we would be only a few years earlier. Those born in 1990 should expect fewer grandchildren than they might have been planning for.

So why, if extreme poverty is falling, driven partly if not largely by the falling number of children born into poorer families, have concerns over poverty and inequality been rising? Why are we so worried about the rising cost of living when there has been a slowdown in the growth of the number of mouths to feed? The simple answer is that the overall number of human mouths continues to rise, not least because the old are living longer. The world's population is not set to peak for another sixty years, in 2086 (revised down to 2084 in July 2024), despite the near continuous fall in birth rates that has been taking place since 1968, and has accelerated downwards even faster more recently.

But there are other reasons, and more complex answers. Few people really know quite why they worry about what they worry about, or why some people might be less prone to worry. Often what news is available, and the way it is framed, directs people's worries. For example, in some places people are more often told that they should expect to be rich, that riches represent success, and that life's highest aim is to have more than most others, and so are greatly disappointed when that does not happen. The message 'work hard and you will have more than most people, you will be rich' is guaranteed to make most people think they have failed. Unless they see through the message.

When we had much greater fears than the possibility of not being better off than most other people, we worried less about trying to become rich. My mother can remember my grandmother being frightened when she heard on the radio that the first atom bomb had been dropped on Hiroshima. My mother remembers asking my grandmother what an atom bomb was, and my grandmother replying that she did not know, and had no idea where Hiroshima was, or who might have lived there. But both the mother and the very young child knew it was something to fear. War was not a crisis for my mother, however: she had been born in war; it was normal for her.

People were told to fear people when the book *The Population Bomb* was published in 1968. The book foretold a time of great famine in the near future, and encouraged its readers to prevent other people having large families, so as to protect themselves from the threat of overpopulation. Readers of *The Population Bomb* might not have known much else about the places where apparently too many people were being born. They usually did not understand why it was said we would never be able to feed these extra mouths. These arguments turned out to be false once the children were born. But the lasting legacy of the book was to create a widespread fear about overpopulation.

The fact that population growth rates are now falling faster than we ever imagined possible does not, in the short term, alleviate the concern about 'too many people'. Nor does knowing that in some of the poorest countries of Africa, when the COVID-19 pandemic hit in 2020, pregnancy rates fell precipitously, and have since continued falling faster than was previously predicted. This fall was particularly marked among the youngest women of childbearing age, because of a sudden rise in modern contraceptive use. Greater uncertainty about the future after 2019 actually *reduced* the number of births, rather than increasing them, as often occurs during a crisis.[12]

The idea that rising inequality and poverty are a product of our rising numbers worldwide is wrong-headed because global inequality has in fact fallen in recent decades. It fell most in the years when the world's population was rising the fastest in absolute numbers: in the 1990s and through the millennium, as more and more people living in China rose up through the global income distribution. Global income inequality continued to fall, even as it was rising *within* many countries at this time. The latest figures show that it fell from a global Gini coefficient of 61.8 in 2013 to 60.1 in 2018.[13] Part of the fall could be attributed to China's population growing so slowly that income per person could rise even faster there.

Just because population growth slows, that does not mean that most people are necessarily better off. That depends on how resources are distributed among people. It is thus not simply demographics that determine which people get to exploit others and keep them poor, nor is it just economics or some secret of sociology. It is also the art of politics, including particular theories of economics and sociology, that help a few people to exploit others. A wider more diverse education does the reverse, helping us learn to live together better and to be less fearful of others.

Fewer children being born in poor countries – as well as some very poor countries, such as China, becoming better off – is key to the post-1968 decline in extreme poverty worldwide, and to the most recent trends. The number of babies being born in rich countries also fell quickly during the COVID-19 pandemic. A detailed study in Spain showed that this fall in births accelerated after 2019, because of the rise in economic uncertainty.

The fall in children being born in Spain was greatest in younger and poorer mothers, those most likely to be affected by that uncertainty. There was also a fall in births to older mothers, some of whom might have been likely to turn to medically assisted reproduction, which was less available during the pandemic. And there was simultaneously a fall in very young women giving birth, as unplanned pregnancies decreased due to fewer conceptions occurring 'immediately after the introduction of stay-at-home orders in March 2020'.[14] Furthermore, there are as yet no signs of a rise in births after the end of the main wave of the pandemic, or the many subsequent waves. So there was no rise that would make up for the children who were never born during the worst of the pandemic.

Despite births falling worldwide, and that fall accelerating after 2019, for some decades to come there will be more and more people on the planet. So does this inevitability mean that we will continue to feel poor and fear poverty and inequality in the coming decades, even if the absolute and most basic measures of the quality of the lives of those who have the least of all continue to improve? The situation can, in fact, change quickly: it can worsen quickly; so too could it improve quickly.

The cost-of-living crisis that began in 2022 hurt us not because of rising prices, but due to so many people living in poverty as a result of high inequality and of rising prices further constraining their ability to exercise choice about where to work and live. This cost-of-living crisis has three implications that matter greatly for the future: it reduces how free we are (liberty); it affects how we see and treat each other (equality); and it constrains how well we can act collectively (fraternity).

When you cannot afford to eat, you are not free. But there is more to life than just eating. You are not free when you cannot afford to send a message to a loved one. A first-class stamp in the UK in autumn 2023 cost £1.25: as much as it did, adjusted for inflation, when postage stamps first appeared, and were priced at 1p. Of course, we are now less likely to use letters to communicate with loved ones – not least because they are too expensive, but also because they require far too many people to deliver them and use up far too much paper, which has become more precious (as the price of wood rises). Today, it is rather when you cannot afford a phone that you are not free. Even in the best-off places, poverty caused by inequality, and exacerbated by rising prices, takes away liberty. Think, for example, of France, where in the national elections of July 2024, the far right was held at bay. Why was it that France surprised the world and yet again refused to turn to the far right, as the UK had done between 2010 and 2024, electing Conservatives that were too far-right ('reactionary') to be members of the European Conservative grouping (European People's Party – EPP), and as the US did when it elected Donald Trump in 2016 (and would do again in 2024)?[15]

The French have it good. France has one of the lowest levels of income inequality in Europe, and thus in the world. When the issue of France's levels of inequality is being discussed, some suggest that the country is so much more equal than most other European countries because of lower inequality before taxes, further bolstered by higher social transfers, including higher average welfare payments than in most of the rest of Europe and a higher level of redistribution among citizens than in almost any other country, worldwide. The favourable position of France can be explained by lower inequality in labour income among the employed, by a higher effective workforce participation of the French working-age population, by a relatively lower number of inactive people with no income, by comparatively low gender inequality, and by what some claim is the lowest inequality in income from wealth – income from charging interest, from lending to others – in Europe.[16]

France's earlier retirement age of sixty-two helps it ensure its high economic activity rate. (That retirement age will rise to sixty-four in 2030, in a move that the left-wing coalition that won the greatest share of votes in the French national elections in 2024 has called to be rescinded.)

There is enough useful work for everyone under age sixty-four, but if you spend so long living in retirement, you have to have a pension you can rely on. If pensions are reliable, the incentive to try to hoard as much as you can earlier in life, to try to amass too much by working too long, is diminished. Amassing more is always done at the expense of others because holding money means holding a right over others' time and labour.

France practises greater redistribution than is seen in the majority of the rest of Europe, and social benefits are higher and slightly more targeted. If they were not, France could not have such a low level of reported income inequality, as measured by the Organisation for Economic Co-operation and Development. The low income inequality of France sits alongside, at most times, the highest public spending levels in Europe, as measured and reported by the International Monetary Fund. However, even these official reports, which if read correctly imply how well France does, suggest there is still great room for improvement. But you have to read reports on inequality carefully, because what often comes across as kind words can hide ill intent.

Towards the end of 2020 the Office of the Prime Minister of France published a report that suggested: 'Increased targeting of certain deductions and benefits would make it possible to reduce the volumes transferred without increasing inequalities, or to reduce them further without increasing the amounts of money transferred between people.'[17] In other words: less money for the poor and lower taxes for the rich. No wonder people became so agitated in France after 2020.

In a 2022 report on poverty in France published soon after the official numbers were released, Oxfam showed that nearly 11 million French people were poor and that 17 per cent of the population was living below the poverty line. The charity revealed that poverty in France remains multifaceted, differing in intensity for different groups, and is highest for the working poor. Women are more impacted, especially when experiencing long-term unemployment. Furthermore, the UK-based charity suggested, this situation has been becoming worse in France almost constantly for twenty years, after having generally improved between 1996 and 2004. The Oxfam report offered fifteen recommendations to reduce inequalities by revising France's tax policies and its wealth redistribution system. It proposed, among much else: further increasing the salaries of public health workers and teachers; strengthening social benefits; fighting tax evasion more strongly; taxing the rich more, and more thoroughly; and implementing a climate crisis wealth tax.

Surely both these accounts cannot be simultaneously true? Can France be the country in Europe with the lowest wealth inequality and low rates of income inequality, and yet still have seen poverty rise over twenty years (in most of the years since 2004)?

Oxfam criticised the official statistics provided by INSEE, France's National Institute of Statistics and Economic Studies:

In 2019, INSEE counted 9.2 million people living below the monetary poverty line [in France], to which must be added about 1.6 million poor people who escape the statistics. Not to mention the fact that INSEE's statistics concern only metropolitan France, while the monetary poverty rate in the DOM [the overseas departments of France, Martinique, Guadeloupe, French Guiana, and Réunion] is two to five times higher than in metropolitan France. Thus, the poverty rate in France is officially 14.6%, whereas poor people actually represent at least 17% of the population. Poverty is not only characterized by a lack of money. In 2017, the European Union defined an indicator of material and social deprivation that covers, for example, energy insecurity, food insecurity (not being able to eat properly) or digital insecurity (not being able to afford internet access). In metropolitan France, 21% of the population is in monetary poverty or material and social deprivation.[18]

It is indeed simultaneously possible for France to be one of the best places to live in Europe and also for things to have become worse in France over the past twenty years. That, of course, is a sobering thought. It also explains why, both worldwide and in France, these are issues that are highest in the minds of most people when they are polled. In the January 2023 *What Worries the World* Ipsos report, more than seven out of ten French people thought that the country was heading in the wrong direction, with 44 per cent putting inflation as one of their top three concerns, 29 per cent citing poverty and inequality among them, but only 12 per cent listing unemployment as a key worry. That is compared to 49 per cent in Spain and 41 per cent in Italy listing unemployment as a top-three concern.

Bearing in mind ideas of liberty, ask yourself – given how bad the situation was – why did the French reject the far-right politics of Marine Le Pen in July 2024? How did they feel free enough to do that, given all these concerns and how bad the situation in the country appeared to be just two years earlier, in the spring of 2022? Why were the French, unlike the British or the Americans, able to stop the far right from taking power?

In March 2022, in the run-up to that year's French general election, the far-right leader Marine Le Pen announced that she would ensure an extra €150–€200 a month for each family by cutting VAT on fuel and raising tax credits. She endlessly repeated the slogan that people were 'having to choose between eating or heating': a phrase that elsewhere – in the UK for example – was used by the left.[19] Despite the French government having strictly capped the increase in gas and electricity prices that people had to pay, providing extra financial aid for the poorest households and ensuring that there was a 15-cent reduction per litre of fuel, it was still widely recognised that an impoverishment of many groups within the population was occurring. This was something that the French far-right seized on in an attempt to secure power – however, they failed to do so that year.

It did not help the politicians in power in France to insist that there was still plenty of evidence that the French standard of living had risen greatly since the 1990s, particularly for pensioners. Whereas in the 1970s it was French pensioners who made up more of the ranks of the poor, by 2022 it was the country's unemployed who were poorest, along with unmarried women in employment. Great inequalities among different groups of French pensioners remained, however, most obviously to the disadvantage of women, to those with fewer years in paid employment, to those paid the least while in work, and to those who had done the most labour-intensive work during their working lives, formal manual labourers (including many farmers). The proposal and then enforcement of the rise in France's pension age promised yet more hardship for those who had the least.

You might think it would be better if people knew where they stood, and were told that in France, income inequalities are lower than average for Europeans. And it certainly would be better if it were more widely known outside France. However, regarding the perception of income levels and wealth inequalities, at least one study suggests that even in France there are great misperceptions about the nature of inequality, and not in the direction you might think. People in France think they are *more* equal than they are. Low-income households overestimate their standard of living and do not realise that they are not well rewarded. While high-income households tend to underestimate their position in the hierarchy, thinking they are not as well-off as they are, which affects their views on inequality and what taxes they should pay. Even so, in France, like almost everywhere in the world today, people are more likely to identify poverty, inequality, and the cost of living as a current crisis than any other issue.

In France (as in all rich nations that pay unemployment benefits and institute other transfers to ease poverty), as the better-off become wealthier, so the cohort of those who favour reducing unemployment benefits grows. Those who think they should receive more than others, including many people who are in fact quite poor but not unemployed, would (when asked and on average) often happily see unemployment benefits cut. Even in France, many people think that this would lead to a drop in their taxes, making such a cut personally worthwhile. They are unlikely to think of themselves at risk of unemployment, or that any benefits they might receive would be useful. This is despite almost no one in France thinking they are in the best-off quintile. As one report dramatically put it: 'It's a scoop: there is no rich person in France! . . . When the French are asked to position themselves on the income scale, hardly anyone ticks the ninth or tenth decile box.'[20]

You are not free when you are ignorant. If you want to understand why the far-right rose in France, the simplest answer is that enough people thought they were being unfairly treated and that the migrants and poor were better off than them. Cost-of-living crises can be engineered to achieve this. However, if you want to know why the left won the most seats in the French Parliament in July 2024, it is because fewer people are ignorant in France than elsewhere, and that is partly a product of lower economic inequality in France. At least a few people tick the ninth or tenth decile box in France. In the neighbouring UK, citizens' ignorance about the lives of others in their society is far greater than in France.[21] The US knows itself even less well – it is no land of the free.

Equality

In many places in the world, inequalities have been falling of late. In China, there was a great rise in inequality at the start of the current century, but more recently it may have reached a peak – at least according to the World Inequality Database published by the United Nations University.[22] In India, however, inequalities are still rising, and as Lucas Chancel put it recently: 'This is quite spectacular. Policy choices in India over 2016–2021 led to huge economic degrowth for the poorest households (−53% drop in incomes) and huge growth at the top (+39% increase), as per this large household survey. That's "shining India", for the few only.' Indian officials might dispute this.[23]

Poverty is the leading cause of premature mortality worldwide, and the principal driver of poverty is inequality. Poverty and inequality have been a majority concern for a long time. But that concern is because fewer people now see this crisis as inevitable. People often characterise an issue as a crisis because they want it to change and believe it can be addressed. For some people, what may be chronic issues aren't cited as big concerns because they consider them inevitable. A third of the world's people have put inequality in their top three greatest concerns for around a decade. Academic research, and the advocacy of groups such as Oxfam, play a large part in it continuing to be seen as important, but so too does the reality of the lives of most of those who are not in the top 10 per cent. So what should we think about the future prospects for less, or more, economic equality?

Fantastical extrapolations do exist, and at times some of them dominate the global discourse. They range from the bleak belief that the world's billionaires will continue to pull away from the rest of humanity at an ever greater rate, to highly optimistic suggestions that continued economic growth will bring almost all of the world's poorest people out of poverty in a few decades. Neither of these extreme scenarios is likely. It is more likely that inflation will serve to reduce wealth inequalities worldwide by destroying a part of the overall value of wealth.

Around the world, wealth inequalities are almost always higher than income inequalities. Nevertheless, even if wealth inequalities do fall with inflation being a little higher than in recent decades, poverty will remain entrenched because those who benefit from widespread poverty, those for whom poverty provides a cheap workforce and willing borrowers, are unlikely to give up their current economic power without a struggle. But it is just as likely that there will be a struggle. Most young people in the world are now literate, and increasingly highly numerate, and because of access to the internet, people around the globe can now know what is possible and is already occurring elsewhere instantly in way that was impossible just a few decades ago.

Unfortunately, the scope to manipulate the masses has also never been higher. In India, one factor at play is mass manipulation of the population by the current ruling party and its politicians. According to the January 2023 Ipsos survey, just under a quarter of all adults in India rated poverty and social inequality as one of their three key concerns. By December 2023, that proportion had fallen to 19 per cent! The only other countries where the proportion was that low in both months were the US and Saudi Arabia. All three countries tolerate very high levels of inequality. Getting people to overlook an issue, even if it has a major impact on where they live, is one way of allowing it to remain a problem. Nevertheless, in the summer 2024 election in India, just as in France, the political right did worse than had been predicted.

It is not easy to predict how much people in any particular country may be concerned about any one issue, or if they can be fooled or not. Simply knowing how bad that issue is, as compared to the situation in other countries, does not help much. People appear to be more unaware of inequality where it is worse, sometimes because they have been taught that high inequality is somehow natural and good; or that they are told to believe in a caste, class, or aristocratic system as being worth maintaining. Meanwhile, people in countries such as Sweden, France, and Norway, which have low inequality, are greatly concerned about it.

Concern for issues can rise even when the issue is being addressed; especially if the way in which inequalities are addressed is by a levelling down. In the UK there has been a form of de-gentrification in recent years that has hardly been acknowledged as yet. Here is how one commentator explained it:

> The south-east [until recently the most affluent] has seen the biggest fall across the country in disposable income since 2019, with a gap opening up between median income and house prices that far outpaces the rest of England. More recently, some of the country's most expensive mortgages were among those hit hardest after the Truss [2022] Budget. Nor is the county [of Surrey – traditionally the richest] immune from the cost-of-living crisis. Throw in rising unsolved crime levels and a cripplingly expensive commute into the capital, and it's not unreasonable to talk about a wave of de-gentrification taking place not just in Surrey, but across the Home Counties.[24]

Despite the reduction in inequality that levelling down produces, it is initially the poor who suffer most, because even though they may experience the smallest fall in their standard of living, they have the most limited capacity to absorb the impact. In the UK in April 2023, surveys revealed that a third of all adults, the poorest third, were saving money by cutting the amount of healthier food they were eating; a third were spending less time with friends, and a quarter less time with family. A sixth of those surveyed said these changes were already affecting their health, and those who worked said it impacted how well they were able to do their job(s).[25]

Although these numbers are shocking, it is often what people tell researchers that hits home the hardest: 'I'm finding it hard to sleep and just running numbers around my head'; 'I can barely afford to exist'; and 'I'm frightened to think what is next' – they say.

What the poorest in the UK are now thinking about the future, or trying not to think about, are the same concerns that preoccupy the majority of people around the world.

Tellingly, in 2023, it was the best off in the UK – those living in a household with more than £60,000 a year in combined incomes – who thought that the government was doing too little to help. In fact, everyone but the very richest thought that the government should do more.[26] While those at the sharp end are all too aware of the challenges they face, those who are significantly more privileged often do not hesitate to complain about any perceived impact on their economically comfortable lives.

In 2023 in the UK, three-quarters of all adults, and 72 per cent of those who had voted Conservative in the 2019 general election, believed that the very rich – those with £10 million or more in wealth – had too much influence on the political system. Large majorities thought it was highly concerning that poverty was widespread while such wealth was still being amassed. More than two-thirds of adults (and 64 per cent of 2019 Tory voters) thought that the UK government should be taxing the wealthy more. The survey these numbers were taken from was also especially interesting because it found: 'Conservative voters are more, rather than less, likely than the average respondent to believe that accumulating wealth in this way is only possible for some people in society.'[27] Conservative voters tend to be older and may have more experience of seeing who actually benefits in the longer run.

To understand more about why people worry so much about inequality, poverty and cost-of-living issues, above all else and almost everywhere, requires understanding how these problems can rapidly worsen at particular times.

In the 1970s and 1980s, what was called the *return on investments* began to fall, for those with money. This occurred first within Western Europe, then across North America, and then in Japan. It happened because making money out of others could not continue to rise as it had, not least because the world's young population was no longer growing as quickly. Some of those with money moved their investments to places where wages were lower, where unions were absent or constrained, or where population growth was still high and thus future consumption was expected to increase – and also into places where environmental controls on what companies could do were weaker, so greater profits could be made. Of course, greater environmental damage took place under weaker regulation.

At first, the growth in foreign direct investments resulted in new fortunes being brought back to the old countries; but only to those who owned shares in those overseas firms. The stock markets of Western Europe, the US, and Japan boomed. Wealth inequalities widened and income inequalities grew, as those with wealth saw their income from wealth grow too. But wealth also grew for a tiny few in the places where some of this money had moved: to Brazil and much of the rest of the Americas, especially from the US; to India and many of the other former European colonies; to Eastern Europe and Russia; and to China, from Western Europe and the US. Within all those places inequality grew, even as it fell worldwide. In recent years, investments into China from North America and Europe have fallen, while those into China from other South-East Asian countries have risen.[28]

What happens as a result of these movements of money? Sharply rising inequality leads to fears among those at the top that something will break. Top firms employ chief risk officers to tell them what they must do to survive, plan and strategise against crises, and to suggest ways in which the potential crisis that might change things forever can be guarded against. But they should look within their own group, within the elite itself, for where the greatest threat may lie. Revolutions do not often come from the grass roots. In 2024, the political right was blocked from outright victory by better middle-class perspectives on the current cost-of-living, inequality, and poverty crises, both in France (spectacularly) and in India (more mutedly).

At the very end of this book, I discuss Figure 8.1, which demonstrates that it is not just political scientists who know that inequality matters greatly, but also (and perhaps more) those who study society directly – sociologists. In contrast to the sociologists, however, are the economists, many of whom produce a competing narrative, a near-constant stream of work, that casts doubt on the idea that inequality is a significant problem. For example, it is often claimed that inequality is not becoming worse precisely in those places where it has indeed been increasing.

On 2 December 2022, in a programme titled 'Understand: The Economy' broadcast in the UK on BBC Radio 4, a claim was made that inequality in the UK had been falling since the 1990s. A listener commented and on 2 March 2023 their complaint was dismissed by the Executive Complaints Unit (ECU) of the BBC: 'A listener complained the presenter Tim Harford had suggested inequality in the UK was not getting worse and should not be thought of as a problem. The ECU considered whether the programme met BBC standards for due impartiality.'[29] This was despite Mr Harford's comments at the end of the programme, when he said: 'Next time you hear somebody complaining that inequality is getting worse you'll know to ask them which measure they are using and you'll be able to call them out.'

So, what had actually happened to inequality in the UK? Harford was comparing the median incomes of the top and bottom quintiles of the population, using statistical measures that completely exclude the poorest tenth and richest tenth of all people. If you ignore the best-off 10 per cent of people in the UK, who take about 40 per cent of income every year – as the BBC did, based on Harford's chosen statistics – you could indeed claim that inequalities have fallen among the rest of us.

Conservative chancellors have used the same method as Harford in most of the UK budget speeches of the past decade. But the take of the top 10 per cent remained stubbornly high, and even rose between 2010 and 2019. Those of us living in Britain were at peak income inequality when the pandemic hit, and that particular crisis did little to dent it. It was only when the pandemic began to subside in 2023 that inequalities *might* have begun to fall – we do not yet know. The complaint had nothing to do with wealth. Harford was using a very odd, flawed measure of income inequality.

Why would the BBC uphold the suggestion that 'income inequality has been coming down since the 1990s'? I suspect this is because they and their presenters simply believed it to be true. But how could they believe it to be true when it was so easy to see that it was not? The reason they could believe it was that among a very small, very tight circle of people, mostly living in London (and a few, like Harford, in Oxford), this myth had become accepted as truth. As has already been mentioned in relation to India, it is not only the level of inequality that matters, but whether we accept it as an inevitable and unchangeable condition of life. Sadly, some people see inequality as desirable because they think they are worth more than others.

The UK has an abysmal record on inequality, save for a few remarkable decades from the late 1930s to the end of the 1970s.[30] So if you have a rose-tinted view of British history before the 1930s, and its politics since the 1970s, you might believe that high inequality is not a problem, but an indication that some people deserve more than others; that 'tall poppies', as Mrs Thatcher called people like her, should be allowed to grow even taller.

Harford's programme is just one of many examples where establishment organisations, including the BBC, suggest that inequality has not risen, and is not something the public should worry about. Poverty and inequality never feature as subject areas on the BBC news website banner; instead, various wars, the cost of living, and the climate are its staple news topics. Other establishment organisations accept that inequality has increased, but essentially say we just have to live with it.

One reason levels of inequality and poverty are so often ignored by commentators is that it can be difficult to be sure whether they are currently rising or falling. One source suggests that recently, the take of the best-off 1 per cent in the UK may have fallen to 13 per cent of all income, a third of what the entire top tenth take. However, Britain's 1 per cent may have also become better at hiding their income and not declaring it for tax. In Sweden, by contrast, taxation is a far more public affair: anyone can find out how much tax any other individual paid last year, and it is consequently far harder to avoid.[31] What any long-term graph of income inequality shows is that inequalities were terrible everywhere in the nineteenth century, except for a time in the US.

In most Western countries, inequality is now higher as compared to the best times in living memory. So most of us, rightly, worry. Humans are sensitive to slights. They may not know just how much the rich are taking, but they know what they themselves cannot afford.

Fraternity

Today, even in the most equal and fraternal of countries, there are threats to cohesion. In Finland, for example, when the best off are unhappy with their lot in life, a recent report notes that 'the wealthy may strategically retreat from public life and employ other means of political influence'.[32] But others among the very wealthy in Finland, the top 0.1 per cent that are the topic of that report, may also help to protect what has been achieved there.

Finland gives us reason to hope that the richest do not always try to increase inequality and take more for themselves. It is when people have hope that the future will be better. It is where people know that low inequality means that the society they have is better than people in most other countries have, that they are both more fraternal and less affected by inequality and poverty. The rising cost of goods is better shared out among people in a country with more equal incomes, like Finland.

Hope is alive while people refuse to accept their lot, and challenge conservative economists who try to tell them that inequality is not a problem. But not all economists have been so misguided. In 1978, Jan Drewnowski published 'The Affluence Line', which would later become the key academic work on how much is enough: it described a way to calculate the monetary level above which an individual's personal 'consumption need not and should not rise'.[33]

Drewnowski was born in 1908 and died in the year 2000 at age ninety-two; in 1978, he was working in The Hague. He wrote: 'The high incomes and affluent way of life are not incentives to anything that is useful to the society. The opposite opinion is one of those fallacies which are hard to dispel, but the sooner this is done the better.' Despite articulating the problem and providing a theory as to how the affluence line could be determined, however, he did not suggest an actual line.

A generation later, in 2005 in the UK, political theorist Maureen Ramsay reviewed all the evidence she could find, and suggested that the maximum wage in that year should be set at £100,800, or ten times the minimum wage, a sum that was back then only surpassed by 1 per cent of the UK population. She suggested: 'The idea of a maximum wage is a modest proposal because an upper bound on income does nothing to limit personal wealth; it only ensures that wealth would be accumulated less rapidly.'[34]

These proposals slowly rose in popularity to become the subject of ever greater debate, especially on the European mainland after austerity was introduced in the wake of the 2008 financial crash. In 2016, Ingrid Robeyns, then working in Utrecht, explained: 'In a culture where material gain is not the leading incentive, people may also work hard and harder due to commitments, challenges they have set themselves, or intrinsic joys, esteem, or honour.'[35]

Robeyns proposes that we ask ourselves: What does it matter if the very greedy are not willing to work more? Their work is often harmful, from landlordism to playing the stock market, and their profit comes out of the pockets of others. Most academic papers on this issue produce very similar estimates of what a reasonable maximum income should be: around £100,000 or €100,000 a year, with the figure remaining after taxes and housing costs being roughly half that.[36] In Brazil in 2006, researchers suggested that in order to reduce the country's extreme poverty, incomes should be brought down under an affluence line, a figure just under that received by the top 1 per cent richest of the population. The figure was constructed using data from 1999, and those who set it argued that a monthly household income of R$2,170 per capita would be enough for anyone.[37] With inflation, today's figure would be R$10,000 a month, or US$4,000 at purchasing-power parity (£48,000 a year). You may be shocked that the suggested maximum is as low as this, but it is many times what most people in Brazil currently have to live on.

So, how much is too much in Europe or the US? In 2018, Robeyns and her colleagues used data from the Dutch population to identify this figure for the Netherlands. It is interesting that so much work on maximum incomes has been done there. It was the richest place on Earth before Britain's ascendancy. It is also where capitalism began: the Dutch have had a long time to think about how much is too much.

When surveyed in 2018, Dutch people typically believed that no one in the Netherlands could justify having wealth over €2–3 million. On precisely where the line should be set, Robeyns said: 'Women place the riches line at a lower level as well as younger people, and people with lower education. The exception is the relatively small group of people with only primary education, who set the riches line at a higher level.'[38]

The majority of Dutch people find it relatively easy to distinguish between a family that is 'rich' and a family that is 'extremely rich', with a total wealth of about €2.2 million being the most common cut-off between these two groups in the early 2020s. There are specific criteria that help to identify a family as being extremely rich. According to Dutch survey respondents, this includes having a second house or a swimming pool, or savings of at least €1 million.[39]

Perhaps not surprisingly, very affluent people think the line should be set at another – higher – level; not at €2.2 million, but at €1 billion, a sum that is gradually becoming understood as an amount that no one should ever be allowed to acquire. In 2023, the philosopher Julian Baggini wrote: 'A billionaire ban should not be viewed as an extreme measure by anyone who recognises that it is only possible to get extremely rich by extracting more wealth from society than you could ever create by yourself.'[40]

Allowing some people to amass extreme wealth condemns millions of others to live in poverty and debt. At the extremes, the wealth of a few causes entire nation-states to become highly indebted. When interest rates rose in the early 2020s, it was noted that: 'In the current environment of strong interest rate hikes, low-income countries have to spend a high share of their government revenue to service their debt. In Pakistan and Egypt, 50 cents out of every $1 of government revenue goes to interest payments on debt.'[41]

Because it is so hard to defend the holding of a large amount of wealth, or receiving very high income in a year, the very well-off try to avoid talking about it. As soon as you start pointing out how little most people have to get by on, it becomes extremely embarrassing to discuss one's wealth. For example, some four out of five people in the UK think that those working in the early-years sector should be paid more. Most of these workers are nursery assistants, and in 2023 their average hourly pay was £7.42, far below the minimum wage. This was only legally possible because so many of them are young and on an apprenticeship. However, one in ten people in the UK thought it was fine to pay them this little. Of those, a quarter surveyed also agreed with the statement: 'If people don't like the wages that are on offer in the early years sector they can find work elsewhere.' This rose to 34 per cent of all Conservative voters, and more men than women within that group.

A sample of British people were consulted on the statement: 'Increasing wages is important to ensure that children are given the best quality care and education.' The results showed that it was people aged between eighteen and thirty-four with no children and household incomes of £35,001 to £45,000 a year who were most against higher pay for childcare workers.[42] Of those who said that £7.42 an hour was too high, the overall age group with the highest score was thirty-five to forty-nine (16 per cent, compared to 11 per cent for eighteen to thirty-four year-olds). And in respect to incomes, 20 per cent of those in the £70,000–80,000 bracket said the pay was fine or too high, closely followed by those on more than £100,000 (18 per cent)!

Studies such as these help to show us where the limits to fraternity currently lie. It is easier to sympathise with people you see as more like you. But it is also possible to change our views of each other. A growing number of people in a wide variety of countries hold views that challenge the principle 'look after your own', and their attitudes appear to be permeating, now more widely than before. Often such views are presented as new, rather than as part of a long-standing trend, constantly being rediscovered.

In 2023 Daniel Chandler published a book that the former chief economist of the Bank of England, Andy Haldane, greeted as 'energising and timely'.[43] David Miliband, who had been Britain's foreign secretary under New Labour, labelled its message 'clear, brave and compelling'. In *Free and Equal: What Would a Fair Society Look Like?*, Chandler writes approvingly of Belgium's €500 annual limit on individuals' donations to political parties, and suggests that the figure ought to be a little less than that worldwide, with each state matching or exceeding individual donations. Chandler also writes in support of the introduction of universal basic income. He asserts that there is no evidence of economic detriment from very high taxes, but worries that tax rates of over 75 per cent on incomes of over $500,000 a year might encourage tax avoidance. He describes inheritance taxes for billionaires of 80–90 per cent as part of 'our first priority' but shows that – combined with decent income taxes on capital – 'a seemingly low annual wealth tax of 1–2 per cent could see some people paying most if not all of their capital income on taxes'.[44]

Why were so many of Britain's great and good drawn to these ideas, including people who had not advocated such policies so vocally before 2023? One reason might well be that times have been changing rapidly.[45] They might also have been reassured by the fact that Chandler distinguishes his ideal from socialism – although socialism has many meanings. At its heart, it means to be social, to be willing to share.

One simple problem, created and maintained by a selfish minority, is that the rich don't pay much tax. In the UK, only four of the top twenty richest families appear in the list of the hundred families that pay the most in tax. As the article that revealed this explained: 'The vast majority of those in the higher echelons of the Rich List are foreign oligarchs living in the UK, who while multi-billionaires, appear to be paying very little in UK taxes.' This suggests that trying to attract international oligarchs to Britain doesn't benefit public services much, and that the supposed economic benefits of bending over backwards for these people (who are often pretty unsavoury characters) are much less significant than the politicians, lobbyists, and think-tanks that they fund proclaim.

If anything, the key insight from the publication of the rich list is that we should be looking at ways to ensure that such residents make a much more substantial tax contribution in return for being able to enjoy their wealth in the UK. Recent proposals to scrap the non-dom (tax avoidance) status in the UK have now led to action – a positive start in this regard.[46] Whether viewed in combination or separately, the cost-of-living, inequality, and poverty crises are now people's greatest concern worldwide. In one way or another, these economic issues have been with us for a long time – as long as we have been human – but at times of great inequality they rise up our collective agendas, and we see clearly that such problems have as much to do with too much wealth for the few as too little for the many. As the Christian socialist R. H. Tawney put it in 1913: 'What thoughtful rich people call the problem of poverty, thoughtful poor people with equal justice call the problem of riches.'

The problem of riches – what actually makes those costs of living so hard – need not be always with us, and certainly need not worsen and become the next great crisis. Underlying the fear of those costs-of-living is the fear that the rich will take more and more in future. It is a real fear. It is not an impossible outcome. But since this is our current global priority, uppermost in the majority of minds for the 2020s, then we should collectively tackle those who cost us a decent living. The first step to dealing with a problem, is identifying it.

3

Sharing the Work

> *A note to let you know that I accepted yesterday a Voluntary Severance offer and will be leaving the university. I will be unaffiliated and unemployed, but hopefully . . .*
>
> Anonymous, 2023[1]

The second-greatest crisis of the 2020s, according to worldwide polls, was a combination of issues concerning work, unemployment, and immigration. How might we share tasks, the labour to be done? Will there be enough work for us, and for those we care most about, in the very near future? Will others take away what we believe to be our opportunities, or our work – our jobs? Are we, or might we soon become, surplus to requirements?

Unemployment is the largest of this set of fears, but I have also included fear of immigration within this chapter, because in many peoples' minds these issues are linked. In the richer parts of the world, immigration rises to its highest levels in those affluent places where greater inequality increases the demand for cheaper labour, and so people arrive searching for opportunity. But most areas that are home to recent migrants are those closest to places that others have had to flee because of war and other disasters. The overall crisis discussed in this chapter is about whether in future we will be better able to organise ourselves so that we feel valued for what we do and confident that where we currently live will remain a place we can call home. In future, can we collectively become less afraid of an imagined Other, and of not being needed, or will this fear grow?

This is not a new crisis. Exhortations to accommodate others, to be hospitable, and to show kindness to strangers, are found in almost all ancient religious teachings. For millennia, people have tried to teach each other to be less fearful of newcomers. For millennia we have known that such fears are not well founded, which is why those precepts continue to be taught.

Can we find work that is rewarding and safe, and that can keep us occupied and productive until we wish to retire? Or is the idea of security increasingly a pipedream for the large majority, even of the middle classes, across the world? While the greatest crisis today is how we will get by, the second (this one) is about what we might usefully do – and who might prevent us, or our children, or friends, or neighbours, or wider family, or even our entire town or city, from doing it.

These two crises that currently most concern people around the world are clearly closely related. The first is about the cost of living, inequality, and poverty – and in this book they are combined into one issue because they are so closely connected. In this chapter, I will do the same: combining concerns that are so closely connected that they can clearly be seen to be a part of the same greater problem. Statistically, according to the pollsters, we are looking at the third-greatest and twelfth-greatest fears of people worldwide and combining them into the issue of *work*. Around three in ten adults (29 per cent) surveyed globally in 2023 said unemployment was among their top three concerns. The twelfth-greatest concern was immigration, with just over one in ten (11 per cent) putting it in their top three. By July 2024, the former percentage had hardly changed: some 28 per cent put unemployment in their top three greatest concerns. Immigration had risen to be the seventh-greatest concern, however, with 17 per cent saying it was what they found most worrying about the country they lived in.[2]

Numerous examples from recent history show how the issues of migration and unemployment are related. At the end of the nineteenth century, attempts were made to bar immigration from specific countries into the US; similarly the 1905 Aliens Act in

Britain was an effort to control the influx of Jewish people fleeing the Russian pogroms; and prior to 1917, passports were required for migration within the Russian Empire. These were all reactions spawned by fear. Those fears rose again across the rich world during the Great Depression of the 1930s, and again in the 1980s, as a result of global recession. We are now in another great recession, although there is geographical variability in its depth, severity, and the extent to which it is acknowledged as an economic recession.

The boom industry of one age becomes the slump industry of the next. These booms often involve the arrival of many migrants, who often continue to arrive in years when there is less to go around. They may be coming because of ties established in earlier, better times, or because the situation they are leaving is worse, or perceived to be worse, than the one in their destination.

The portrayal of an influx of migrants as a *threat* can be a way to deflect attention from inequality and poverty, and it is often tied in with concerns among the well-off and powerful that their own living standards could be slipping.

It was not until the end of the eighteenth century that ideas of overpopulation became common. It is only when the nature of work changes that we worry about there being too many of us to share it. Stories about overpopulation have often been about the number of people being born, as well as the number of migrants; for example, the poor harvests that immediately preceded the French Revolution helped ignite the idea, expounded by some members of the elite, that there were too many people in the country. The peasants were revolting, it was suggested, because there were just too many of them, and that was the reason they were hungry. The notion of *surplus people* was another way to understand a problem that was otherwise attributed to the heartlessness of a privileged few, Marie Antoinette in particular, who may (or may not) have said, 'Let them eat cake.' A view of the French Revolution as a power struggle between two competing groups of elites, despite being less familiar, is likely closer to the truth than the argument that it was an uprising from below.

In the nineteenth century, the work of Thomas Malthus gave a scientific slant to the prejudice against supposed surplus people. His fantasies, a reaction to revolution in France, were also the result of his unusual perspective from living in or near the richest and largest of cities. Malthus worked in the grand buildings of the East India Company College, just north of London. His workplace is now a boarding school, Haileybury.[3] Malthus was not just affected by his proximity to the teeming multitudes of what was then the world's largest city; he was also preoccupied with maintaining his status and that of his peers.[4] He worried that there were too many children and not enough food to feed them for the current order to prevail. Malthus believed there were insufficient jobs to employ everyone being born, as there was a limit to farmland, and farming was all that he could envisage for the masses. Today, as birth rates drop in many countries, fears over immigration have replaced fears about those hungry, apparently ever-multiplying babies. Immigrants drive down salaries, we are told, and take away jobs. We still find it hard to imagine otherwise.

In truth, however, immigration does not cause unemployment; it is unemployment that causes emigration. People leave areas where there is little opportunity, and they move to places where they think there are more options. If there are no better options when they arrive, they usually move on again. The great majority of people, however, do not emigrate, either because of social ties or because they cannot afford the journey and its potential negative outcomes. This is one reason why jobs remain scarcer in some places than others. The jobs go, but the ties don't, and so folks will remain in an area at least one or two generations after the reason to be there has gone. Eventually a town becomes a ghost town; a remote village that once provided livelihoods is abandoned.

We do not have to worry about there being too many people in future. On 11 July 2024 the United Nations released its latest central population projection, one that will not be updated for another two years. It revealed that the human population of the planet is set to fall in the year 2084, earlier than previously thought because we are now having even fewer children. The only reason why our numbers still grow worldwide is that we continue to live longer, so more of us are around at any one time, even if fewer are being born. Already, across the large majority of the world, there are dwindling numbers of young adults, which means fewer people to do the work that needs to be done.

Automation helps: it takes away monotonous tasks. Artificial intelligence has been helping us for decades. Mechanical looms can be seen as an early version of AI. The calculating machine was certainly a form of artificial intelligence, as, more recently, was the barcode scanner. AI for many years has been doing much of the work of translating documents, albeit by drawing on a vast corpus of work by human translators. All of these innovations have reduced the need for repetitive, if often highly skilled, work. No one today laments that our children cannot make use of their nimble little fingers in textile factories, or that we can no longer make a career out of being adept at doing long division by hand. Students at my university can now produce tutorial essays using AI, ones which, with a little judicial editing, can fool any tutor. One day we may be clever enough as a species not to ask them to write such essays anymore.[5]

There are fewer and fewer of us needed to do repetitive work. So, will work now become more interesting? In future, if work is not interesting, but has to be done by a human, it is hoped that we will pay a high price for such labour – given the diminishing supply of people. However, none of these predictions offer any succour to those concerned about their jobs right now, or to those who fear that artificial intelligence and other forms of automation will rob their children of opportunity.

Step back a little. If people tell you they are concerned about the slight changes that migration, in and out, makes to the balance of people living in any one area, ask them to think about the entirely predictable short-term influence of the decline in birth rates, worldwide, on that balance. Suggest they think about what we know about how even small changes in birth rates can have big effects on the opportunities available to people. Migration often evens out our problems. It is usually a search for greater security, sometimes also for adventure. After all, fears for the future come partly from a sense of jeopardy in the present. Work does not often set you free or make you happy; and neither does your pay, the subject to which we will turn next. But going somewhere different – doing something different – can be invigorating.

For a person who has just been made redundant, the claim that work does not set you free will sound trite. Not having enough income to live on makes you miserable, but having more than enough does not make you happy – and security often matters more than money. A sense of economic security comes through feeling, and being, safe. As economists Richard Easterlin and Kelsey O'Connor – associate editor of the *Journal of Happiness Studies*, no less – have explained: 'Countries can have rising, constant, or falling trends in happiness.'[6] But the positive trends tend to follow other factors, such as policies for reducing fear, increasing solidarity, and finding purpose – all of which increase happiness.

Easterlin is that rare academic who has two phrases named after him. The Easterlin Paradox is the term for his finding that people don't become happier as the place they live in gets richer; at least, this is the case if wealth is measured using economists' methodologies. The second is the Easterlin Effect or Easterlin Hypothesis, which suggests that if you are born into a smaller birth cohort, it will be easier for you to find a good job and other opportunities later in life.

All else being equal, if you are born in a place where the number of children is falling, and where inequalities are neither high nor rising, and the standard of living is generally high, your lot in life may be easier. Worldwide, this is the situation for the majority of people being born today. The advantages include everything from being able to find a home to starting a family and choosing a job you prefer. The mechanism is simple: there are more homes per person as the number of people falls, and often just as much or more work to be done, not least in providing for the elderly but also as we invent new kinds of work. Universities are now a mass industry. They employed only a tiny number of people worldwide, when I was born.

All is never equal, however, and birth cohort effects are just one of a plethora of impacts on our lives. Studies produced in the 1990s claimed that the Easterlin Effect had become less pronounced, perhaps because, by then, more people had to take any job they could, no matter how bad the pay.[7] This pressure, and the apparent absence of the small-birth-cohort benefit was a result of rising economic inequality, which reduces the positive benefit of belonging to a smaller birth cohort (the studies were undertaken in the US). Those with power and money might still exploit you, even if there are fewer of you, and even if each of you might be more valuable due to the growing scarcity of younger humans.

In many of the richest places on Earth, there have never been so few people being born. Furthermore, in the very large majority of the world today, young adults' birth cohorts have never been so small in comparison to how many older people there are. In a minority of the richer parts of the world, the size of families has been falling for three or even four generations. The young have never been so well educated. So, we are left with a perplexing question. Why does youth unemployment persist where there are so few young people, especially as they are so capable? Recent surveys show that never before have so many young people felt surplus to requirements, and are struggling to gain meaningful employment, or hold on to any job at all for any reasonable length of time. So it is no wonder that the search for work is the second-greatest crisis of our times.

Unemployment and jobs

Within Europe there is a huge variation in the extent to which people fear unemployment. In December 2023, unemployment was one of the top three greatest concerns of 40 per cent of people in Spain, 25 per cent in Italy, 15 per cent in France, 13 per cent in the UK, and just 9 per cent in Germany. By July 2024, those percentages were very similar (35 per cent, 33 per cent, 10 per cent, 14 per cent, and 8 per cent). So, a fear of unemployment, coupled with concern over immigration, features high overall, but can also be very geographically specific, and can rise or fall quickly over time. In Spain and Italy people now have very few children, partly because of uncertainty about the future, and partly due to high youth and younger-adult unemployment in those two countries.

The international numbers fluctuate, occasionally quite substantially in a short space of time as other worries rise, or folks are told that their country's economy is doing better. Factors such as a change in government or even a football win may alter the national mood. Additional reasons for fluctuations are chance and sampling error. But the total proportion of people who place unemployment as a top three concern remains fairly steady, so that the global figures change much more slowly and by far less than local measures of concern over jobs. A small part of that reason will be that as jobs are lost in one part of the world they are gained in another; although that is not the key reason for the significant variations among nations on this issue.

Concern over unemployment is not just about being without work. It is also about the repercussions on individuals and families of not having work. In some countries, those without work are well looked after by the state. In other places, work is plentiful partly because the state ensures near full employment. In the UK and US, by contrast, unemployment is low because people have to work, even if their work does not help them to escape poverty. Most poor families have working parents. In March 2023, when people in Britain were asked to list three things that mattered most for government spending, the NHS was cited by more than two-thirds (69 per cent); cost-of-living support by nearly half (49 per cent), and social care by a quarter (25 per cent).[8] No other issues were as important to those surveyed.[9]

In the same month, March 2023, when people in the US were polled, their second and third top government-spending priorities were increasing the size of the military (43 per cent) and increasing aid to the poor (43 per cent); but their top priority was reducing government spending (57 per cent).[10] People's priorities often reflect their media consumption. Tell them that their country's military is too small, even if it is the largest in the world, and many will say it needs to be larger. Explain that huge numbers of their compatriots are poor, not just those they can see with their own eyes, and concern for the poor grows. Tell them that government is too big and they will ask for it to be smaller, while simultaneously and paradoxically asking for two areas of government spending to increase. It is not hard to hold contradictory views, especially when the views you hold are given to you by others. All of our views are in one way or another given to us by others. Right now, I am influencing you and I, in turn, was influenced by others. You and I both have individual agency to decide what we pass on, but usually not as much as we might believe.

Within a country, people's views are highly variable. While almost half of US citizens may have thought in the spring of 2023 that more should be spent on the poor, another quarter said that 'government should provide less assistance'. The latter group were more likely to be Republicans, but Republicans' views also vary greatly by both age and income. Younger and lower-income voters are more likely than older and higher-income Republicans to say that the government should provide more assistance to those in need.[11] Generalisations should be treated with caution. Some people with great privilege have very little fear of unemployment for themselves and those close to them, and a few even see it as a useful way to ensure that the poor are willing to work.

If you are not afraid that you will never again find work, it can come as a shock to discover how many people in the world list unemployment in their top three concerns. But unemployment is a very rational fear. In the recent past, in living memory, there have been times of far too little work. This has nothing to do with a fear of artificial intelligence, but the mundane reality of factory gates shutting permanently, or work-from-home job opportunities drying up, and in many cases disappearing for good when opportunity moves elsewhere around the globe. It is a fear of being left behind.

Sharing the work available is the second-greatest worry of people around the world, because the fear of unemployment, or of only being able to secure a low-paying and precarious job, or several temporary jobs, is so real for so many of us. The fear that the good jobs are gone, or going, is also the fear of poverty. The fear is also about having no, or very little, personal value; of being redundant.

You can force people to work: you simply starve them into it. In the rich world, the US and UK excel at this. Some 2.5 million *more* people were in work in the UK in 2019 than in 2008, a third of them self-employed and one million of them on zero-hour contracts. Such contracts hardly existed in 2008. This increase in employment was achieved by increasing fear, and it certainly has not increased happiness.

In the 1980s and since, Detroit has become the most famous of thousands of American industrial centres that have turned into semi-ghost towns. Today, almost one in ten jobs in the wider (greater) Detroit area is in tourism: people come to see it shrink! The report documenting this also claims: 'One can visit Detroit and the once bustling but now abandoned resorts of the Catskills and decide for oneself which is creepier.'[12]

In the US, if you do not work, and particularly if you do not work in a well-paying job, then you will not have adequate health insurance, and you may simply die if you fall ill. It is not just *you* who may die through being unable to afford life-saving care; if you do not have private health insurance, your children may end up at the back of the queue in the hospital or will never be allowed into a 'good' hospital. And it is not just you who will go hungry, but your children will too. No wonder official unemployment rates are so low in the US. Many people work because of fear.

To understand why getting work is such a great concern for so many people in the world today, consider the strange and extreme example of the UK.[13] Well over thirty years ago, Prime Minister John Major asserted that British people had little to fear: that in the 2050s the country's citizens would still be playing that odd English game, county cricket, in which nothing much happens and no one really cares what the result is.[14]

When Major made his observations on fear, the country he led was in a crisis over its status as a member of the European Community, and he complained about the metaphorical knives of his Conservative political colleagues repeatedly stabbing him in the back. Britain was just emerging from the sustained mass unemployment of the 1980s, and youth unemployment was especially high. Unemployment was the fate of far more of the children I went to school with than of their parents or grandparents.[15] One of the strategies politicians used to counter the widespread fear of unemployment was to claim that there was something exceptional about the UK – and to pretend that people were arriving to take our jobs and that this state of affairs was worse than it was in other countries. Throughout my lifetime, anti-immigration rhetoric has risen and risen. Thankfully so has anti-racism.

Even when unemployment fell to some of the lowest levels ever recorded, the British never stopped worrying about it, or about immigrants. Perhaps talking about cricket was an attempt to soothe fears of an uncertain future. Sixteen years after Major's paean to a somewhat imaginary vision of Britain, Prime Minister Gordon Brown attempted a similarly patriotic approach with the slogan: 'British Jobs for British Workers'.[16]

Let's be clear: when it comes to levels of employment, immigration is completely beside the point. Lack of work can cause emigration, but it does not attract immigrants. In fact, Britain is exceptional for all the wrong reasons. For many decades now, it has had the lowest social spending in relation to average earnings in Europe, and, for the affluent, the lowest tax regime of any large country in Europe. That is a key reason why most people in Britain are so badly off when they are out of work.

Unemployment is greatly feared when the consequences of being unemployed are so bad. But just 14 per cent of British respondents listed unemployment as one of their greatest fears by July 2024, because there are now other things that they fear more – not least being forced to do low-paid work. It could be argued that the British are not good at sharing – or, more plausibly, that the political landscape has made them worse at sharing than they should be. The same is true for many people in the US.

The principal way in which we share resources is through taxation. How we choose to tax work affects what other work is done. It is tax policy that mostly determines not only levels of inequality, but also the number and quality of public sector jobs. The crisis of not sharing the work includes not employing enough people on public money to do what most needs to be done: to maintain a healthcare system, an education system – to maintain and renew the social fabric. These are the people who administer and maintain social housing; employ too few of them and social housing falls into disrepair. They are the people who provide social care to elderly people, to the sick, and for children in trouble. In decent societies, public servants tend to us when we are sick or lost. They clean our streets, tend our parks, watch over our safety, design the master plans for our cities, and ensure our roads are as safe as they can be. They make sure our water is clean to drink and always available, and that our food is not adulterated. Reduce the size of the state, and you reduce the civility of a society.

The UK is the example I will use to illustrate concerns about sharing the work because it is the place I know best, and because it illustrates what happens when fear is fostered, and how (apparently) near full employment is not a solution to a crisis when so much of that employment is coerced. Today the UK has very little unemployment; however, because it experienced mass unemployment in the 1980s and high unemployment for many years in the 1990s, there is latent fear that can be targeted. Politicians dealt with the lack of jobs by reducing the power of unions so that new jobs could be very badly paid. When membership of the European Community became a further barrier to reducing rights at work (and to damaging others' living conditions), the campaign to 'take back control' by those who already had the most power grew stronger, and significant members of the rich and powerful argued for Brexit.

Many people in the UK have a great fear of unemployment even if they do not list it among their top three. There is a general sense that if you lose your job, the state will not look after you. The social failures of Brexit are, in one sense, just part of a long history of social failure in a UK dominated by England, and an England dominated by the richest – people who typically have at least one home in London (but only in certain parts of London).

The powerful and wealthy who supported Brexit promised there would be work in future if immigrants could be kept out, taxes could be kept low, and the UK remained wary of its European neighbours. The British government that came to power in 2024 has continued its predecessor's tradition of acquiescence towards the rich and powerful, and promises a better future if immigrants can be held back, even if it no longer intends to fly some of them to Rwanda. It has continued to advocate low taxing and low sharing, and remains cautious over interacting too much with the strangers across the narrow English Channel. The UK has come to epitomise a wider crisis about sharing out the work. Despite its anti-immigrant rhetoric – in fact very possibly because of it – the new 2024 government found itself dealing with some of the largest and most numerous far-right riots in British history within a month of taking office.

The British have been told that their taxes are high and have risen in recent years to new heights; but what rises there were mainly affected the poorest, and taxes are still lower than almost everywhere else in Europe. Taxes rose both because the population was ageing, and because of mismanagement. Both as I write now, in 2024, and when I wrote at the time of the Brexit referendum in 2016, no other large European country levied *as little in direct taxes* as the UK. While income tax is relatively low in Britain, however, the poor pay very highly in indirect taxation, including through VAT and taxes on some goods they consume.

But the UK's poor had so little money that those taxes did not raise enough to sustain a well-functioning state. Things slowly fell apart from the 1980s onwards. The British establishment blamed foreigners – immigrants and the European Union; the latter was held responsible for allowing immigration and imposing weird EU rules – rules that mostly existed in the imagination of journalist-turned-politician Boris Johnson.

Thus, the latent fear of unemployment in the UK and US – two countries where other fears are greater, but being out of work is still a huge concern – is primarily because benefits are so low. You have to take any job on offer. The same is true in the vast majority of poorer countries worldwide, but less often in rich ones. Germany and the Netherlands, for example, whose citizens have the least fear of unemployment, have a relatively high tax take from the very well paid, as compared to the taxes raised on the same highly paid groups in the UK.[17] But where those two countries also differ from the UK is in the taxes still being levied at normal rates on the low paid, most of whom are not as badly paid as their counterparts in Britain. Therefore, in the Netherlands and Germany, far more people contribute through work taxation, and get more back from the state in return: not just more in terms of being insured if they become unemployed, but in the fact that state education is so good that there is almost no private school sector. In those countries your children will not have to leave their school if you lose your job. In those countries there is less fear, and the work is more equitably distributed.

Politicians try to reassure their electorate that nothing much is changing for the worse, and, at the same time, that the future will be better. Despite the long shadow of old fears, we have a tendency to remember the past differently, and more positively, than the reality. The past was often not very wonderful at all – and we can be persuaded to see places as unique, when their circumstances are actually much more like those of other places. The

UK may be unusual within Europe, but there are other places very like it elsewhere in the affluent world, with similarly high levels of inequality and callousness. Our crises usually have much in common. Even countries where those polled tend to respond more positively about their current situation, or feel it is improving, have many problems. There is no place that is entirely safe from worries, and even our rose-tinted recollections of the past can be punctured if we look back more carefully. All this fear is very understandable when put in context.

In the UK, the great rise in inequality of the 1980s was begun by a surge in unemployment, and it reached a plateau with another recession and a shorter period of high youth unemployment in the 1990s. Similar trends occurred elsewhere, but were managed differently. These events created a fear that made people compliant; it is a fear whose shadows live on in social surveys. In the UK a seventh of all adults routinely list unemployment among their three greatest concerns. In the US, even more people greatly fear unemployment: a sixth of all adults there listed it in their top three worries in 2023 and 2024. An engineered rise in inequality in both the US and the UK during and after the 1980s was not just useful to encourage people to take any jobs on offer but has also been used to stoke fears of immigration, and the fear that immigrants would take people's jobs and homes and swamp their communities.

Immigration

The beginning of 2024 saw a flurry of articles published about the number of elections to be held around the world that year. One writer predicted: 'This time around, it will be a contest between competing fears of rising temperatures, immigration, inflation, and military conflict.'[18] He was referring to an analysis that suggested temperature rises would be a key electoral issue – but the data had been gathered in response to the survey question: 'Which of the following issues has, over the past decade, most changed the way you look at your future?' In other words, the survey made a distinction between what was most important to respondents and what 'most changed the way you look at your future'. Furthermore, the study showed huge geographical variations:

> Voters in Germany, for example, felt immigration was the most transformative crisis (31%), whereas in France it was climate change (27%). In Italy and Portugal, both of which were badly affected by the 2008 financial crash and ensuing Eurozone crisis, a plurality (34%) of respondents said worldwide economic turmoil and the rising cost of living were paramount among their concerns.

The specific way a question is asked matters greatly. When trying to identify the greatest crisis today, so as to prepare for the next crisis, we have to consider the framing of the questions asked in surveys such as these.

People's concerns about unemployment are often reflected in what they say about 'the economy'. Unequal countries are all, without exception, unhappy countries. A local crisis that apparently affects only one place can often be better understood as a symptom of a significant global crisis. Temperatures are rising around the planet. But immigration, inflation, and (at times) military conflict all give rise to more local, immediate fears. The fear of immigration is a fear of losing out. The fear of inflation is a fear of being poor. The fear of others – of losing control of your country's borders, of being unable to 'take back control' – is a fear of imaginary monsters.

To return to our UK example, in the years leading up to the 2015 decision by Prime Minster David Cameron to hold a referendum on withdrawing from membership of the European Union, the UK had faced a series of challenges.[19] Since 2011, however, only four issues were ever mentioned by a majority of people polled by YouGov as one of their top three greatest concerns: health; immigration; the economy; and the UK's membership of the European Union. The focus on just these four was remarkable, given the 416 YouGov polls that asked questions about fears and their importance in this period.[20] These four top issues are shown in the graph in Figure 3.1. Apart from isolated periods when Brexit, and then the COVID-19 pandemic, became the key issue, the economic situation and immigration were clearly and consistently the main concerns for most people – and the only two ever-dominant main concerns.

The UK is an illustration of the crisis caused by not sharing out the work that needs to be done. For the British, it was not just 'the economy, stupid', it was 'those immigrants'. For many decades, immigration had been the first or second most salient issue at the time of any UK-wide general election (see Figure 3.1). Only the economy could supersede it, although prior to the global financial crisis of 2008, it rarely did. But the *economy* really meant the threat of unemployment or very poorly paid employment. Even then, the economy only topped the polls through to 2013, after which immigration and people seeking asylum once again became the greatest concern of the highest number of voters.

The UK had fared spectacularly badly in the global financial crisis of 2008, because of earlier financial deregulation – the so-called Big Bang of 1986 – that had diverted so much investment into finance, and subsequently because of British politicians continuing to favour the banking sector, including unerring support of financiers becoming filthy rich by the New Labour government of 1997–2010. But the public were told that all of this mattered less than the number of immigrants. The reasons why roughly half the population of the UK believed that immigration and asylum were one of the three most important problems facing the UK in the period 2011–15 have been covered by many studies of racism, populism, and journalism.

By 23 June 2015, only a minority of the British public listed 'the economy' as one of the top three issues that most concerned them. As Figure 3.1 shows, immigration fears rose to first place in the year before the 23 June 2016 referendum.

If you believe in securing power while intervening to improve the lives of people as little as possible, and if your aim is to divert attention away from rising inequality and the real reasons for

Figure 3.1: 'Tick up to three issues' – what people care most about, UK, 2011–24

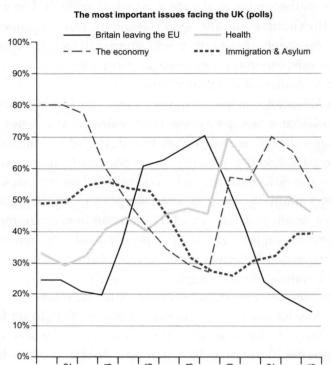

Source: Data series as accessed on 18 July 2024 from the YouGov archive: yougov.co.uk/topics/education/trackers/the-most-important-issues-facing-the-country

growing problems in schools, housing, and health, then you will both blame and condemn immigration. And you will especially persecute asylum seekers and label them 'illegals'. You will also try your hardest to make people afraid of the very small boats in which the desperate people you have demonised attempt to land on British shores, once all safe routes have been closed to them.

In summary, those politicians and their paymasters who wanted a minimal night-watchman state had learnt over the course of a century that blaming immigration for problems was beneficial to their cause.[21] Because we do not have data for 1905, when the antecedents of the British Union of Fascists stoked similar fears, or data for the 1930s, when Oswald Mosley was the fascist leader (and when unemployment first rose to record highs worldwide), we cannot be certain that the strategies in the lead-up to the Brexit referendum caused the highest level of incitement to hatred ever seen in the UK. But it was recently very high indeed because the haters were (by their logic) successful.

The UK offers a particularly sobering account of how right-wing politicians use fear of immigration to get what they want. Brexit was one example. But Brexit was not caused simply by a social failure to welcome other people coming to help the UK economy function; nor was it the direct result of Britain having become the most unequal large state in Europe (by income), and then becoming the most unequal of all, apart from Bulgaria. Instead, Brexit reflected a combination of crises coming to the fore: fears over the results of high inequality; concerns about sharing out work fairly; and a terror – fired up among some British people – of immigrants.

Rising terror of immigration in the UK was partly the result of people having already experienced for eight years falling living standards, and incessantly being told the myth that curtailing immigration by leaving the EU might solve that. In the event, Brexit helped both prolong and then accelerate that collapse. The actions taken during the brief forty-nine days of the Liz Truss government of 2022 mean that the current UK pay crisis is very unlikely to end any time soon. Even by 2027, real wages will still be lower in Britain than they were in 2008 – as the British trade unions (TUC) predicted in 2022 and again in 2023 – because until September 2023 prices were still rising faster than wages and inflation was not slowing as quickly as expected.

As a result of manufactured fears about immigration, it will take many more years than British politicians hoped to get the state back to the level of prosperity it had enjoyed in 2008.[22] In the meantime, they are blaming immigration. One type of immigration is apparently such a problem that in July 2024 British Prime Minister Sir Keir Starmer decided to commit £84 million to measures including 'taking the smuggling gangs down' – as if politics were a game of football where hard tackles are laudable.[23] A few weeks after he made that statement, far-right racist riots spread around the country, resulting in thousands of arrests and the attempted murder by arson of hundreds of asylum seekers housed in temporary accommodation. The so-called crisis of immigration and asylum is a fabricated bogeyman – a highly effective one for the far-right.

Without immigration, of course, the failing British state would have been even worse off. Britain is not a failed state, but it is a good example of a rich state that is failing on many fronts.[24] Were it not for immigration, the UK's health service would be even more inadequately staffed, the population would have declined, schools would have neither enough pupils nor enough staff in all employment grades to run them well, and most new housing would not have been built or maintained.

Just because a crisis is fabricated does not mean it is not real in people's minds. Nonetheless, after Brexit, immigration into the UK rose, especially from outside the EU. This more than compensated in absolute numbers for the declining in-flow from the EU, but it did not compensate for the skills lost.[25] Whether the UK will gain from this shift in the long run is doubtful, as fewer new arrivals are being given rights to stay and settle. Similarly, how far the new immigrants will benefit is also not yet obvious; nor is it clear to what extent the places that they have emigrated from will stand to gain or lose. But, in the summer of 2024 and sadly, probably, for some years to come, arriving or just living in the UK could be a terrifying experience, especially if your skin is not white or your accent is not local.

What we can say, with certainty, is that net immigration to the UK has not fallen, as was promised by the Conservative government, 'to the tens of thousands'. It did not fall at all in the wake of Brexit, although net immigration would have fallen if more people with UK passports had been able to emigrate and take jobs in mainland Europe. The influx to the UK is further proof that calls for migration controls in affluent countries such as the UK are always trumped by the real demand for people who will more willingly and ably do the often poorly paid, insecure, difficult work that locals do not usually want to do or cannot afford to do because they can't live on the wages – and by coming they replace the children that were not born in the UK in the past.

For decades it has been relatively easy to predict future net migration into and out of the UK simply by looking at the national record of births.[26] According to that pattern, the main reason for the recent increase in immigration is that it has been compensating for the years in which birth rates were lower than replacement rates (in the 1980s and 1990s). Figure 3.2, below, illustrates how birth-cohort size in Sweden influences immigration and emigration in the long term. Similar accounts exist for other countries in Europe, North America, and elsewhere in the more affluent parts of the world. Because they do not realise this, some pundits tell stories about migrants that simply are not true: about why they come, what they contribute, and what happens when they don't come any more.

One of the promises made by those arguing for Brexit was that it would secure a better economy for future generations. After the vote in June 2016, I travelled around England and gave roughly one hundred public talks on Brexit, almost all in areas in the south of the country where a majority of people had voted to leave the EU. What I learnt was that the elderly, who were those most likely to attend the talks, said they voted to leave not for themselves, but for the sake of their children and grandchildren. They could not see these generations having a better future unless something changed – and they were offered only one option for change: vote to leave the EU. Because most of them did not live in marginal seats, their participation in general elections was unlikely to have an impact. If they voted Conservative there were almost always enough other Conservative voters where they lived for their vote not to matter, as the seat was hardly ever marginal. Although in many places that was no longer the case by July 2024 – to the shock of many.

Since Brexit, the UK has continued to languish economically. In contrast, by 2023, more than a dozen EU or single-market members were richer or far richer than the UK. In terms of GDP per capita, measured using purchasing power parity (PPP) for comparability, at the time of writing these were: Austria, Belgium, Denmark, Finland, France, Germany, Iceland, Ireland, Luxembourg, the Netherlands, Norway, Sweden, and Switzerland. People in those countries are unquestionably better off than their counterparts in the UK, and in each case the gap with the UK has been widening continuously since Brexit.[27] In fact, the entire Eurozone had become 3 per cent better off than the UK in real terms by 2023, despite including a great many countries poorer than the UK in terms of GDP per capita. By the summer of 2024 the UK appeared (from the perspective of mainland Europe) to be in a state of disarray, and according to some commentators in the US, to be on the verge of civil war.[28]

So why do people still move to the UK, despite its increasing poverty, despite its framing of immigration and the sharing-out of work as crises, and despite its recent riots and deteriorating standards of living? There are both short-term and long-term reasons. The former are more obvious: people come because they are fleeing a war; because of the long-established reputation of the UK as a prosperous land; because they already have family or friends there; and because they have learnt English, perhaps among many other languages, and cannot face having to try to learn one more and never really fitting in.

The longer-term reasons are more interesting. Migrants to countries such as England and Wales come because they can fill holes in the social fabric, with the right aged people to make a place work. Who comes and stays, and who is born in a place but leaves, make up the current patterns of migration that reflect past patterns of births or of not having children. In 2009, I used a quantitative extrapolation to create this theory to understand such patterns for the UK, but it is easier to understand if we take a simpler example, Sweden, which has the longest high-quality record of data in the world on births, deaths, and, by implication, migration.[29]

Figure 3.2 shows two lines. The higher line shows how many children in Sweden were born each year since the early 1750s, with the number of births given on the right-hand axis. The lower line shows how many people, net, of that single year's birth cohort entered and left Sweden between the time of their birth, and their death. The graph ends in 1910, as almost everyone born in 1910 is now dead, and so we have a complete record. What you can see is that as births began to rise in Sweden, more of those born in the higher birth-rate years emigrated. Look closely, and you will see

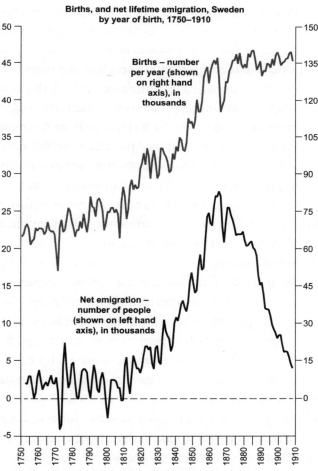

Figure 3.2: How size of birth cohort influences immigration and emigration

Source: The Human Mortality Database, accessed 18 July 2024 from mortality.org. Note: the migration figures have been adjusted by one pass of binomial smoothing to allow for timing differences.

that for those born in unusually small birth cohorts, such as in the late 1860s, fewer (net) left.

Sweden, like the UK, became a net-immigration country shortly after 1910, but that is not shown in the graph as those birth cohorts are not yet complete.[30] In short, people tend to leave a place when there are more of them than needed, and settle in a place where there is space for them. This is what humans have always done. What is new is the stoking-up of a fear that too many people will come to places where, for many decades, not enough babies have been born for that community to cope without immigration in the future.

Fear of immigration resulting from the belief that there are mass exoduses of people from particular areas of the world is not just a creation of the political right. Environmentalists and sometimes even those with more progressive politics stir it up, often inadvertently, when they express concerns about the near future. Take this example from historian Adam Tooze: 'Climate modelling from 2020 suggests that within half a century about 30% of the world's projected population – unless they are forced to move – will live in places with an average temperature above 29°C. This is unbearably hot. Currently, no more than 1% of Earth's land surface is this hot, and those are mainly uninhabited parts of the Sahara.'[31]

The implication here is that almost a third of humanity will soon live in such conditions and so millions of people are about to move to escape. But the population levels cited here are *projected* – figures reached largely by how many people will be born in a place if nothing else changes. Those who can move are only ever a small minority – there is almost never an exodus of huge numbers of people.

Tooze's story of a triple inequality crisis continues with what, at first reading, is a lament about the unfairness of who is causing the most pollution. On closer inspection, it also looks like concern about these *others* coming to where *we* live; that is not what he is saying, but it is how some might read it. When it comes to how much pollution each human in the world contributes towards enhanced global warming, as Tooze explains: 'Those at the very bottom of the pile barely register at all. Mali's per capita CO_2 emissions are about one-seventy-fifth of those in the US. Even if the lowest-earning third of the global population – more than 2.6 billion people – were to raise themselves above the $3.20-a-day poverty line, it would increase total emissions by a mere 5% – that is, one-third of the emissions of the richest 1%.'

Imagine doing this same exercise in 1823 rather than 2023, when Tooze was writing – but of thinking of a less restricted future for the poorest third, or even of them being like the rich. What if the poorest inhabitants of a European city had each owned as many horses as the rich: how on Earth would all those horses be fed? Where would they be stabled? What would be done with their dung? Hearing all these questions, you might have swiftly concluded that the only way to avert societal breakdown would be for all those poor people to have fewer children. But what you should have concluded was that horse-drawn travel within cities was as unsustainable then as the motor car is today. For most cities in the world, something entirely new would soon be moving the majority of people around – public transport.

In 1823, Thomas Malthus, mentioned at the start of this chapter, submitted an entry to the *Encyclopaedia Britannica*. It was based on a text he had written many years earlier, *An Essay on the Principles of Population*. He had been adapting it to try to make it stand up to various critiques, and at this time he was working on changes to what would become the essay's sixth edition. Within the very first draft of the essay for which he is known, Malthus had argued: 'Natural inequality of the two powers, of population, and of production of the earth, and that great law of our nature which must constantly keep their effects equal, form the great difficulty that appears to me insurmountable in the way to the perfectibility of society.'[32] His was a simple message: that there was some natural law limiting human numbers, as if we were rabbits running out of grass to eat on a small island. The reality turned out to be rather different.

We can look back at Malthus for a lesson in the dangers of making assumptions about the future based on the way things are now. He compared English wealth with Chinese poverty in the first edition of his essay. Of course, he had no ability to prophesy – there was no reason why he should have foreseen the much later economic decline of England or the rise of China. Similarly, he could not have known how effective both contraceptives and farming techniques would become. In 1973, just half a century ago, China was home to the largest mass of the poorest people on Earth. Imagine what might have been said about China's future then, had we known just how much global temperatures would increase between 1973 and 2023? Would we have made a similar statement to the one that Tooze made in 2023, about China in 1973 – warning of the harm its rise would cause?

Tooze claims that the poorest on the planet are powerless: that they are being bypassed, and that this is new. But they may not be as powerless as we think. The poor may not make up the vast majority of humanity in the near future. Look to China to see what is possible in terms of lifting people out of poverty. Escaping poverty does not mean becoming rich. It is not about being able to travel by plane. Only a tiny minority in this world ever fly, let alone in private planes. Tooze concludes:

> This is the historic novelty of the current situation. As we run ever closer to the edge of the environmental envelope – the conditions within which our species can thrive – the development of the rich world systematically undercuts the conditions for survival of billions of people in the climate danger zone. They are not so much exploited or bypassed as victimised by the climactic effects of economic growth taking place elsewhere. This violent and indirect entanglement is new in its quality and scale.

What is also quite new, and which Tooze overlooks, is how few children both the rich and the poor are having, and how the supply of young labour is shrinking. Having fewer children – having that choice – means the poor being personally a lot more powerful than before.

Tooze's claim is easily countered. He writes of 'entanglement' that is either direct and violent, or indirect but with equally if not more devastating consequences; however, such things are not very new. From the deaths of tens of millions in the Americas following the introduction of Old World human diseases, through to four hundred years of transatlantic slavery and the British-made famines in India in the nineteenth century, and the twentieth-century impoverishment of Africa, or the great famine in China at the end of the 1950s, the severity and scale of the impact of the decisions made by one set of humans on another set, often far away, has always been staggering. What is new is the very rapid demographic shifts we are living through, as well as how widespread knowledge of the current imbalance now is.

Telling your political supporters that there is not enough to share around and that you will make sure they are prioritised is an age-old ploy. In the spring of 2023, when a survey was held in an atmosphere of growing racist rhetoric, some 40 per cent of British Conservative supporters agreed that even genuine refugees should not be allowed to have their case for asylum considered by the UK. It is possible that some of them did not understand the question. It is also possible that some British Conservative supporters did understand and agreed with it all the same – that some thought that refugees simply meant black people and they were happy with any form of racism. It is likely that some had been conditioned to respond as they did by the news and TV channels they consume, and what their friends, family, and neighbours say. But what matters most when considering this crisis is that more than two-fifths of the British public believe the assessment of refugees' claims to be an indulgence. It is important to note that the UK receives trivial numbers of refugees as compared to most European countries. This is not about numbers, but about fear of the future.

When it comes to the great concerns of our times, one person's worry may be another's hope. If the UK had a better system of social security, then more people would be able to be unemployed for some time. The furlough payments of 80 per cent of salary introduced during the pandemic for those who could no longer work are, in some European countries, simply what you receive by right, for a time, when you are out of work. If we in the UK planned better, then we would have some idea of what shape our cities would take in future. We could even plan for a higher total population than we have now, living in cities where there is less need to use cars. You may think this utopian, but that decline in car use has already occurred in Japan over the past half century.

For many people, immigration is a boon, not a curse. For those seeking a better, different life, whether safer or more adventurous, moving to live in another country is a huge decision, and rarely taken lightly. Migrants choose a destination they believe is worth the effort. In many cases, immigrants make the place: almost all the major cities of the world only continue to exist and are restocked in this way. London has always been a city only sustained by immigration.

Many industries rely on migration. The short-term movement of people is the bedrock of tourism. Medium-term moves make possible the continued existence of many universities (including my own). Long-term migration is now almost always necessary if a large new enterprise is to work (or an old university is to have enough new employees); the local area can rarely provide enough new workers. The UK exploits migrants by allowing them to be paid less and, since the year 2023, has (now legally) treated many as guest workers. There are many examples of countries with larger-than-average immigration rates that have formal systems of exploitation: the local population would not tolerate their own children being treated that way.

There is a web of migrant exploitation around the world, from the South Asian guest workers who make it possible for the oil states in the Middle East to operate, to the Mexicans and others from Central and South America who clean and tidy the US, to the migrants from Africa that Europe increasingly relies on to do the most essential of jobs: running the basic infrastructure of its cities, harvesting its crops, and looking after the old. Everywhere, security guards tend to be immigrants. Countries in Eastern Europe draw in migrants from even further east.

This global web of exploitation of hopes, dreams, and fears is made up of individual human lives, not waves of migrants – the lives whose value we pay lip service to. If we really believed all people were created equal, we would not tolerate the poor treatment of so many; and we would not re-enact this treatment on others, often just a few generations, or just one, since we too were immigrants.

Treat people too badly, and when better opportunities arrive, they leave, or others do not come at all. Rarely do people recognise their own behaviour as poor treatment of others. Often the local population demands that incomers should be grateful for having been allowed to arrive in the first place. And often they are not aware why the migrants stop arriving.

When I began writing this chapter in 2022, the number of Chinese immigrants to the UK was falling: 'There were approximately 124,000 Chinese nationals residing in the United Kingdom in 2021, an increase from the 103,000 Chinese nationals residing in the United Kingdom in 2008. The highest number of Chinese nationals residing in the United Kingdom was 147,000 back in 2017.'[33] The next crisis could very well be the one that occurs when migrants no longer come to the places they so recently came to in such high numbers. As I finished writing this chapter in August 2024, we were wondering how many overseas students would watch the news of race riots across the UK and decide not to take up their university places in the autumn.

What was the effect of the number of Chinese nationals living in the UK, mostly students, increasing so much in the decade before 2017? To what extent did their arrival reduce or increase fear? In Sheffield, where I lived for ten years before 2013, the arrival of students from China and a handful of other countries transformed it from being a city in decline when I arrived in 2003, to one in which a new Chinese quarter had sprung up by 2017 and more money was being made from serving overseas students than from the historic industries that founded the city. The same can be seen in other northern cities such as Newcastle and Manchester. However, the highest density of Chinese residents in the UK, who increasingly are not students, is in the so-called Silicon Fen of Cambridgeshire. The recent turnaround – the sudden decline in migration from China to the UK – could be expected to have just as big an impact: as negative in its effects on the local economy as the influx was positive. If it is more than just a temporary blip, it could be the most unexpected of new crises for a place like Britain. As with all nascent possible crises, we can only wait and see.

Places that do not receive migrants quickly turn into places from which jobs begin to disappear, despite the locals' reluctance to leave. We need to be better at understanding the connections between people coming and a thriving economy. We need to understand that the sharing of jobs is easier when people can move around more freely. If this could be made clear, the fear of unemployment might be appeased not by barring immigrants but by inviting and welcoming them.

It is not hard to imagine such a state of affairs, because it is already happening in a number of places. There may be a future in the UK and US, not just in Southern Europe, in which one of the most pressing concerns is that no one is arriving from elsewhere, while the young are leaving for brighter prospects – for fears, among other things, over unemployment. This is one of the reasons adults are so concerned about their children's education. Concerns about other people taking our jobs are often at the heart of the fear of immigration, as if immigrants only reduce the availability of work in an area and do not also grow the economy, and along with it, the local job market. The end result is a terror of migrants caused by a spiral of fears that have become increasingly difficult to allay.

Artificial intelligence

The crisis of sharing the work is not just about immigrants taking our jobs. Some of the stories being told about work, and sharing it out, are distinctly far-fetched. One extreme describes a world in which robotics and artificial intelligence have so significantly reduced the amount of work that needs to be done that billions of people no longer need to labour. At the other extreme, some predict a future in which most people will have poorly paid, insecure, and difficult jobs that they hate, as in the frequently cited example of car washing by hand having overtaken car washing by machine in the most unequal of rich countries.

The reality may be that migration, instead of reducing the availability of work, will help to create balance by allowing people to move into regions where their work is most needed. It may produce demand in those regions, for new jobs that might be better paid, more secure, and also more interesting, while reducing the competition for work in areas where too many people are chasing too few jobs. But what if that new demand were met more and more by machines?

Will the robots take away work? The short answer is almost certainly *no* – because new technology never removes the need for net (in aggregate and as a whole) human labour. Furthermore, artificial intelligence is no longer really new: 'There have been no major breakthroughs in the academic discipline of artificial intelligence for a couple of decades. The underlying technology of neural networks – a method of machine learning based on the way physical brains function – was theorised and even put into practice back in the 1990s.'[34] As Stephen Wolfram explained at the end of his book *What is ChatGPT Doing . . . and Why Does it Work?*, AI might never work much better than it does now, because it doesn't scale up well. The AI we have developed to date is not capable of becoming significantly cleverer. Because we recognise the possibility that a new iteration of it might scale up, however, we entertain fears of how we will one day be replaced by machines.

Of course, artificial intelligence hypothetically has a much greater utility. We will find it useful for things we have not yet imagined. Already we are told that hardly any of us will need to type in the near future – we will just mutter our thoughts into a machine and grammatically cogent text will appear. But just as some people prefer to use a pen than type, some of us will still want to type and avoid the machine's (often mistaken) corrections. And remember, AI only *appears* to think like we do. We may not think better, but we always think differently; whereas AI is a mimic, like an American mockingbird.

All new technology influences how things are made and services are provided, and how capital circulates. Karl Marx's oft-repeated comment – 'The hand mill gives you society with the feudal lord; the steam mill society with the industrial capitalist' – is the kind of phrase that artificial intelligence is likely to regurgitate, as it has been repeated so often (the words of AI are rearranged bouquets of others' literary flowers). In very recent years, it has been proposed that AI will give us something new; but AI is no more determinist than was the hand mill or steam mill, neither of which changed much on their own. It was people and their greed, avarice, sociability and compassion that used and shaped the impact of these new tools.

The sharing out of the work that needs to be done is changing, and is likely to continue to change because so much no longer needs to be performed by humans – including spell-checks, grammar-checks, identifying people from photographs of their faces, and even listing trite but plausible comments on the implications of AI. But what would it take to reach a point where unemployment is no longer in the top three greatest concerns worldwide? How likely are we to leave that as an inheritance to our dwindling numbers of children?

John Maynard Keynes's famous 1930 essay about what our grandchildren may inherit mentioned such a possibility in its predictions for 2028. His predictions came to pass for the era of the grandchildren he never had: 'We are suffering just now from a bad attack of economic pessimism. It is common to hear people say that the epoch of enormous economic progress which characterised the nineteenth century is over; that the rapid improvement in the standard of life is now going to slow down.'[35] Ten years later, at the start of the Second World War, Keynes wrote that workers could no longer expect pay rises: 'We cannot reward the worker in this way, and an attempt to do so will merely set in motion the inflationary process. But we can reward him by giving him a share in the claims on the future which would belong otherwise to the entrepreneurs.'[36] In other words, we can build greater equality.

Is such an aspiration still possible today? Yes, but only through considerable efforts. In Scotland in 2024, we learnt that the use of food banks was no longer rising as it had been. The introduction of the Scottish Child Payment a few years earlier, and then its dramatic uplift to £25 a week for every child aged under sixteen in a household receiving benefits, had a huge effect (it rose to £26.70 a week, later on in 2024). A university student discovered its dramatic effect when writing her final-year dissertation on the correlation between reduced food bank uptake in Scotland and the increase in payments.[37]

In 2023 there was only a 5 per cent increase in the number of food bank parcels provided for families with children in Scotland that year, three times lower than in England or Wales, and nearer five times lower than in Northern Ireland, where the UK government was blocking public funds to force local politicians back to government. This was part of a longer-term trend over the previous five years. The longer-term rise in Scotland of 46 per cent more parcels for families with children was described by the Trussell Trust as being 'significantly lower than any other part of the UK (Northern Ireland – 188%, Wales – 82%, and England – 140%). It is likely that the implementation of the Scottish Child Payment in 2021, and the extension of eligibility from aged 6 to age 16, and the £5 increase to £25 a week, that was introduced in November 2022, has made an impact.'[38] There were hardly any far-right riots in Scotland in the summer of 2024.

We cannot know what the world's children will inherit in terms of work and space, fear of others and the fear of not inheriting a house, apartment, a country, or just a small space, to call home. Of those who are concerned only about the fate of one country, we could ask, to what extent have the immigrants who have arrived in the UK replaced the children who were not born here, and to what extent should we expect this trend to continue? We could then carry out the same exercise in every other country where immigrants are presented as the problem. What are the most pessimistic and optimistic outlooks on employment, and where, between those two extremes, are we most likely to end up? The answers to those questions may well depend on what else transpires, and not least on the hopes of those children themselves and how that motivates them as they become adults.

4
War and a Home

Our country is being destroyed. And the only thing standing between you and its obliteration is me. It's true.

Donald Trump, 2024[1]

Somewhere in Europe, and it could be almost anywhere, an old man sits, afraid. He is afraid of a terrorist attack. He is afraid of there being a conspiracy in Europe where foreigners will take over, and of dying, along with those he loves, from its repercussions. He worries that there will be war again, but especially now, in his region of Europe. He has been made fearful by all the bad news.

What he does not consider are the risks posed to him and his family by his own country's failing healthcare system, its poor road safety, the extremely high levels of pollution in his home town, and the poor-quality food that global companies dump on his country's food markets. He and his family encounter these threats every single day and their impacts are far greater than the minuscule probability of the kind of violence he imagines.

The violence he worries about is certainly possible, but if he were a highly numerate man, and had access to all the data, he would know what the greatest risk was by far, and he would adjust his fears. War, though, to him is an existential danger, as opposed to a slow whittling away of what could have been a good life; and it is happening not too far from him. War is also a threat to what he has been taught to hold dear, to the wider community he imagines he is a part of, to the religion that he grew up with, and to a collective identity that supersedes him and will, he prays, long outlast him.

The old man fails to see a clearer picture, and so he worries much less about the everyday – despite these being the things that he and those around him could act upon and demand to be changed. He could act effectively because the actual harms are closer to home, and local threats are both more palpable and amenable to action. These harms are perpetrated by those he sees as his friends and protectors: by the local political bosses, the middleman profiteers, and big business left unfettered by his national government. It suits them well if he has other preoccupations.

We are most afraid of the things we believe we cannot control, not the things that are most easily tackled by local policies, or the things our own governments do that end up harming us if they distract us enough. Instead, we fear, and some of us fear most, what might come out of the shadows. We may then see our government as our greatest protection from the imagined ogre of war – not as its most likely cause. Imagined threats to our home, as far as we are concerned, are existential threats. We fear the shadows. And we crave safety.

The greatest crisis facing the world today, based on the surveys that are at the heart of this book, is a combined crisis of the cost of living, poverty, and inequality. It is the fear that we, or those around us, will not be able to get by. The second-greatest crisis involves our place in the world: how we share out the work, and the masses of people who we imagine might be coming to take our work and homes away from us. We are afraid of not being wanted or needed, and, for adults of working age, this means not being employed and not being paid. The second-greatest crisis, like the first, is about economic violence.

The third-greatest global crisis in the minds of those surveyed is quite different. It is about physical safety: about both the reality and the fear of crime and violence, and the prospect – or, much more rarely, the reality – of war and other such conflicts. It is about having a safe home and what the threats to your home might be.

It should not, today, be hard to see that there are many kinds of violence that we might be frightened of, and answers to surveys that score violence highly will partly be us expressing some of our wider fears, ones we do not voice often (other than when ticking off our fears). Violence is not innate in humans. Most of us are remarkably peaceful all our lives.

Anthropologists debate our innate and changeable long-term biological and cultural nature. Depending on the context, they sometimes say we behave like chimps, our rather violent primate cousins; at other times, and especially in situations of greater gender equality, they say we tend to behave more like bonobos (closely related to chimps but more loving and less aggressive).[2, 3] People's propensity to commit and support violence is almost entirely a product of upbringing, the circumstances they live through, and the fears they are given.

Today, violence is all around us. Violence is both close and at a distance, and this varying proximity impacts people's concerns for the future. Violence near to home is presented to us every day on the news, its impact greatly disproportionate to our chances of ever being a victim. People can see a great deal of violence on their phone screens, which all too often foreground the worst news from around the world. But it is violence at or near home that the vast majority of people worldwide fear most. The bulk of this crisis is about the fear of violence and the search for a safe home. When most people say they fear crime and violence, they are referring to theft, robbery, mugging, assault, and – at the extreme – rape and murder.

Terrorism is also a fear of many, one almost entirely provoked by the ubiquitous reporting of remarkably rare acts. Few of us are aware of the violence we sponsor, however, when we fund our governments to engage in acts of violence by paying our taxes and voting for politicians who want us to trust (or overlook) their foreign policy. The violence that we inflict on others at a distance, from selling and dropping bombs to impoverishing those we do not see, is not included in the statistics that make this the third-biggest crisis worldwide. But it should be.

Because most people do not live in a war zone, most of us are most afraid of more minor crimes – especially those that involve violence. But we harbour a great fear of far more serious but far less common crimes that can become commonplace in times of war: assault, rape, and murder.

Crime and violence are the fourth-highest concerns of people worldwide. Some 25 per cent of people regularly list it among their top three concerns (this was the figure for April 2022; it was 30 per cent in both June and July 2024), and military conflict between nations is the eleventh most concerning issue, with 14 per cent of people globally placing war in their top three (10 per cent in both June and July 2024). A further 8 per cent of global survey respondents put terrorism in their top three most concerning issues (9 per cent in June 2024, falling to 8 per cent in July). These may not be the paramount fears of more affluent classes and countries, who tend to worry more about climate change, but these concerns, especially over crime and violence, are high among most people worldwide, and highest of all in the two very different countries of Mexico and Sweden. People are slightly more likely to be concerned about crime and violence if they live in the US than across the globe as a whole, while people in the UK are half as likely to be concerned about crime and violence as are those in the US. But this worry became much more pressing for the British in June 2024 – perhaps because the British election campaign of that month was dominated by rhetoric about immigration, falsely framed as being linked to a threat of violence.

In a country like Sweden, with high rates of equality, low poverty, little unemployment, and one of the best social security systems worldwide, it might well be that other concerns are less immediate, and thus crime and violence take on relatively greater importance. Alternatively, or additionally, a single event that occurred shortly before the cited survey was conducted might have temporarily increased people's fear, although that does not appear to be the case in Sweden. Unlike in Britain, where politicians stoked fears of violence in June 2024 and then violence ensued in the race riots of August, in Sweden something a little different has been occurring.

There used to be, and still is, relatively little violence or crime in Sweden. So why are people so fearful of it today? Of all the countries included in the global survey of April 2022, people in Sweden were the least concerned about financial or political corruption (5 per cent); the second least concerned about poverty and inequality (18 per cent); and the third least concerned about inflation (18 per cent). Some twenty months later, in December 2023, those proportions remained quite low. These proportions might all have risen, because the proportion of people concerned about military conflict in Sweden fell from 30 per cent in April 2022 (third highest) to 13 per cent in December 2023 (seventh highest). The proportion worrying about crime and violence, meanwhile, had risen from a very high 56 per cent in April 2022 to a remarkable 63 per cent in December 2023, falling to 61 per cent in June 2024 and 57 per cent in July 2024. That is a very high majority of Swedes who are scared, even if a peak in fear may have passed (although it still stood at 58 per cent in August 2024, and 57 per cent by December 2024).

It does not take long to search out news reports that explain how shocked people in Sweden are about an increase in crime and violence in recent years. Of course, for the vast majority, that fear is largely the result of those reports, since almost none of those who became so fearful were personally affected. In 2023, Swedish Prime Minister Ulf Kristersson reacted dramatically to the rise in violence and shootings that had recently occurred in that country: 'Sweden has never before seen anything like this. No other country in Europe is seeing anything like this.'[4]

The reasons remain unclear as to why violence rose so suddenly in Sweden in 2021 and 2022, and why violence went on to dominate news headlines there in 2023. Rising inequality, poverty, and unemployment in the highest-crime areas are among the explanations that have been put forward. Clearly, something tipped the balance in Sweden in the third year of the third decade of the third millennium; and the changing circumstances made that tipping possible. What exactly caused the increase to occur then, in that place, and in the streets where it did, will take more time to understand, and may only be fully understandable when the fear has subsided as the timing of the fall in fear will in part explain what was driving and sustaining it.

Explaining why something appears to be a greater crisis in one place as compared to another is not straightforward: consequences are not necessarily the clear result of changing social circumstances. Luck and individual agency, far-right political parties spreading alarm, and the harsh reception of refugees from war zones: all this might have contributed to Sweden's rising fear. It is impossible to disentangle all the possible factors, especially during a crisis. But we can at least know what is important in the minds of the people surveyed; we can ask why a specific crisis has not been averted, and whose interests might be served by its continuation.

All crises are connected. Although the recent rise in violence in Sweden has been linked to clusters of high unemployment and immigration within particular cities, researchers have shown that it is not ethnicity but poverty that correlates most closely to the geographical patterns. Their work suggests that a rise in inequality triggered the violence in Sweden, and this is reflected in the circumstances of both victims and perpetrators. Income inequality in Sweden is very low compared to most of the world, but by 2020 it was higher than it had been for decades. Most of the rise in inequality had occurred in just the past twenty years, and in 2008 the poorest tenth of people living in Sweden saw their incomes fall. The situation has hardly recovered since. Income disparities are the most important inequality of all in terms of determining the shape and social trajectory of societies, so we are incredibly sensitive to any slight changes.[5]

~

Geographical variations in concerns over war are even more significant than those over crime and violence, and they are even more affected by events. Doubtless because of the invasion of Ukraine, the three countries whose respondents expressed the most concern about war in the spring of 2022 were Poland, Germany, and Sweden. The least-concerned respondents were in South Africa, Turkey, and Argentina: countries where other issues were seen as more important and war was not a pressing local concern that month. By June 2024 it was Poland and Israel where concerns over war were greatest, and Chile, where the fear had already been very low, had joined the three places where it was least feared.

In April 2022, only 14 per cent of people in Israel listed war as one of their top three concerns, a lower proportion than in Australia and Japan (both 19 per cent), or the US or France (both 20 per cent), or another seven countries where it was mentioned by between 38 per cent and 21 per cent. By December 2023, 36 per cent of survey respondents in Israel – more than in any other country polled – mentioned war as a great concern. By July 2024, that proportion had risen to 45 per cent; and then 50 per cent by August 2024.

In December 2023, 64 per cent of people in Israel said that what they saw as terrorism was one of their greatest concerns. That had dropped to 49 per cent by July 2024. It is not just that the definition of terrorism is often controversial, but also that the word's meaning can change in the minds of people over time depending on events and rhetoric, more so than other concepts tend to. Concern about terrorism is even more variable than concern about war. But all our concerns about anything related to violence tend to be raised when there is a significant amount of unrest or conflict, even in faraway places. In autumn 2023, long before the latest and most shocking phase of the decades-long war on Gaza, people worldwide were generally frightened about the current prospects for peace in the world.[6] They just became more frightened by the summer of 2024, than they had been in many years; and then Israel's soldiers invaded Lebanon in the autumn of 2024.

Events remind us of what we are capable of. As the war in Ukraine has continued throughout 2024, more than a century after the first battles of the First World War in the summer of 1914, fears about war increased among the population of Germany. By June 2024, this became a preoccupation of 23 per cent of Germans, lagging just behind the equivalent figures in Poland and Israel. Part of this terror is about war spreading and the escalation of the use of more and more deadly weapons. Within Europe this fear subsided only slightly in July 2024, to preoccupy 20 per cent of those in Germany and 27 per cent in Poland; but by the end of that month, more general concerns of war spreading from Israel to Lebanon and Iran rose again, especially in late September 2024. The many other wars taking place in less reported parts of the world had far less impact on global sentiment. This can be attributed to lack of coverage, but perhaps it is also because the states involved do not possess nuclear weapons.

Nuclear war is still a fear for many. According to one large survey, in February 2023 almost half of all people in the world thought that nuclear weapons might be used.[7] It is naive to imagine that the nuclear threat has diminished just because war is no longer among the top three fears globally. Ask the question another way, directly, and our persisting collective fear of war, and especially nuclear war, is revealed. This fear might be lingering from the 1960s, 1970s, and especially the 1980s, when fear of a looming nuclear world war preyed on the minds of many, and the last great global conflict was still within living memory. But perhaps we are just as capable today as we were in the 1980s of launching a nuclear war, because many younger adults have forgotten the lessons learnt, and we have now lost almost all our relatives who were adults during the Second World War.

The current war in Ukraine is part of a long series of wars that have heightened the recent global concern about the possibility of a future nuclear confrontation. When a war begins, what can be said about it is limited. Several years after a war has started, commentators start to normalise the story and fit this new war into the long-running sequence of conflicts around the world. This effort to fit wars into a wider understanding of events and global politics might help us to change our human nature and hopefully, in the future, wars will become less predictable, less deadly, and less frequent, as the power and popularity of those who wage war recedes. Fewer people now view any conflict as a just war, or a simple matter of good versus evil.

The ongoing war on Gaza, which escalated with utterly tragic consequences in October 2023, and which was spread to Lebanon by Israel a year later, has led to increased speculation about the future of the world and whether we will ever be capable of building peace. Just as we tend to think that poverty will always be with us, so too is there a tendency to see war as inevitable, or that any series of connected crises is a case of business as usual. But the global situation always changes – fast on the surface, and slower on a deeper level. It was in this context that Ipsos issued an out-of-sequence update to their annual report in November 2023. Its first paragraph read as follows:

> We are releasing this report ahead of COP28 and have found that attitudes towards purpose are declining for the first time in a decade. People are focusing more inwardly on themselves and their world, rather than the broader problems surrounding them. The polycrisis, which includes political uncertainty, climate change, and war to name just a few, has arguably worsened, leading to a lower priority on environmental concern and brand/value alignment among citizens in many countries. Our end of year update reflects this sentiment, and the increasing sense of pessimism we felt as we wrote this report.[8]

The term 'polycrisis' is hardly helpful, but this report was not meant for general consumption. The interim report stated that it was aimed at an audience of 'businesses, organisations, brands, and governments'. The key change since the previous report in February 2023 had been the start of a new phase of the long-running war on Gaza, but the interim report referred to it only in the most oblique way: 'The polycrisis wears on: 2023 has been a challenging year marked by multiple global crises.'[9]

Thus, violence in 2023, alongside the primary struggle of the cost of simply living, reduced what consensus for action ('tackling') could be found when people were asked a somewhat leading question over the climate crisis: 'Should it be tackled?' By June 2024, crime and violence was a major concern of more people than inequality and poverty, when presented as an issue separate from inflation. So this set of crises around violence, especially when combined with worries over war and terrorism has, over the past decade, risen at some times to be the second most important concern worldwide after the cost of living, with poverty and inequality.

It was assumed that those reading the interim report were not primarily concerned about these great crises, but rather about how public perception of them might alter consumer behaviour. Ipsos was presenting what it implied was dire news for 'brand value'. The report was not written for those who consider over-consumption and brand loyalty as signs of the human race heading to hell in a handcart. Just at the moment when many were saying that a new genocide had begun, Ipsos was preoccupied with a different kind of casualty:

> The continued rise of brand/value alignment is another casualty of tougher economic times. Consumers are becoming more cautious with their spending and are less likely to buy brands that reflect their personal values. This trend is more pronounced in developed markets, with a drop of three percentage points to 57% in Great Britain; down five points in the US to 61%; and a nine-point fall to 52% in France.

The implication is that all these crises – uncertainty about the future, high and rising prices, the continuation of the war in Ukraine, and the growing atrocities within Gaza – were correlated with a sudden drop in loyalty to big brands, despite a fall in inflation. The findings were actually based (according to the survey dates) on global sentiment *before* 7 October 2023 – before the latest wave of atrocities within and just outside Gaza – but were interpreted in its shadow.

Clearly, the events of October 2023 in Israel cannot be blamed for a change in global sentiment apparent in a survey taken prior to them. Nonetheless, people were widely, for many reasons, becoming less trusting – of brands, of politicians, of governments, and of the media. The relevant survey was conducted in the two weeks between 22 September and 6 October 2023. Over 24,000 adults in some thirty-one countries, including China, participated in the research; in India, almost 2,000 adults were surveyed face to face. The Ipsos survey has been becoming more sophisticated and more representative, and this one reflected the depths of global sentiment just before the first new shots were fired in the latest of many violent conflicts around the world.

War is the ultimate threat to a safe home. An increase in fears about war, and of terrorism – which is so often associated with war – raises anxiety about violence in general. But it is concerns over everyday crime and violence that drive these issues to be placed third in the global public consciousness in most years, and second by 2024. Routine violence in countries with unstable regimes often looks like war to those of us in safer places. There are no neat dividing lines between a declared war, a warlike situation, street shootings as part of a local battle, or so-called gang-related violence.

With the exception of Sweden, fear of crime and violence is highest in poorer countries: in Chile, Peru, South Africa, Mexico, Argentina, Brazil, and Colombia. These were the seven countries where the fear of violence was highest in December 2023. They are all heavily influenced by the US, and all but one are in the Americas. The US itself is home to some of the world's highest levels of everyday fear, with 31 per cent of survey respondents there putting crime and violence in their top three greatest concerns that month.

In contrast, the countries where the fear of crime is lowest are mostly those further away from the influence of the US, and often – with the glaring exception of one immediate neighbour (Canada) – also physically far away: Poland (5 per cent), Singapore (6 per cent), Hungary (9 per cent), the Netherlands (16 per cent), Japan and Spain (both 17 per cent), Turkey (18 per cent), Canada (19 per cent), and South Korea and Indonesia (both 22 per cent). Understanding the global geography of fears requires a sense of the real rates of crime and violence, how perceptions of these rates may differ, and what else there is to be afraid of; but it is also necessary to consider possible reasons for the results in relation to the American sphere of influence.

The US is clearly crime-ridden, but some of its states and cities are so violent that people from other parts of the country avoid going there. For Europeans, the continuous cycles of apparently gratuitous violence that plague the region can lead us to question the sanity of our American cousins. US Centers for Disease Control and Prevention data shows that deaths from firearms in Texas have been rising particularly quickly, leading one commentator to note: 'If more guns and fewer gun laws made Texas safer, it would be the safest state in the US. Instead, it has rising rates of gun suicide and homicide, and is home to four of the nation's 10 deadliest mass shootings.'[10] Note, however, that Texas is far from the most violent state in the US: in fact, twenty-six states (the majority of states), had a higher firearms mortality rate than Texas by 2021. Texas had an under-average rate of violence in 2021, so even though its record is terrible, it is not an outlier.

A clear argument as to why guns raise fears of violence, as well as actual violence, is so obvious that it need not be rehearsed here.[11] Active shooter incidents in the US have become more frequent in recent years.[12] It is hardly surprising that people should fear criminal violence there, but there is also a fear about much wider violence – especially that involving the state. These fears range from police shootings up to and including widespread legalised state violence: war.

State violence

Violence is now rare in most people's lives – almost certainly much rarer than it was in the lives of their great-grandparents and great-great-grandparents. Some forms of violence are disguised or hidden – including threatened violence – within the home, towards partners and children, through to state violence, which is often presented as legitimate. Incarceration is a form of violence (it shortens lives), as are deaths that could have been avoided had governments cared more, including those labelled social murder. Most concern about violence, however, pertains to events that are more explicitly labelled as crimes in the media.

State violence is not well measured because institutions have little interest in documenting their own wrongdoing. Crime, in general, is not easily measured over time because what is seen to be a crime changes over time, but the most extreme – murder – is not too badly recorded worldwide, and through time.

Incidentally, I happen to live in one of the places in the world that had the highest murder rates recorded in the distant past and which is still a place that produces more (now corporate and political) criminals than most: 'Oxford can be crowned a medieval murder capital due to its population of rowdy youths. In the 14th century, the per capita homicide rate in Oxford was up to five times higher than in major cities such as London or York, and 75% of the perpetrators were [university] students between the ages of 14 and 21.'[13] We often forget that there tended to be far more violence in the past than there is today.

In general, violence has been falling in recent years, although not in all its forms, and certainty not in the US and other increasingly lawless places. There is no guarantee that violence will continue to fall in future. It is even possible that fear of crime may rise as some of our other fears fall, and as our societies age. Just because nothing of great significance happens to most people most of the time does not mean that there is not a crisis when it comes to violence and crime. The crisis people are most likely to refer to is about what they most fear might happen – and hence is about the future.

State violence makes us particularly angry and fearful, especially when it is done in our name. It varies in intensity geographically and over time; but it is always present and is a founding principle of states, which were created to have a monopoly on violence. Between 1990 and early 2024 in England and Wales, some 1,887 deaths occurred in police custody or following contact with the police. This number has been falling very slightly each year since 2017. Since 2013 there have also been 3,329 deaths in British prisons, of which 2,213 were not self-inflicted; and dozens of deaths in immigration centres, most not self-inflicted. The worst recent year was 2017.[14]

After 20 May 2020, the slow death of George Floyd under the knee of a US police officer quickly came to epitomise state violence worldwide. The statistics for state violence in the US are far worse than those anywhere in Europe, or indeed most of the world. Deaths in US custody have risen during recent years: the official count in 2020 was of over 600, higher than for any of the previous four years.[15] The actual number of deaths will be significantly higher — at least double — due to gross underreporting.[16] In Greece, by contrast, careful documentation of evidence shows that the targeting of civilians in peaceful protests by the Greek police peaked in 2019; but when aggregated by year, state violence in Greece has in fact risen each year since 2020.[17]

Although the US is the most afflicted nation in the world when it comes to police violence, the example of Greece shows that atrocities and abuses of power can be found everywhere. There is an international geography to racism, corruption, and violence that is led by the US, but which tends to reflect the degree to which a country's people have been taught to tolerate inequalities. The US and Israel almost always head the international league tables of countries with the worst outcomes associated with violence. The record of Russia has also recently been poor. Occasionally, when the harm being measured is less directly related to violence — for example, whether people lack opportunities — another country such as India or Greece comes out worse (but in this specific example there is no comparable data for the US or

Israel).[18] Most importantly, levels of violence have been rising across the world in recent years: wars, state violence, and everyday violent crime.

In 2018, the World Bank estimated that by 2030 half of the world's poor will be living in countries with high levels of violence, as well as many people in more prosperous countries.[19] It traced the rise in violence to what it called the breaking of a more peaceful lull from 2007, 'when violent conflict began to increase in scope and number of fatalities, particularly beginning in 2010'. Had the World Bank not been based in Washington DC, it might instead have traced the rise in violence back to the 2003 invasion of Iraq by the US and its partners in the so-called 'coalition of the willing'.

The invasion of Iraq was a part of a general warlike trend and a new acceptance of violent methods as being legitimate in some cases. It was a US decision, and only very few other countries took part willingly or made more than a token contribution. From Europe, that coalition included just the UK, with 46,000 troops, Poland with 2,500, and a few other mainly East European states with a minuscule presence, such as 24 men from Moldova.[20] Notably, France, Germany, Italy, Spain, Canada, India, and China declined to take part.

The World Bank, in the context of the overall rise in war and war-related violence worldwide, noted: 'Until recently, the world was becoming more peaceful.' Its researchers were relying on Stephen Pinker's *The Better Angels of Our Nature: Why Violence Has Declined* – published in 2011, just as violence was increasing again, Pinker being unaware of that. However, the World Bank's 2018 report did produce various statistics showing the rise in violence increasing, and it demonstrated that most of the deaths were connected to areas of special US interest; for example, the US government had been supporting one side in Syria's civil war since 2011.[21]

Figure 4.1 is an enlargement of a diagram, depicting data for 2016, that first appeared in the 2018 World Bank document.[22] It has been redrawn to take account of the countries' geographical positions and with additional data for many earlier and later years. It could be argued that the pattern in the World Bank diagram resembled something of a crusade. The redrawn version includes all war deaths between 1989 and 2022, and it depicts a clear global pattern where Muslim and/or black people are disproportionately the victims of violence.

The global fear of war and violence rises as war and violence become increasingly more common. It is not simply the case that wars have been becoming more frequent and more violent, but they are also lasting longer, as for example in Afghanistan. Many are wars where most of the victims are poor and the weapons used are usually made in richer countries.

In Europe in 2016 there were just a few war deaths involving Ukraine and Russia. Seen against the backdrop of all war deaths recorded over more than three decades, the number of deaths in Russia and Ukraine looks small, but they are a high proportion of the deaths of white folk. The year 2016 is under discussion because it is the one shown in the diagram cited above; but the wider data confirm that this year was no outlier.

In Afghanistan during the later years of that very long US-instigated war, a drone fleet began to surveil what Barack Obama in 2013 called 'some of the most distant and unforgiving places on earth'.[23] For people living in those places, however, the US was the most distant and unforgiving place on Earth. It was the country that hosted the World Bank and the International Monetary Fund, and which insisted that Afghanistan roll back its government, privatising its security and road building, resulting in the proliferation of initially ungoverned, and then divergently governed, territories.[24]

The policy of rolling out fleets of drones to try to govern the ungovernable from the skies was dreamed up in the US. But it failed. The last US military plane left Kabul airport at a minute to midnight, local time, on 30 August 2021.[25] Perhaps other events and opportunities were now of more interest to the US? Its war efforts soon focused on supplying weapons to Ukraine and Israel. On 24 February 2022, when Russia invaded Ukraine, the US was

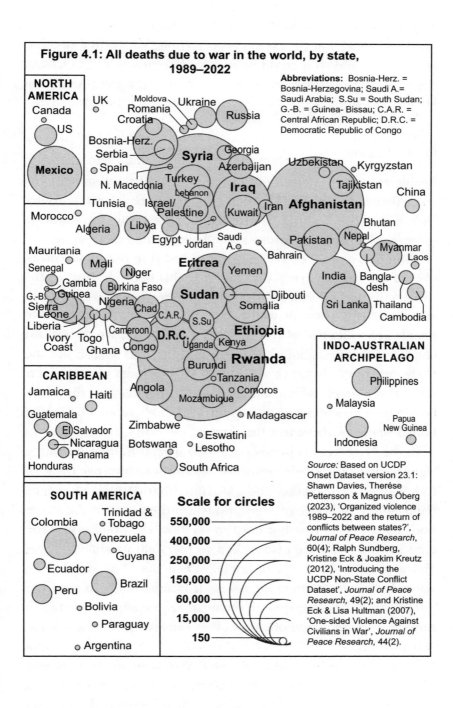

Figure 4.1: All deaths due to war in the world, by state, 1989–2022

heavily implicated in every way except in not having overt 'boots on the ground'. The devastation was terrible; but there was access to Ukraine, and so it could be reported accurately.[26] In October 2023, the decades-long war on Gaza rapidly escalated. Again, the US was involved.

Place of safety

People's sense of safety is not just a product of the degree of violence they have perceived in their community or country, or what they might think about the future threat of war, terrorism, or more local violence. It is also about being safe in their home.

Although a sense of safety is not included in the survey measures of the various crises that organise this book, having a place to be safe naturally fits within this chapter because it is a prerequisite for a sense of well-being. We cannot talk about why people are so fearful of war and other violence if we do not also consider what it is about home that matters, and what is at stake in the fear of not having a safe home. This includes issues as mundane as the supply of housing. Refugees often sleep on the streets beside the native citizens of a country when there are not enough homes made available to either group.

In the Netherlands in 2024, the UN special rapporteur on the right to housing called 'for urgent measures to improve the right to housing in the Netherlands, warning that decades of government policy rather than immigrants are the cause of the "acute housing crisis"'.[27] It is not hard to see how the other crises covered in this book are also linked to fears about violence, war, and a place to have a safe home. When the West wages wars abroad, migration from the places it bombs tends to rise. It is notable that the country with the most acute housing shortage in Europe, though, is the one that takes the fewest refugees fleeing war (the UK).

Around the rich world a new rent crisis grew as the pandemic of the early 2020s appeared to abate. In November 2022, the *Atlantic* magazine published an article that claimed: 'For

Americans to live a productive, prosperous, happy life, homes need to be truly abundant.'[28] It suggested that, given the operations of the free market and the vicissitudes of economic inequality, an enormous number of homes would have to be built in the US for the poor to have access to a decent home, because the rich would want so many homes to live in. The scenarios the article presents verge on the ridiculous, being based on the assumption that there would have to be a huge movement of people into the areas of highest housing demand, before that demand will eventually fall. This would require much more housing to be very quickly built. In San Francisco, for example, estimates of a future workforce, 510 per cent bigger than today, imply an overall citywide population of something like 4 million, compared to the current 815,000.

The *Atlantic* article is based on a 2019 paper by two economists, Enrico Moretti of the University of California, Berkeley, and Chang-Tai Hsieh of the University of Chicago. They have analysed how much of what they refer to as 'productivity' in the US is apparently reduced by the throttling of the housing supply in its biggest cities through planning controls. Moretti and Hsieh suggest that if New York, San José, and San Francisco – just those three cities – had enjoyed the more permissive planning standards of Atlanta or Chicago over previous decades, the US economy would have been roughly $2 trillion bigger by 2009; and that each American household's average annual income would be $3,685 higher.[29] You may well wonder what all this has to also do with crime and violence; but consider how this thinking on the housing crisis might reflect something significant about this country and its notable problem with violence.

To come up with their estimates, economists build complicated models. The ones behind the *Atlantic* article assumed people could move wherever their wages allowed them to, and the housing supply would adjust as needed. They estimated that 53 per cent of Americans would not live where they are currently living if planning laws were relaxed. San Francisco would have 2 million housing units (4 million workers) instead of 400,000. The

Bay Area would be five times its current size, the economists estimated, while the average US city would lose 80 per cent of its population. And New York's population would be a startling eight times bigger than it is now.

This is an example of those misleading futures imagined by people who really should know better. When experts of various kinds advance such predictions about the world of tomorrow, it confirms that some people really believe this is how the world works today. Of course people can have high-quality housing without such free market fantasies. For example, China has 90 per cent home ownership, but in more expensive parts of that country, until the large older population dies out: 'intergenerational transfer has become indispensable for the lucky few young adults to achieve homeownership.'[30] The current crisis of housing in China is not that there are too few homes, because the young adult population has been shrinking for decades; it is a problem of an increasingly unequal distribution.

Where income equality is greatest, issues of safety, violence, and housing tend to be least pressing. Some parts of Europe have achieved good-quality housing for all that would be the envy of people in much of the rest of the more prosperous world, if only they were aware of it.[31] In most of the poorer world, meanwhile, billions live in shanty towns, or tiny concrete boxes in the high-rise equivalent of ancient slums. How we are kennelled alters how we behave.

Housing, as a topic on its own, did not feature as a question in the Ipsos survey, but other relevant questions were included – such as on taxation (the sixth most commonly mentioned concern) and access to credit (including mortgages, the least commonly mentioned issue) – so it makes sense to include these issues here, in the context of wider issues of violence, safety, and of being able to afford a home where you want to live in a society that is functioning well. If you doubt that housing and violence are closely connected, consider those who die in fires when housing is not safe. Violence comes in many forms, not all of them immediately visible or obvious, which is why the term 'social murder' was used to describe the consequences of the fire in Grenfell Tower in London in 2017.

Wars, crime, and unsafe housing are all perpetuated by inequality. To what extent are we made unsafe by allowing others to be so rich? Ben Ansell demonstrated recently that despite wealth inequality rising to a forty-year high in the UK, wealth taxes have collapsed, both because we are taxing wealth less and because evasion has increased. He also explains that the Norwegians and the Swedes have practically abolished inheritance taxation: 'People don't want to do it because they don't believe in it. They don't think it's fair. They might be willing to tax the "very wealthiest" or to consider treating capital gains like income as fairer. But when it comes to taxing property or savings, there's relatively little public support because it gnaws away at many people's fundamental views of desert, effort, and prudence.'[32] An alternative view is that the Nordic countries have worked out that it makes much more sense to tax *income*, including income from wealth. That also helps prevent people becoming so wealthy in the first place. Two diagrams that Ben Ansell uses have been combined to construct Figure 4.2. The main graph shows the share of all wealth in each of four countries that is held by the best-off 1 per cent for the period of 1900 to just after 2010; the inset shows UK wealth distribution over a shorter period, using a different vertical scale.

The inset tells a story of rapidly growing wealth inequality in the UK between the late 1980s and the early 2010s. The best-off 1 per cent went, in fits and starts, from holding 15 per cent of all wealth, and thus fifteen times the mean average wealth holdings, to having 20 per cent just a couple of decades later. The control of assets, principally housing wealth, was becoming more and more concentrated. Fewer and fewer of the 99 per cent were safe, or at least had the safety that is perceived to come through access to wealth – not least being able to afford to leave a place that has become dangerous.

What seems to be a great change can look much less dramatic if you zoom out. Add three more countries – the US, France, and

Sweden – and another eighty years of context (back to 1900), and we now see from the main part of the figure that the norm had been for wealth inequalities to fall – widely and significantly. For the European countries in the figure, we are not yet back to 1950s levels of wealth inequality. But the US has regressed to the 1930s, when it was the second least unequal of the four by wealth. What looks like a great crisis in the UK in recent decades is less extreme than what has occurred elsewhere.

Most importantly, Figure 4.2 demonstrates what is possible. Continued significant, if lower, inequality in wealth can be successfully combined with a more equitable distribution of assets such as housing. In all these countries, the gap between the

Figure 4.2: Share of wealth for richest 1% in four countries, 1895 onwards

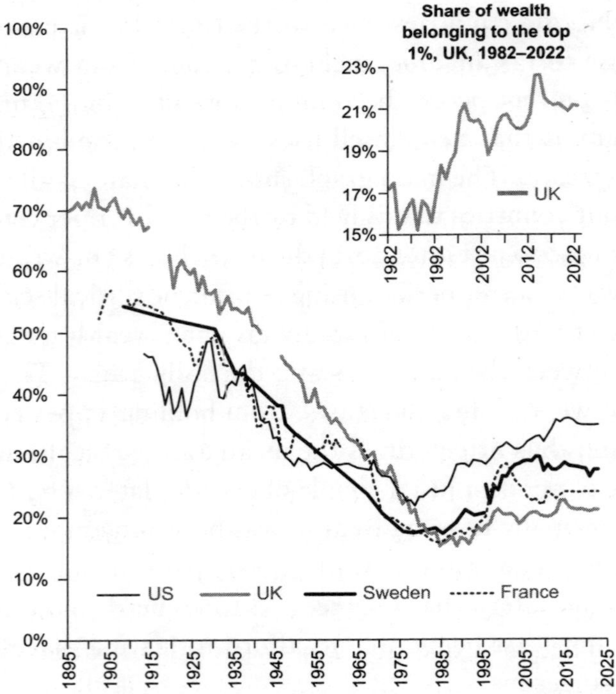

Source: World Inequality Database (wid.world/) and Ben Ansell, 'A Puzzling Inheritance: Why, in a world where wealth matters more than ever, we want to tax it less', benansell.substack, 27 January 2023.

richest and poorest in society in the 1970s and early 1980s was the lowest it had been since these records began. The large recent decline in wealth inequality in France and the much smaller more recent fall in the UK show that the growing inequality trend can be reversed again.

Just as we could choose to be less violent, to reduce funding and support for wars abroad, to learn from those societies where violence is less common and effect gradual change, so too could we choose to spread wealth and safety more evenly. There are numerous people who, for various reasons, want you to believe that peace and justice are impossible – these people are the real problem.

Although the most effective way to promote equality is through income taxation, there is also widespread support for taxing the wealth of the very wealthy – this support is rising across the world, including within Europe, and is strongest in some of the wealthiest places of all.[33] In 2023, '77 per cent of Brits said they would support a 1% annual wealth tax on people with more than £10 million in personal wealth; 74% said they would support a 2% annual tax on people with more than £10 million in personal wealth'.[34] It is interesting to consider who comprises the 3 per cent who consider the jump from 1 per cent to 2 per cent to be too much. This matters, as the 2 per cent rate would raise £22 billion annually, whereas the 1 per cent rate would raise only £11 billion.

A majority of the very well-off would even be in favour of taxing some of their own wealth, at least when they are asked in a particular way. Another 2023 poll found that 68 per cent of people with over £1 million 'to invest' supported the introduction of a net wealth tax of between 1 per cent and 2 per cent of total assets for those with more than £10 million, while 66 per cent of people with assets over £10 million – those who would be affected by such a tax – agreed that this was a good idea. However, that proportion fell if the question were asked slightly differently, with only 52 per cent of those with assets over £10 million supporting higher taxes on their own investable assets (not on their more general illiquid wealth) and only as long as the revenue generated provided better public services.[35] This is fair enough. Who would want to be taxed to support a war machine if they thought, just for a minute, about what that meant?

Individuals brought up in more egalitarian societies, and almost certainly those brought up in families aspiring to equality within society more widely, are more likely to favour redistribution.[36] In contrast, those brought up in the most unequal of societies, and especially in the most acquisitive families, are the most likely to say that their wealth has been achieved through their own choices and hard efforts, rather than luck. This is especially true of the richest 5 per cent of Americans, although 'the top 1 per cent were unique in emphasizing both choices and genes as causes of those traits'.[37] It is very telling that a significant proportion of very rich people really do think they are special, have special genes, and have somehow been chosen to be rich.[38]

In a way, those who believe they have been chosen, via what some call their 'God-given genes' might be right about the genes (if not the god having given them): their families may have (repeatedly and over many generations) stepped or trampled over others to achieve their status to result in where the respondents to these surveys now find themselves to be. It is possible that there really are a few people who are especially, maybe even genetically, selfish: more willing to promote war as a means for getting what they want, and unperturbed by seeing countless other people homeless, or working for little reward until they die.

Fortunately, many people are now working to amass the evidence that in the war against inequality, there is an enemy within – the rich and selfish. Paul Piff, professor of psychological science at the University of California, has for some time been disseminating new scientific discoveries in this area.

> What we've been finding across dozens of studies and thousands of participants across this country is that as a person's levels of wealth increase, their feelings of compassion and empathy go down, and their feelings of entitlement, of deservingness, and their ideology of self-interest increase. In surveys, we've found that it's actually

wealthier individuals who are more likely to moralize greed being good, and that the pursuit of self-interest is favourable and moral.[39]

If you are rich, how do you keep the poor at bay? You promise them the sunlit uplands: 'The expectation of high future earnings can offset a negative shock in the present.'[40] You promise those with less both security in peacetime and victory in war. You lie. You try to hold on to your unfair share. You claim there is no alternative.

The high income of a few is as big a problem as that of the high wealth of a few in terms of social well-being. Well-off people everywhere tend to underestimate how rich they are; but in more unequal countries, they are even more likely to do so. In the UK, in 2022, most people with incomes between £80,000 and £100,000 a year described themselves as being on about average earnings. This reflected their limited understanding of the society they lived in. In March 2024, the then UK chancellor suggested that an income of £100,000 a year was too little to live on in a specific county near London.[41] In reality, the average income of people in full-time work was much less than half this amount, even there, and the average family was much worse off than that, because not all families have at least one full-time earner.

These examples of ignorance among the very rich come from the UK, but they can be found all over the world. It is not just that people in many countries do not understand the wider society they live in; they also often do not even understand the situation of their closest family and friends. As the 2022 survey cited above shows, British people appear to be particularly ignorant of the situations of those nearest to them; most of all the richest of the British! People in Britain in 2022 were more than three times as likely to describe their family and friends as being better off than them, as opposed to worse off: '39 per cent of respondents think their social circle is, in general, better off than they are, only 11 per cent believe their friends and family to be worse off on the whole.'[42] Of course, that is not possible.

Just as many of our family and friends tend to be a little worse off than us as there are those who are a little better off. However, we may have a tendency to more often overlook our friends or family who are worse off than us, and this tendency appears to increase in likelihood as we climb the income scale. To quote again from the survey, '43 per cent of those with a household income of £100,001–£120,000 consider their social circle better off than they are, while virtually no one in that group considers it worse off (57 per cent say: "about the same")'. These findings allow us to understand why so many people at the very top feel they are badly off. It is no wonder that they are angry and afraid, including of people in other countries, and unaware of so much that is around them; these beliefs partly explain why many people are willing to sanction various kinds of aggressions up to and including wars in other countries if they think that might protect them. There is a group that supports US military intervention abroad: it is the very rich, and especially rich men (the military-industrial complex is another term for this). It is always the rich who start wars – if you find this hard to understand then ask yourself: how could the poor start a war?[43] But women are not without their blind spots, and they are now more likely to work in senior positions in the weapons industry, to fight in wars, and to be political leaders than they were during the mid-twentieth century, when the term 'military-industrial complex' was coined.

Women are slightly more likely than men to underestimate the social position of their household (despite usually knowing their husband's income, for those that are married to a man) and then to think they are badly off. This is perhaps surprising and is almost certainly not due to women being poorer. Women tend to be better connected socially, but that does not mean that they are better informed about actual household income (especially when men conceal their full earnings more often); conversely, it might mean they are more interested in these comparisons. Almost every rich man has a rich mother, and women, because they often live longer than men, inherit most of the world's riches – except in a few countries where inheritance passes almost entirely only to men.[44] Rich women tend to pass more of their wealth, in general, on to their sons. Both men and women with money help maintain climates of violence and fear and the social structures that make economic inequality and its many correlates, including robbery and mugging, more likely.

How do the very affluent get away with it? Their children almost never have to fight the wars they support. They have more wealth than they could ever actually use, more homes than they can live in, more clothes than they can ever wear out. They get away with it because we have been taught to respect those with more, especially men with more. We have been conditioned by extreme patriarchy: 'Patriarchy means the individual property will be defended by men, often in wars, but enjoyed by women as well. This type of social organisation has steep hierarchies, almost always headed by men, but also maintained by women.'[45] We don't live in a social vacuum, none of us are immune from societal influence – we are worried about how we compare to others, about how others see us, and at the same minute we worry about TV reports about whatever the most topical war in the world currently is. All this is connected to housing, wealth, and inheritance. What will our children inherit? How might we move them from the country they live in, to get them to safety, to get more money to be safe from violence? The very rich also ponder over where might be a safe place they could flee to, if needed.

Our view on many issues tends to be dominated not just by our social position, but also by what is happening in the time and place where we live. So, readers based in the UK and US may well think that the future is likely to be even more unequal than the past, because that is the current prediction in those countries. This was demonstrated in a report from a Resolution Foundation publication of 2020, which showed the change in the share of ten groups of UK families, sorted from least to most wealthy.[46] It depicted a hollowing out of distribution, with decile groups five and six being almost 1 percentage point less wealthy by 2016 as compared to where they stood in 2008. The same figure for individuals is even more stark, with the even better-off group of decile seven most badly affected. The pooling of wealth among family members slightly mutes what has happened. In short, the poor had little wealth, and so nothing much to lose, while the very rich became much richer, and the middle, in the UK (but also in many other countries) saw their position worsen as they were paying more in rent (mostly to the rich), or having to borrow (mostly from the rich) a huge amount for a mortgage.

The very rich are always a burden, rarely a blessing. The excessive incomes of the richest people most damage the life and the life chances, safety and security of the majority, and of all our children and grandchildren. The rich are most unaffordable where inequality is highest. In the most unequal of affluent nations in the past four decades or so, the consensus has moved far from the idea that we should provide decent and affordable housing for all. Housing is now almost entirely subject to market forces, which of course gives disproportionate power to the better off.

When the rich are allowed to become even richer, their ability to pay increases, which drives up house prices and makes housing generally expensive and often unaffordable for the many, especially younger people and families. Such concentration of wealth leads to multiple property ownership, which restricts supply and makes housing unaffordable for local people, especially in coastal and rural areas. It accelerates gentrification and social segregation in urban areas, leading to 'postcode inequality' and the monopolising of the best local services, notably schools. It perpetuates the buy-to-let market because landlordism obtains higher returns than those offered by high street banks' savings accounts, or from many other forms of investment. It drives housebuilding towards unaffordable luxury developments, which give higher returns on investment, and away from spending to build affordable housing. Then the wealthy help their children and grandchildren onto the property ladder via the bank of mum and dad (or granny and grandad), further restricting the supply for everyone else.

The housing system in the most unequal of affluent countries, the ones with the highest income inequality and lowest public spending as a proportion of GDP, and where the rich are taxed the least, is also the most inefficient. As the best-known data analyst at the *Financial Times* explained in 2023:

> Anglophone planning frameworks give huge weight to environmental conservation, yet the preference for low-density developments fuels car-dependent sprawl and eats up more of that cherished green and pleasant land. Ultimately, whether the goal is tackling the housing crisis, protecting the environment or boosting productivity, the answer to so many woes in the English-speaking world is to unburden ourselves of our anti-apartment exceptionalism.[47]

Anglophone countries are also the readiest to support, encourage, and start wars, to make weapons and profit from the arms trade. That is why this chapter has connected violence so closely to the search for a safe home: they are two sides of the same coin.

Moral decline

Most politicians, everywhere they have been asked, tend to think that the general public, on average, hold political opinions significantly to the right of those they actually do. This was first realised in 2013 in the US, and then later in every other country surveyed. The lowest bias was found among politicians in Wallonia in Belgium, where just under two-thirds took this view. In Germany, over two-thirds of politicians thought the general public were more right-wing than they actually were; and 86, 91, and 92 per cent 'of all politicians in Switzerland, Flanders and Canada' believed this to be the case.[48]

Why do politicians consistently overestimate the conservativeness of public opinion in their country? In the US, the Republicans do it more, but elsewhere our representatives on the left and right are equally likely to do so. One suggestion has been that conservative members of the public tend to be more vocal and attention-seeking, and that they contact their elected representatives more often. A second suggestion is that politicians are more inclined to take such voters seriously because they tend to be better off and apparently better educated, although 'politicians with less-privileged backgrounds can be less susceptible to inequalities in exposure'.[49] A third hypothesis focuses on the impact of the media, which is typically controlled by the rich, and has a vested interest in presenting the public as holding similar views to the rich and powerful owners of newspapers and TV channels.

It is not only the old who think there has been some form of moral decline, of the kind that right-wingers talk about. In Finland, the very small number of young people in the country's most right-wing party were considered dangerous as far back as 2011 because of a particularly worrying social characteristic – isolationism: 'The most frightening in this is that the supporters of the *Perussuomalaiset* the [far-right Finns Party] do not even want to discuss but rather stay at home. This is a revolution of the silent men.'[50]

The 'silent majority' is a term frequently used to describe an imagined conservative group. But huge effort goes into constructing consent for the kinds of immorality that justify wars, inefficient use of housing, and the concentration of wealth. The state often spends a large amount of money to manufacture such supposedly innate views. Loyalty to a certain way of thinking has to be constructed. In a detailed analysis, two sociologists concluded that the 1953 Coronation of Queen Elizabeth II was almost universally accepted and 'a great act of national communion'.[51] But could this reading have mistaken apathy, submission and obedience for consent?

Social scientists argue intensely about how evidence should be interpreted, and the theories and morality behind that. Economists have developed a kind of morality within the discipline that is self-serving, even cultish:

> Economics is not perfect, but relying on it is better than not. Economics is a science – yes, like physics. Calling it a moral science is not an oxymoron. It helps explain and predict things that would otherwise be puzzling. And not only that. It upholds the promise of improving our own lives and of making the world a happier, better,

and more just place for us and our children. This is particularly true when it comes to the poor and dispossessed.[52]

The author of these lines, Erik Angner, ends his missive by claiming: 'Economics really can save the world'.[53] His response to those on the political left who question his beliefs is: 'society can't be run off of unicorn fluff' – being simultaneously insulting and ignorant, characteristics which help to undermine his case. Who would take seriously an economist who believes in unicorns (let alone their fluff!)?

Public life has been corrupted when the view prevails that money is God; that the market is omnipresent and all-powerful. Look closely and we see that of course people have a huge number of moral concerns, but the views of the majority differ from those of a significant section of the rich. In fact, most people *are* worried about inequality as a moral problem; they see the super-rich becoming more powerful than national governments, and do not welcome that. Between 2018 and 2023, and particularly in the worst years of the pandemic, a reversal in public views took place across many parts of the world: 'Back in 2018, when asked to pick the most powerful from a list, the public were more likely to say governments (33%), rather than the very wealthy (29%), were most powerful.'[54] By 2023, '39% of the UK public rank the very rich as having the most power, compared with 24% who say the same about governments.' Although these figures are from the UK, they are very likely to apply more widely.

A moral decline can be seen in the most unequal of affluent nations; but it is not what is normally referred to as such. It is a decline in the morality of the better off. It is possible to believe that the three major political parties of England are very different, and to select graphs and data that demonstrate a few trends that highlight these differences; but it may be more accurate to say that they are far more like each other than are many of the political parties in Europe. The Liberal Democrats, of course, were in the Conservative coalition that preceded the decision to hold a referendum on leaving the EU. It was not their plan to contribute to that outcome, but they did so by aiding the party that contained most of the politicians who wanted that referendum.

There is an almost endless stream of examples that can make the case as to why violence, crime, housing, and general moral decline is a great crisis of our times; but I will now draw this chapter to a close by referring to one last piece of evidence. Some graphs were published just before Christmas 2022 in the *Financial Times* to highlight apparent political policy differences between Labour and the Conservatives, and the outcomes of those differences.[55] Two years later, though, the two parties and the trends in the graphs did not look that different. Similarly in the US, the Democrats and Republicans have much in common, especially when viewed from a small village in a war-torn country that has just been hit by rockets made in the US. Within the US in late 2024, the two candidates vying to be president appeared to be very different to each other; but not to those dying in the small village far away from where the key decisions were being made.

There have been some significant leaps involved in this chapter as the discussion shifted from war to housing across a nation in crisis. I could have added health services that are falling apart or becoming obsolete (see Chapter 5 for more on this). Yet each of these situations involves deaths that would not otherwise occur. Does politics in a state such as the UK or the US really change when the party in power changes? If you can access a copy, look at the graphs in the *Financial Times* report I mention, closely.[56] They show that NHS waiting lists fell in 1997 and 1998, despite the Labour Party sticking to Conservative spending plans for its first two years in office. Perhaps the waiting lists peaked in 1997 in part because of the huge 1919 birth cohort, the largest the UK has ever had, by far, which was then aged seventy-eight. In 2024 the Labour Party began doing the same as it did in 1997 – sticking to Conservative Party spending plans. These are the kinds of contexts in which people worry that they have little power. It does not matter how they vote, they might think. Whoever wins will go to war, support despots abroad, fail to protect citizens at home, and insist that everything must be dictated by the market. It is a crisis indeed if voting differently will not end it.

5

Cradle to Grave

Forty-five percent of people have not felt true happiness for more than two years and 25 percent don't know, or have forgotten, what it means to feel truly happy.

Oracle Global Report, 2022[1]

When, in spring 2023, it was announced that for the sixth year in a row Finland was the happiest country in the world, followed by Denmark and then Iceland, not everyone was convinced. These rankings were based on people's answers to the Cantril ladder question: *Think of a ladder, with the best possible life for you being a 10 and the worst possible life being a 0; how (all things considered) do you rate your current life on that 0 to 10 scale?* Finns, on average, reported 7.8. At the bottom of the international league came Lebanon and Afghanistan with averages of 2.4 and 1.9 respectively.[2] Israel, bordering Lebanon, came fourth from the top.

Perhaps Israel coming fourth appears strange, but the survey had been taken in the years 2020–22, and Israel had fared relatively well in the pandemic, achieving widespread and early vaccination and suffering few deaths. Fifth was the Netherlands, and sixth Sweden, both of which had also seen a relatively good pandemic. Sweden had demonstrated that strict lockdown was not the most effective response to events.[3] Seventh was Norway, eighth Switzerland, ninth Luxembourg and tenth New Zealand. The last of these demonstrated that it was possible to cut yourself off from the world for a couple of years and remain happy – at least in the short term, before the economic realities of self-imposed extreme quarantine isolation – and the impact of the collapse of in-migration on the economy – hit home.

What most of the countries that topped the international happiness tables had in common was that they tended, with a couple of notable exceptions, to be socially and economically more equal than almost all other countries. That mattered far more than the way they had handled the pandemic.

On 21 March 2023, Branko Milanović, a somewhat sceptical economist, tweeted: 'How to explain that Finland, Iceland and Denmark are the top three happiest countries in the world, but are also No. 10, No. 1 and No. 9 in per capita consumption of antidepressants? Do you take an antidepressant before you answer the question on happiness?'[4] Within a day, 3,000 people had liked his comment and 788 had retweeted it. Only one person quietly dissented. Andreas Backhaus replied: 'Apples and oranges', alongside an image of where Branko had presumably found of the rankings of the tenth, first, and ninth for consumption of antidepressants. Backhaus is a population and development economist working as a postdoctoral researcher at the Federal Institute for Population Research in Germany. It is interesting to consider why he was the only one to spot the flaw, whereas so many thousands of others simply assumed that Milanović was making a sensible point.

The flaw was that only twenty-nine countries were compared in the ranking that Milanović had used to try to claim that Finland, Iceland and Denmark had some of the highest uses of antidepressants in the world. Furthermore, Iceland topped the list because its data included prescriptions from hospitals, for which the state reimbursed the cost of drugs, as well as the purchase of over-the-counter drugs which were almost certainly not as strong as the antidepressants that required a prescription to access. Hospital prescriptions were not included in the data for some countries, including Canada and the UK; and more significantly, the US and almost all poorer countries in the world were not included. Of course, few people in poorer countries would have been able to afford these drugs; but the US has very high levels of antidepressant use. Had Milanović taken these points into account, his quip would have been less convincing to those not already on the lookout for a pro-growth and happiness-sceptical economist's statistical sleight of hand.

Why would Milanović have wanted to undermine the suggestion that more equitable countries are happier, or that social fairness is one of the main routes to people becoming happier? I have written about that before, so won't waste more words on it here.[5] But clearly his suggestion – that the Nordic model does not increase happiness – is one that is welcomed by many people, especially those who do not see greater equality as a desirable social, or political, outcome.

In March 2024 the next annual set of happiness statistics was released. Finland topped the happiness league table again, and in fact moved up even higher in absolute terms. Average 'life evaluation' in Finland was 7.74, some way above Denmark, in second place at 7.58. Israel moved down a slot to fifth with 7.34 (the survey was taken before autumn 2023). Again, people who look at these figures might wonder how Israelis could, on average, report such high levels of personal happiness despite what has been happening in the Occupied Territories and Gaza for decades; perhaps the large majority of Israelis before October 2023 were unaware or did not understand? Or did not care? In March 2025 it will be interesting to see if the people surveyed in Israel (those who are included) are still so happy. The French dropped down to twenty-seventh (more on that drop below).[6]

Happiness depends on a great many things. For example, it is unlikely that people in more equitable countries rate their current life highly simply because they are living lives more like their neighbours. What is much more likely is that we are seeing the wider benefits of living in more equitable affluent societies: that is what so many studies find, and this is especially the case when it comes to how we are cared for, and health care above all.

Care and health

Who looks after us if we fall and our family cannot pick us up? Who helps when something happens to us that those closest to us do not know how to deal with? What if we have no friends or family, or if the remaining members of our family do not care, or lack capacity? What is the safety net, from birth to death, beneath us? How can those we love and care for be protected after we die, or if we cannot help? And what about everyone else: the neighbours and strangers in our cities and countries?

Maintaining social programmes has featured low down the list of key concerns surveyed by Ipsos in recent years. It is an abstract phrase that offers little purchase. By June 2024, it was a top three concern for only 7 per cent of people worldwide. However, combined with concerns over health care, which 23 per cent placed in their top three, how we are cared for overall from the cradle to the grave was the fourth-greatest set of concerns around the world, and that is even before we include related issues such as education. Who will take care – of us, our children, and our elderly – was the greatest concern after how to get by, what to do, and the apparently perennial fears of crime, violence, and war.

On its own, health care was the seventh-most mentioned concern in the world in spring 2022, a measure that was influenced by the enduring COVID-19 pandemic. Worry over access to health care has been the top concern of the population of China for many years.[7] That is partly because Chinese governments have relieved their people of so many other cares – including how to get by, what to do, crime, and violence – but it is also a reflection of enduring problems in the healthcare system in China, and the frequency with which payments have to be made to access it. Globally, by June 2024, worries over health care had risen to be the sixth-highest individually measured concern. The population of the world was ageing. Post-pandemic, many health and care systems were struggling. In truth, some had been struggling or unfairly managed for decades.

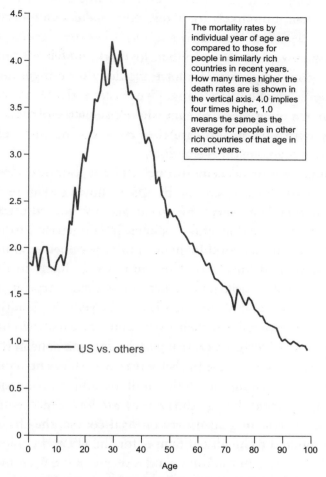

Figure 5.1: How much more likely people are to die in the US, by age, 2020s

The mortality rates by individual year of age are compared to those for people in similarly rich countries in recent years. How many times higher the death rates are is shown in the vertical axis. 4.0 implies four times higher, 1.0 means the same as the average for people in other rich countries of that age in recent years.

Source: Derek Thompson, 'America Fails the Civilization Test', *Atlantic*, 21 April 2023.

The country that spends the most overall on health care in the world, with the least measurable beneficial effect, is the US. It has given the world ample proof that when you don't maintain social programmes, people die early. Children in the US are twice as likely to die in any given year as their counterparts in comparable affluent nations, and young adults are up to four times more likely to die.[8] The disparity eventually shrinks with age, as death is finally inevitable for us all. But a seventy-year-old in the US is still

50 per cent more likely to die in any given year as compared to their contemporaries in affluent countries, and an eighty-year-old is 30 per cent more likely to. Those who make it to ninety in the US are no better off than their peers in other rich nations, despite being a more socially selected (and so, on the whole, an extremely affluent) group; a group who have avoided the younger deaths of their poorer neighbours. A ninety-year-old in the US is generally richer than a ninety-year-old anywhere else on the planet, and yet the very expensive health care they receive is no more effective than care elsewhere, on average.

A simple measure to demonstrate just how poor health care and general health outcomes are in the US is shown in Figure 5.1. For every individual of every single-year age group in the US, their chance of dying in that year is shown in comparison to that for everyone else in the world living in similarly affluent countries. In their first year of life, US babies are twice as likely to die than those born in other affluent countries. The same is true at age one, two, three, four, and so on: each and every year those born in the US are at greater risk. In their early teenage years, the chance of dying becomes even greater, rising each year: someone in the US is three times as likely to die in the year they turn twenty compared to those turning twenty in all the similarly affluent countries elsewhere in the world. By age thirty, they are four times as likely to perish before reaching age thirty-one! Of course, the chances are small compared to historical figures for the US and compared to poorer countries. But what would you pay to reduce by many times the chance of your loved ones dying at age thirty?

By the time Americans reach the age of one hundred – the tiny few that do – they have the smallest of advantages over their cohort of contemporary centenarians in the rest of the rich world, as Figure 5.1 shows. So, for all of that greed and not sharing (more politely termed 'concentration of wealth'), they gain a 1 per cent additional chance of not dying in their hundredth year. An almost entirely worthless reward.

Sadly, most Americans do not know the extent of the failure of their health and social care systems, combined with all the other factors that determine whether people in one country are more likely to die in any given year than in another. In June 2024, only 24 per cent of Americans listed issues of health care in their top three greatest concerns. Far more people did so in twelve other countries that month, including 40 per cent in the UK and 43 per cent in Canada, both countries with far better healthcare systems. The underlying reason for the US's bad health outcomes is that most care is commercial (private), and so accessible only to those who can pay, not to those in greatest need. Paradoxically, and very sadly, health care is considered one of the four greatest crises not in those countries where it is worst but in the ones where people appreciate its importance. People in other affluent countries worry that their health care, drug use, road deaths, and social collapse might deteriorate to the extent that they have in the US. Look again at Figure 5.1. It is how a country at war might look. But the war in the US is a war of the very rich on the poor.

The rich in places of great inequality are a burden we cannot afford, and arguably even one that they themselves cannot afford, as their lives are improved so little through their riches. Their excessive incomes damage the lives and the life chances of everyone else's children and grandchildren, and do not even help the rich to have happier or longer lives than they would otherwise. With regard to health services and older-age care provision, the fact that the richest people in places such as the US can command an excess of services, before others who have far greater need, has undermined the breadth and quality of care available to the vast majority of people via Medicaid and Medicare.

As Figure 5.2 demonstrates, three large European countries had lower life expectancy than the US in the early 1960s: Germany, Italy, and Spain. Germany's was also lower in the late 1970s and early 1980s. At that time, East Germany (included in the entity charted here) was a separate country and suffering due to the Cold War and blockades of goods; fear of war led to very high expenditure on arms and armies in what was then the Eastern Bloc. From the early 1990s onwards, however, the US saw much less progress in health as compared to the other seven large affluent countries shown in Figure 5.2, despite having won the Cold War, despite the collapse of communism in Russia and the Soviet Union as a whole, and despite its huge increase in average affluence. The US had greater wealth and income per person than any of the other seven countries shown, but its wealth was far more poorly shared out among the country's citizens than in any of the other seven.

US life expectancy flatlined and in some years even fell in the decade after the financial crash of 2008. But most importantly of all, when the pandemic that began in China in late 2019 spread around the world in 2020, the US was far less prepared than its peers to deal with the implications. Despite its being home to a relatively small proportion of very old people (who were at greatest risk of dying from COVID-19), the number of people who died early in the US, per capita, increased significantly in 2020, 2021, and 2022. Overall, over two years of life expectancy were lost. The next worst outcome was in the UK where the effects of austerity and pandemic combined. By 2023, people across the US were living five years less than those in Australia, on average; four years less than those in France, Italy, and Spain; three years less than in Canada; and two years less than those in Germany and the UK.

It is little wonder that we are preoccupied with fears about how we will be cared for by the state, especially those of us in places where care is already poor or is being systematically undermined – and especially in places where politicians argue for introducing more US-type private health care.[9] Failing health care is an entirely human-induced crisis, and one that (as always) is as much about what might happen as what has happened. In the UK, the National Health Service has been partially privatised. In Germany, where by contrast there is a stable (although tiered) healthcare system receiving funding of €1 billion a week more than that in the UK, stalling life expectancy is connected to the influence of hundreds of thousands of war refugees arriving from Syria. It is not the sign of a new local crisis, but of a country playing a disproportionately large role in tackling an existing but more distant crisis.

Figure 5.2: How the US compares in terms of life expectancy trends over time

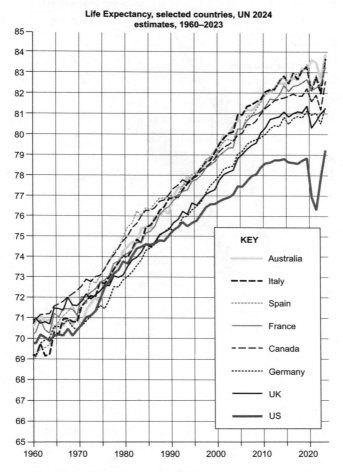

Source: United Nations, Department of Economic and Social Affairs, Population Division (2024). *World Population Prospects 2024*, Online Edition. File GEN/01/REV1, accessed October 2024.

The effect of not having a National Health Service is stark; 'the average American has the same chance of a long and healthy life as someone born in the most deprived town in England'.[10] It is not just the lack of public health care that leads to such poor outcomes in the US; slightly higher income inequality and less solidarity in the culture also take their toll. People die younger in more individualist societies, even the richest of all. As can be seen

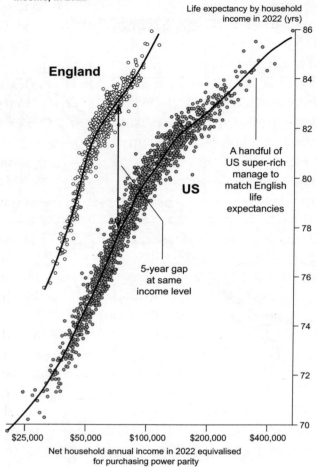

Figure 5.3: Life expectancy in US and England, by household income, in 2022

Source: Redrawn by hand from data first shown in this way by John Burn-Murdoch, 'Why are Americans dying so young?', *Financial Times*, 31 March 2023.

from Figure 5.3, the best-off people in England live as long, if not longer, than those in the US despite having four or five times less annual income. The poorest people in England live five or even six years longer than their counterparts in the US. Even someone whose longevity is average in England lives five years longer than their counterparts in the US.

You could look at Figure 5.3 and read it as implying just how well the English do. On average, they live five years longer than people on the same income in the US, and a year or two longer than people receiving twice their salaries in real terms. But it is only in comparison to the US that England looks good. Compare the English to almost any other set of affluent people in the world, and their health record is revealed to be abysmal.

When journalists working for *The Times*, the UK's paper of record, were confronted with the evidence of their country sliding down the international health ranks, they found it extremely difficult to produce a list of what Britain was good at: 'Obesity is one league table on which Britain ranks highly, beating all our European peers. Only the Maltese are fatter than we are.' Malta may be the capital of obesity, but it has had one of the most remarkable rises up the international league table of life expectancy; by 2020 it had the sixth-highest life expectancy in the world out of two hundred countries, while the UK was thirty-sixth.[11] The *Times* journalist tried to blame 'a lack of education about healthy ways of living', and advocated breaking up the public health service and encouraging people with disabilities to do paid work.

Everything is connected when it comes to care from the cradle to the grave. So let's now jump from the health of adults in different countries, and their obesity levels, to consider the chances of newborns. The two are linked superficially, in that very overweight mothers are more likely to have complicated births. There is a deeper connection too, in that people living in more unequal, and thus more frightened, affluent countries are more likely to get fat; and these are the same countries where health services are likely to be poor – also because of high income inequalities.

In 2021 in the US, the number of women who died during pregnancy or shortly after rose by 40 per cent in just one year, to 1,205, compared with 861 in 2020, and 754 in 2019. As a journalist in the *Wall Street Journal* explained: 'The increase pushed the maternal-mortality rate to 33 deaths per 100,000 live births, the highest since 1965, compared with 24 in 2020 and 20 in 2019.'[12] These women had not suddenly become fat. Some had died because complications in pregnancy were not properly addressed as they would have been just a year earlier – because health services in the US were failing more often as the pandemic continued. The main cause of the rise, however, was an increased risk of maternal suicide shortly after giving birth. Life was becoming more hopeless. The UK also saw maternal mortality rise due to an increase in suicides just before and after birth.[13] These two countries were outliers amongst affluent societies.

Elsewhere, the headline issues tended to be less extreme, with a very different set of problems appearing in France, a much more equitable country. Even though the situation is much better than in the US and UK, there are still great concerns over health care within France. With 11.2 per cent of its GDP going on healthcare expenditure, France spends more on the sector than almost all other European countries.[14] Yet the French consider their healthcare system to be in a state of collapse, making this one of their most important concerns in the June 2024 Ipsos poll. A quarter of all French people listed concerns over health care among their top three, many more than were concerned about unemployment (11 per cent) or climate change (19 per cent).

Within France, growth in public spending has been very low in recent years. While such growth had been 2.4 per cent annually for the Organisation for Economic Co-operation and Development (OECD) as a whole, between 2013 and 2018 it was only 0.8 per cent per year for France, on average. While public spending was increasing in absolute terms in France, it was growing less quickly than needed. The low growth convinced some politicians in charge of some sectors to believe they had to make savings. Indeed, while France leads the OECD in comparisons of healthcare spending, the opposite is true of hospital spending (3.6 per cent of French GDP compared with a 4.1 per cent OECD average).

Just as parts of the French hospital network were shrinking, the French government was not increasing funding for health in line with rising needs. Insufficient resources were leading to poor working conditions in hospitals, with many staff resigning. This led to a shortage of care assistants and nurses, as well as of doctors. The number of procedures being performed over a set period by a general practitioner per inhabitant fell in the same short period of time, from 4.8 in 2000 to 3.9 in 2017 (this is a better measure than the presence of doctors).

There are also medical deserts in France, mainly in rural areas, where healthcare support is hard to find. Other factors contributing to the health crisis in France include an ageing population, the rise in chronic diseases, and more expensive technical innovations being harder to fund. While France has a high life expectancy, its figures for healthy life expectancy are poor: 5 per cent of the adult population suffer from diabetes, and the country has a preventable death rate of 158 per 100,000, which may be partially explained by high levels of alcohol and tobacco consumption.

In 2022, a report from the Senate Committee of Inquiry into the State of Hospitals in France highlighted problems that had been exacerbated by the COVID-19 crisis.[15] The report also covered poor working conditions and low job attractiveness for carers, lack of freedom and autonomy for hospital staff, and hospital overcrowding. The empirical evidence for this included vacancies, bed closures, and additional working time (the need for overtime), staff moral measured as low, as well as staff leaving mid-career, and recruitment difficulties. The report's recommendations included giving hospitals greater freedom and autonomy in the way they were organised, and adapting funding sources. In France these are all considered very serious problems; but policymakers in the UK and US might dream of facing such situations. A crisis is less of a crisis when important remedies have already been identified.

A great deal of what is currently seen as a healthcare crisis in France was predictable and is theoretically not that hard to deal with if the right systems are put in place at the right time. Following the boom in births that started at the end of the Second World War and lasted until the early 1970s, the French population is now ageing. The consequences of this have been much debated in the French media.[16]

First, there will be an increase in dependency, with an additional 20,000 people needing to be housed and cared for in specialist establishments every year for many years to come – and at considerable cost. Another consequence is a shortage of labour, due to a decline in the number of younger people in work. Finally, there is the challenge of locked-in savings, because even though retirees save more than younger people, they are more likely to be homeowners and thus they usually hold the majority of their capital in illiquid forms. Groups such as the Petits Frères des Pauvres, an association that supports the elderly and isolated, are calling for public policy to take proper account of the ageing population, and they point out that by 2050, one in three people in France will be aged sixty or over.[17]

In 2022, a journalistic investigation made startling revelations about the inhumane treatment and living conditions of the elderly in the EHPAD (Etablissements d'hébergement pour personnes âgées dépendantes) of the Orpéa group, the sector leader.[18] In the aftermath of this scandal, a parliamentary bill (*PPL bien vieillir*) sought to meet the challenge of the demographic transition. Among the proposals was the allocation of new financial resources for autonomy, with the creation of a territorial public autonomy service in each district (decentralising many decisions), and increased staffing levels in EHPADs.[19]

Unsurprisingly, partly as a result of concerns about health care, France does not rank highly in happiness ratings. These concerns combine with others that affect well-being. In part due to this, in the spring of 2024 France ranked only twenty-seventh in the world happiness rankings, down from the twenty-first place it had held in the spring of 2023.[20] French society was in flux. In the general election of early summer 2024, the far right was again held at bay. In fact, the left won the most votes and began to negotiate with the diminished centre over who would govern the country into the autumn. In the event, the shrunken centrists tried to form a government with the smaller group of right-wing politicians. At the centre of this debate in France, as with so much of our politics in affluent countries, was the question of who cares. The political centre and right appeared to have most in common, over both caring less.

Who cares about education?

We worry greatly that other people do not care enough; that they may not be educated enough. For example, although climate change is a much lower priority in most people's thinking than all the issues so far discussed in this book, it is the health implications of future climate change that tend to be most worrying. At the start of summer 2023, the *Financial Times* ran a story that opened as follows:

> Phoenix, Arizona, where maximum temperatures have now exceeded 40°C for 26 successive days, is America's fastest growing big city. I fear that one of the reasons for such irrational behaviour is that most discussions about climate change continue to emphasise the risk of much worse things coming down the tracks. This is understandable, but a permanent focus on the future can blind us to what is already happening. We instead insist that life simply goes on, that we're adapting. The thing is, for a growing number of people, life does not go on at all. It's all very well saying that Arizona has always been very hot, but there are degrees of very hot. Between 1970 and 1990, an average of 16 people per year died from 'exposure to excessive natural heat'. Between 1990 and 2015, the average rose to 38. In 2020 it was 210, and 2022 came in at 257.[21]

These heat-related deaths comprise a tiny subset of all who had really died of this cause: in these cases, a medical examiner made the decision to declare extreme heat as the direct cause of mortality. The article reported that some of the deaths were of 'people who suffered severe burns when their skin came into contact with pavements superheated to as much as 82°C (180°F)'. The rise in heat-related mortality in Arizona is partly because there are now far more people living there who are not used to heat than has formerly been the case. There are also far more older people in general due to the baby boom following the Second World War. Furthermore, there was greater economic inequality and poverty that exacerbates these issues in the US by 2020 than in earlier decades, forcing more to live on the streets or in poor housing. The facts outlined in the quote above are extremely shocking. However, all those other factors just mentioned will account for a large part of the most recent rises in heat-related deaths, alongside the impact of the rising heat. Furthermore, and in addition to the overall undercounting, this is a larger issue than the raw numbers imply because heat-related deaths are more likely to be undercounted in areas where health services are stretched. In this way, one crisis – how the state cares for us, or not – is related to another, the climate crisis.

One reason why we do not, on average across the world, worry much about the climate crisis is that although news stories about deaths caused by climate change might be shocking, the numbers are still relatively small, and for many pale into insignificance in comparison to mortality caused by poverty and inequality, and crumbling health and social services. In addition, there is the everyday issue of just getting by. Is there an adequate school for your children? Are you able to pay for and access decent housing? Issues of social provision from the cradle to the grave constitute much greater crises in the minds of most people worldwide because they are current and remain unaddressed for so many. Why worry so much about what might go wrong in future, if today your children's or grandchildren's school is too expensive, too far away, disorderly, or underfunded? Or if the home where you are bringing them up is unfit to live in through no fault of your own? You might think adults bear most responsibility for their homes, but it is the country they live in that most determines their quality. Similarly with the provision of education, and no reasonable person would blame a child for the education they receive. Think about state education: why we have it, and what it does.

The perennial crisis of state services, and of how we are cared for (or not) by each other from the cradle to the grave, always revolves around how we view each other. When we viewed many children as a source of cheap labour, how they might be schooled was less of an issue. Over a century ago, education was expanding in most affluent states, not only because industry needed more literate and numerate workers, but also because it was thought that a better educated workforce would become a more docile and compliant electorate.

It is our politicians who determine how our education systems are funded, how well or poorly resourced most of our schools are, and whether young people will be plunged into ever-growing debt if they attend university. It is our educational systems and societies that produce these politicians – our representatives (as they describe and legitimise themselves). Thanks in many ways to the politicians of a past generation, the young are now the most educated, most literate, and most numerate generation ever to have lived. But we do not yet teach them enough of what they need to know to avert these crises. This is largely because we, older adults, are still so unsure about how to resolve them ourselves.

Services such as education are often said to be in crisis because of the speed of change, and the speed at which our thinking changes.[22] It is hardly a surprise, therefore, that there is always controversy about education, as we often do not know, and certainly do not agree on, what the truth actually is that we are trying to teach. Schools are as much about teaching children to conform, to accept their future place in the society they are born into, as they are places to foster thinking and learning.[23] We tend to want our children to believe what we believe, rather than to question it. But that reductive approach to education is always, thankfully, contested.

For the elite of the world, the standard of a child's education is thought to be linked to their parents' ability to pay – either through school fees or having the money to live in the catchment areas of the best state schools (in the US these are called public schools).[24] In countries with high income inequality, it is easier to sustain demand and support for inequality in education, including the allocation of more funding to school boards in some areas than in others, or more money and other resources for selective state grammar schools across Europe than is fair (given their easier workload), and a great deal more money for private schools in places such as the UK. All these decisions perpetuate divisive, unfair, tiered educational systems.

The very affluent in more unequal societies can more easily avail themselves of extra tuition and extracurricular activities that ease their children's progress to university. Their children can have private tuition and revision classes, and they can take as many exam resits as are necessary to get into the university of their choice. And the rich can help their children take on low-paid or free internships to get a head start in the job market, leading to opportunity hoarding for the best-paid jobs. Even in the most equitable countries, such as Finland, very few working-class children go to university. There is always a risk that it will not work out well, that it will not be beneficial; and with no cushion of family wealth to fall back on, that is a high risk. Thus, everywhere we look in the world, there is enormous inequality and very often corruption in education, especially in those places where it is seen as a sifting or sorting mechanism to best identify the supposedly most able.

It is sometimes claimed, particularly in more unequal countries, that government spending on education disproportionately benefits poorer people. In one study of income inequality it was claimed: 'In Australia, the biggest expenditure items – health and education – are somewhat redistributive to lower-income individuals.'[25] As better-off people tend to live to much older ages, however, and make more use of health services as they age, this is hardly ever true of health services when measured in terms of impact over time. Similarly, if paradoxically, even in countries with large private health sectors, public health care still tends to favour the rich who live longer.[26] Likewise, even in countries where few affluent children use state education, government spending on education tends to benefit better-off children the most, as they are much more likely to attend better-functioning (labelled 'the most successful') state schools, more likely to gain higher qualifications, and also to go on to higher-paid jobs, and go on to university, and likely be better rewarded in their later careers. This is the case in almost all countries ever studied, even the most equitable.

The economists whose comments on the Australian data are cited above, assumed that government spending on health and education were spread equally, to benefit every adult and child. This led to their conclusion, which was later publicised widely, that Australians had a real income *equality* as high as France.[27] A more nuanced analysis finds that to be false. For example, people born after 1957 will not receive state pensions until age sixty-seven in Australia.[28] By contrast, in France the pension age is now still around sixty-four for people born after 1968, and lower for older people. As the poor die earlier, disputes over pension age become part of the crisis of state care. University-educated children are also more likely to be able to afford to retire earlier – the unfairness accumulates.

French school education at first glance is what many of those of us living in the UK or US might assume to be equitably provided state education. However, as with health, when we ask if there is an educational crisis in a relatively equitable country such as France, many will claim that there is, despite that country having a better education system than most. France has a higher-than-average number of children per class (18.5 compared with 13.5 across the European Union as a whole in 2019), and also a higher than average number of hours being taught per subject, but a low teacher salary, at €29,065 in 2019 for a secondary school teacher, compared with €59,935 in Germany, for example. These two teaching positions are not strictly the same, because Germany's education system is more tiered than that of France (and this is a higher tiered teacher in Germany). Nevertheless, there are huge differences even between neighbouring European countries in terms of what is considered fair. Public spending on education is fairly high in France. In 2018 it stood at 3.3 per cent of GDP for primary and secondary schooling, and at 1.1 per cent for higher education, while the tuition fees for attending public universities in France, as in most of mainland Europe, are extremely low – usually minimal.[29]

Out of France's 869,300 teachers, 726,800 are in the public sector and 142,500 are in the (so-called) private sector.[30] The private sector in France is so highly subsidised by the state that in other countries it would be viewed as a part of the state sector, but it is selective. We can see this when considering a pupil's social position index (SPI), which provides information about their social, economic, and cultural conditions. In October 2022, the French education authorities were required to publish the social position indices of secondary schools, based on the average SPIs of their pupils. This showed a social divide between the country's private and state schools, with a concentration of the most advantaged pupils in private schools, particularly in large towns. Only 3.3 per cent of the 10 per cent of secondary schools with the lowest SPI are private establishments, compared to 60.9 per cent of the 10 per cent with the highest SPI. It is no wonder that when such statistics are revealed, many people say that there is something wrong with education, even in France – wrong enough to amount to a crisis.

There are also major regional disparities. It is a great disadvantage not to be a child of elite parents living in Paris. This is because these most advantaged students are the ones most likely to perform well, and their concentration in (the so-called) private education reinforces the inequalities between private and public education. Note that in France, private education is 73 per cent funded by the state and local authorities; yet remains highly discriminatory.[31]

France's elite higher education institutions known as the *grandes écoles*, mostly state funded but with selective entry, are frequently accused of encouraging the social reproduction of unfair advantage (sometimes called 'privilege') by further accentuating social inequalities in academic success, particularly through the competitive entrance exam. This is not a new problem. For children born between 1959 and 1968, their father's socio-professional category was very strongly correlated to the probability that they would enter a *grande école*. Less than 1 per cent of children of blue-collar workers ended up in one of those institutions, while around 20 per cent of the children of French university professors did.[32]

Another 2018 report shows that France's school system is, in fact, more unequal than those in most similarly developed countries, with schools largely failing to address the impact of social inequalities. In France, only 17 per cent of adults whose parents do not have a higher education diploma go on to obtain one, compared with 73 per cent of adults whose parents have a higher education diploma.[33] All these divides were exacerbated when the COVID-19 pandemic reached Europe in 2020. Different countries took very different approaches to the shutting of state schools.[34] Social scientists will study the lasting effects of these decisions, including on social mobility, for decades to come.

Social mobility in France (and Belgium, incidentally) is lower than might be expected given its level of income equality; it is higher than expected in Denmark, Finland, Sweden, the Netherlands, and Switzerland. The number of teenagers having children, almost always at age nineteen, is higher than might be expected in France, as it is in New Zealand and the US. Poorer French children do much worse at mathematics than their equivalents in comparable countries. More people in France perceive that opportunities are unfairly distributed than their peers in comparable countries, given the overall level of income equality. This perception is even more common, albeit likely for somewhat different reasons, in the Netherlands and Greece. In France, education is the key culprit. All these findings are based on the most recently available statistics, those of July 2024.[35]

French economist Thomas Piketty deconstructs the myth of an egalitarian French education system by showing that the choices made in allocating money have led to sharp increases in educational inequalities.[36] Pointing to the 10 per cent drop in spending per student between 2007 and 2017, he notes that the allocation of public money is three times greater for students in selective streams than for those in other streams, where there is a greater concentration of socially less advantaged young people. He explains that France is the only country where private schools and colleges are almost entirely state-funded, and they have the right to choose their pupils, which contributes to high levels of social segregation. And yet, there are still those who argue that France's school system is based on merit and rewarding hard work, rather than on underlying notions of social determinism.[37]

In March 2022, France's minister of education, Pap Ndiaye, declared that he was 'a pure product of the republican meritocracy, of which the school is the pillar' – implying that he is special and had been sought out for his personal brilliance.[38] On 2 June 2022, Emmanuel Macron launched pilots for 'the school of the future' in Marseille, an initiative focused on mathematics that provides funding for participating schools to undertake innovative projects, and began rethinking allocation mechanisms to send money where it was most needed.[39] The dangerous idea that selecting some children to receive more educational resources, other than those suffering some deficit that requires addressing, is increasingly going unchallenged in France.[40] This is just one example of a significant part of the overall crisis about how we care, and for whom, particularly as selective education teaches children through its very existence that not everyone is equally deserving of care and attention.[41]

In the past it was easier to spot those who believe we should be dividing up our children and that many of those whose families are poorer should never be born. An advocate of eugenics sounded an alarm just over a hundred years ago, in the context of US education and society: 'It is estimated that if the present trend continues, in 50 years from now every other child born in this country will either die in infancy or be unfit for self-support, thus being a burden upon society.'[42] Crises of wrong-headed thinking in education are nothing new. Far fewer children should be born poor, rather than the poor be prevented from having children. We do not have too many children.

State housing and political corruption

The echoes and initiatives about housing and schooling crises that travel back and forth across the Atlantic, and also over the Pacific, and very locally too, are now continuous. In April 2023, *UnHerd* magazine, founded in 2017 by British right-wing Conservative activist Tim Montgomerie, released a report on the 'declining Blue Wall'.[43] There was trouble, it revealed, in Surrey – a county that had until recently been the most affluent of England, and was once one of the best-off parts of Europe. A short extract illustrates this well (excerpted at greater length on page 46, the text bears repeating):

> The south-east has seen the biggest fall across the country in disposable income since 2019, with a gap opening up between median income and house prices that far outpaces the rest of England. More recently, some of the country's most expensive mortgages were among those hit hardest after the Truss Budget. Nor is the county immune from the cost-of-living crisis . . . it's not unreasonable to talk about a wave of de-gentrification taking place not just in Surrey, but across the Home Counties.

Much has changed in recent decades in the UK: child poverty is now higher in Surrey and other counties in South-East England than in Scotland, which had for decades been one of the poorest parts of the UK. England now suffers from a growing lack of adequate homes. As the Resolution Foundation explained in 2024 (most of the UK, of course, is England): 'UK homes are more cramped, and less conveniently located for jobs, than in many comparable countries. Adding insult to injury, the UK's housing stock is also the oldest in Europe (four-in-ten homes were built before 1946), and one of the most poorly insulated as a result.'[44] British homes are also the most expensive of any large country in Europe.

France is more typical among affluent countries, at least in the context of housing, but that does not stop housing from being considered in crisis there. Closely coupled to the housing crisis is the question of who ends up with the most wealth in each country and how its distribution is often, although not always, becoming more skewed.

In France, inherited wealth concentration has been on the rise. In 1970, wealth that had been passed down represented 30 per cent of total wealth, compared to around 60 per cent of all wealth in France today. The median inheritance is now around €70,000, but 40 per cent of households receive an average inheritance of less than €8,000, which reflects major and growing inequalities in wealth. Between 10 per cent and 25 per cent of French people pay inheritance tax, but 79 per cent are opposed to taxing inheritances from wealthy parents who they consider have worked hard all their lives. French people who inherit younger usually inherit less: in the early 2020s, 53 per cent of heirs under the age of thirty received less than €8,000. In fact, single people are in the majority at each end of the scale, typically receiving under €8,000 or over €100,000, with couples more often found in the intermediate brackets.[45]

When it comes to housing in France, in addition to wealth inequalities, there are major generational divides, much to the detriment of young people, and these have worsened in recent decades. In the past few years, housing has become the highest-cost item for French households, ahead of food, transport, and health. While the baby boomer generation benefited from affordable property prices in the 1970s, enabling a sharp rise in home ownership among that cohort, lower interest rates and longer borrowing periods in the 1990s increased demand and led to higher prices. Increased borrowing by younger adults enabled homeowners to become richer, as rising prices, particularly in cities, made it harder for younger adults to buy a home without borrowing enormous sums of money. There are also major generational inequalities in access to social housing, as residential mobility is very low.[46]

According to INSEE, home ownership in France is highly concentrated within certain groups. A quarter of households living in France are multi-owner households, and they own two-thirds of all the country's housing stock held by private individuals. Some 3.5 per cent of all households own at least five homes, but they also own 50 per cent of all rented accommodation held by private individuals. The typical profile of multi-owner households is as follows: well-off or fairly well-off, older than average, and married, with their main residence being on the outskirts of a town. Half of them own more than one rented property, and those properties are typically in the centre of large towns.[47]

In terms of international comparisons, 2020 OECD data shows that in France, 29 per cent of low-income tenants spent more than 40 per cent of their income on rent in the private sector, which is below the OECD average (36 per cent), and well below the equivalent proportion in the UK (53 per cent) and in Italy (35 per cent). This proportion is higher than in Austria (19 per cent) or Germany (15 per cent) – two European countries with much less of a housing crisis. On the other hand, when it comes to overcrowding within housing among low-income households, France comes out better with a rate of 16 per cent, just below Italy (23 per cent).[48]

In the European Union in 2020, 8 per cent of households and 32 per cent of poor households were overburdened by housing costs. In France, the proportion of poor households overburdened by housing costs increased by 15 per cent between 2020 and 2021. In Germany, the problem is even more acute, with a 39 per cent increase, partly due to having accepted more poor refugees in recent years. Other countries have also seen a small increase. These include Slovenia (+5 per cent), Belgium (+4 per cent), Estonia (+4 per cent), and the Czech Republic (+3 per cent).[49]

Homelessness has steadily increased over the past decade in all EU countries except Finland, where the number of homeless people is falling. Finnish policy on homelessness is ambitious and based on the construction of affordable housing and the adoption of the Housing First model. This consists of offering homeless people permanent rental accommodation and needs-based support as part of the National Programme to Reduce Long-Term Homelessness. Finland is proof that political will and long-term effort can dramatically reduce homelessness, a social issue which is often seen elsewhere as an unsolvable, permanent problem.[50]

Faced with the growing need to provide emergency accommodation, France introduced a five-year housing plan (2018–22) that reformed access to housing for homeless people, based on the Housing First model.[51] Why don't other states address their housing crisis by imitating Finland's example, as France is doing?

Many people have highlighted obvious solutions to the crisis. These commonly cited solutions include bringing urban land under democratic control, strengthening the planning system, and making sure that the state owns a decent proportion of land overall. Private landlords should mostly be squeezed out of the market entirely; this is best done by strengthening rent controls, providing more secure tenancies, and taxing wealth more effectively, as was once the case in countries like the UK where income from wealth was taxed at the same level, if not higher, than income from labour. The well-publicised arguments of the private sector that its continued prosperity is essential to solving housing problems now ring very hollow. The counter-refrain is becoming more familiar: 'True public housing – affordable to all at the point of need – must be our central goal.' But such missives almost always end with some version of the age-old conundrum that 'who might deliver this . . . is a question without an answer'.[52] In Finland, an answer has been found: the state, supported by achieving greater equality and political advocacy – each building on the other over time.

So why is so little of value done to address the housing crisis in so many countries, despite such good examples from elsewhere? Corruption is the simplest answer, and it is worth noting that financial and political corruption was cited by 26 per cent of people in July 2024 as among their top three greatest concerns. Our politicians are too often corrupt. In many countries, many elected representatives are also landlords (and landlords as a category are often corrupt in terms of both their finances and in the low quality of the service they provide). So it is important to consider corruption in the context of the overall crisis of state care, a crisis ranked so highly by people worldwide.

In 2022, and still by June 2024, financial and political corruption came fifth in the greatest concerns for people around the world. Education was the ninth most mentioned issue (tenth in 2024); moral decline (mentioned also in Chapter 4) was the fourteenth (twelfth in 2024); and the rise of extremism was the sixteenth (fourteenth in 2024). Corruption is included in the group of concerns combined in this chapter because of its links to concerns about health care, ageing, taxation, and the maintenance of social programmes in general, including education, housing, and in wider public life.

Among countries surveyed worldwide, financial and political corruption is of least concern in Sweden, Japan, Germany, and France, and is of greatest concern in South Africa, Malaysia, Peru, Colombia, and Hungary. It is not that difficult to link the concerns that citizens have over the corruption of their politicians, or their financial sectors, with how well or poorly a country is educating and housing its young people. The extent to which some claim there may be an ongoing moral decline can be linked to increasingly widespread forms of extremism and support for greater authoritarianism in the very near future, especially in the most economically unequal countries.

Even though people in France and other countries like it may view corruption as a minor issue overall, it is an everyday topic of discussion when it comes to perceived links between networking and corruption, and especially given the links between elite French secondary schools and politicians. There is Nicolas Sarkozy, for example, born into a very wealthy family in Paris, educated at a private Catholic school, and charged with corruption in 2020; in 2021 he was sentenced to three years in prison, but had to serve only one of those years, and spent it at home rather than in prison. Sarkozy passed the baton on to François Fillon, having endorsed him to be president in 2016. In 2017, while Fillon was a presidential candidate, *Le Canard enchaîné* uncovered the fact that he had hired his wife Penelope as a parliamentary attaché, and that her fictitious employment continued for several years, to the tune of €600,000. Both were later convicted.[53] They both received prison sentences of several years, which were substantially reduced; Penelope did not spend a single day in prison.

In the wake of this scandal, France passed a law on ethics in public life with the aim of preventing favouritism and corruption. Among other things, it prohibits the hiring of family members (ascendants, descendants, and spouses) by members of the French government, parliament, and local authorities; requires the presentation of invoices for the reimbursement of actual expenses to members of parliament; abolishes the parliamentary reserve for the allocation of subsidies to avoid 'clientelist abuses'; and demands that the president's assets be verified at the end of his or her term.

Corruption in public life and its impact on health, housing, education, and procurement in general is a great ongoing concern. In one of our possible futures, the world will become ever more dominated by politicians and financiers drawn from more exclusive schools and universities, including those who have paid to take postgraduate degrees in learning how to be a world leader at the most elite of global universities. Some will be the leaders of housing associations that pretend to be providing social housing while actually behaving like giant private landlords. Others will run private universities or private hospitals to increase their personal profit. To some, this would be a technocratic paradise in which we are mostly governed by our betters, for the common good, with the market deciding who thrives and who struggles. Others see this as a road to serfdom for the majority; a plausible candidate for the next great crisis.

Roughly a third of people worldwide agree with the statement: 'Regardless of who is officially in charge of governments and other organisations, there is a single group of people who secretly control events and rule the world together' – or they did when asked in August 2020.[54] This is usually described as belief in a conspiracy theory. However, the wording of the question is ambiguous. If you consider 'the most powerful people' in the world as a single group – the ruling class, the elite, or the 1 per cent – it would be harder to suggest that you were engaging in a conspiracy theory if you were to agree with such a claim – particularly if you think (or have learnt through experience) that key decisions are almost always made in secret by the rich.

Leaders tend to avoid open debate on the subject of whether to go to war with another country, for example. Central bank interest rates tend to be set by groups that, at least initially, discuss their decisions in secret, even if they later publish them. Almost all the policies of all the political parties in the world are at first formulated in private meetings. In some cases, a hugely momentous decision might be made by only a couple of people.

The question of who runs the world matters, because answering the question above positively is often seen as a belief that the world is 'secretly run from the shadows by persons unknown', a conspiracy theory that YouGov (who ran this survey) describes as stemming from the late eighteenth century, while noting that 'it could be argued to be older'. Crucially, this survey question does not ask people if they think the world is *run* by 'persons unknown'; it asks if the people you think have most power: 'secretly control events and rule the world together', which does imply an unlikely degree of coordination between those separately in charge of, say, China, India, Europe, Russia, and the Americas.

If you see the ruling elite of the separate parts of the world as being remarkably similar to each other and made up of people who tend to share common interests – almost all tending to be older men, for example – then it might not be unreasonable to agree with this statement. Although, as you can tell from my caution here, while I have some sympathy for people who hold conspiracy theory beliefs, I would want to reply to this question with a short essay rather than just ticking a box. We all suffer from paranoia at times, and some groups have far more reason to do so than others. Occasionally there *are* conspiracies – as the cases of corruption in recent French politics illustrate; more often there is a collusion of likeminded interests among the very rich and very powerful.

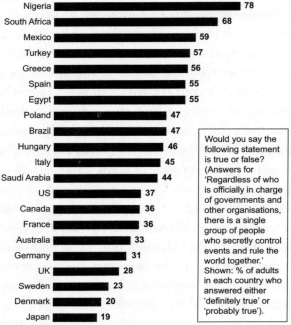

Figure 5.4: Adults who believe a single secretive group rules the world, 2021 (%)

Country	%
Nigeria	78
South Africa	68
Mexico	59
Turkey	57
Greece	56
Spain	55
Egypt	55
Poland	47
Brazil	47
Hungary	46
Italy	45
Saudi Arabia	44
US	37
Canada	36
France	36
Australia	33
Germany	31
UK	28
Sweden	23
Denmark	20
Japan	19

Would you say the following statement is true or false? (Answers for 'Regardless of who is officially in charge of governments and other organisations, there is a single group of people who secretly control events and rule the world together.' Shown: % of adults in each country who answered either 'definitely true' or 'probably true').

Source: Connor Ibbetson, 'Where do people believe in conspiracy theories?', London: YouGov, 18 January 2021.

If you look at the geographical distribution of people who ticked yes to the question of whether there is a single group who secretly control events, they are concentrated in countries that are poorer and less equitable (Figure 5.4).

Examining the answers more thoroughly for the UK, the 28 per cent in Figure 5.4 comes from summing two totals: the 5 per cent of people who thought it was definitely true, and the 23 per cent who thought it was probably true. A further 28 per cent thought it was probably false, and 28 per cent thought it definitely false, with some 15 per cent responding 'don't know', which might be the most sensible answer of all. After all, if these meetings are being held in secret, how would we know?

A true conspiracy theorist might add all these figures up and wonder why they amount to 99 per cent and don't include the

1 per cent – but of course this is the effect of rounding up (honestly – I am not trying to fool you – rounding errors are not a conspiracy). Notably, in the YouGov study that underlies these claims: 'China, Saudi Arabia and Egypt were excluded from some combined country samples as YouGov only conducts certain types of research in these countries.'[55] Could it be that in some places (perhaps China, Saudi Arabia, and Egypt) it is particularly obvious that – regardless of what public body is said to officially be in charge of governments (and other organisations) – there is a single group of people who secretly control events together? A particular coterie within the ruling party, the royal family, or the military may, for some very long periods of time, always be in charge, regardless of official claims for great openness.

Even in the most equitable and democratic of countries, there needs to be vigilance when politicians meet in private with those who own newspapers and large businesses. In Finland, the non-English-speaking country I have studied the most, it has been clear in recent years that orchestrated attempts were being made by some well-funded groups to stir up racial hatred on social media. Yet it is also the case that: 'conspiracy theories have a very strong emotional appeal – at least to some people. Some believers in these theories like to think that they are impartially choosing their belief because they are more rational, more intelligent, or more open-minded than all those benighted, deluded "sheeple" out there.'[56]

Public services tend to be better provided in those countries where fewer people believe that a secretive elite controls events and rules the world. There is a telling international pattern here. In Canada, for example, a minority believe the following statements are true or do not know if they are true: 'The 1969 moon landings were faked' (29 per cent); 'The AIDS virus was created and spread around the world on purpose by a secret group or organisation' (29 per cent); 'The idea of man-made global warming is a hoax that was invented to deceive people' (31 per cent); 'The US Government knowingly helped to make the 9/11 terrorist attacks happen in America on 11 September, 2001' (40 per cent);

'The truth about the harmful effects of vaccines is being deliberately hidden from the public' (44 per cent); and 'Humans have made contact with aliens and this fact has been deliberately hidden from the public' (49 per cent). Canadians have better health, education, and housing systems in place than their neighbours to the south enjoy. They also more often believe that they, and not a shadowy elite, hold power, but only by a single percentage point more than their neighbours in the US. It may also shock you how many people, even in Canada, subscribe to these beliefs; but we should ask more carefully why they do, rather than simply dismissing them as ignorant.

A majority of Canadians believe (or do not doubt) the following two statements: 'Members of Donald Trump's election team knowingly worked with the Russian Government to help him win the 2016 US Presidential Election' (76 per cent); and 'Regardless of who is officially in charge of governments and other organisations, there is a single group of people who secretly control events and rule the world together' (53 per cent).

The same pattern is found in Brazil, where the two majorities are 62 per cent and 59 per cent respectively, and the other standard public statements (on the moon landing, AIDS, and so on) are distrusted by a majority. Exactly the same patterns appear in the following countries: Spain (78 per cent and 70 per cent); Italy (75 per cent and 64 per cent); Germany (67 per cent and 50 per cent); and France (52 per cent and 54 per cent) – although in France, 58 per cent doubt they are being told the truth about vaccines. This last pattern is also found in Japan: 72 per cent believed (or did not doubt) the statement about Trump and Russian influence, and 50 per cent believed (or did not doubt) the existence of a group secretly controlling world events, with 58 per cent distrustful of vaccines. In Greece, the figures are 70 per cent and 68 per cent, although the Greeks are evenly split over whether aliens have made contact (50 per cent saying definitely or probably not), and only 46 per cent of Greeks think there was definitely or probably no US involvement in 9/11.

Like the French and Japanese, the Greeks are more distrustful of vaccines. Similarly, in Hungary these proportions are 65 per cent and 60 per cent, and a majority also entertain the possibility of alien contact having occurred. The US is very similar to Hungary, where 61 per cent and 56 per cent believe or do not doubt the claims about Trump and about the secret global group, with a narrow 51 per cent majority not doubting that there has been alien contact, and 52 per cent unsure whether we have been told the truth about vaccines.

In Sweden, 76 per cent believe or do not overtly doubt the allegations of Trump's officials colluding with Russians, but only 41 per cent believe or do not doubt that the world is secretly controlled by the powerful. Denmark is similar: 78 per cent and 37 per cent. In Mexico, Nigeria, Poland, South Africa, and Turkey, there is, perhaps understandably, more distrust. And despite YouGov claiming not to have asked these questions in Egypt and Saudi Arabia, answers to them were nevertheless reported in their data tables, although very large numbers of those respondents opted for 'don't know' to most questions (which might be a sensible answer to many questions in those countries in case you are being individually monitored!). The countries in which the questions were not asked, and no data recorded, were actually India, China, Indonesia, and Thailand.

The only two countries where the pattern differs significantly are the UK, where 80 per cent do not doubt the Trump allegations (they think his initial election to become president was a Russian stitch-up) but 45 per cent think secret control by the powerful was unlikely, and Australia, where the figures are 78 per cent and 48 per cent respectively. What is it about the UK and Australia that makes the suggestion that the powerful might sometimes collude more of a taboo than elsewhere? I'll leave you to look for the clues (hint: Rupert Murdoch and his media interests) – but beware of being labelled a conspiracy theorist![57]

The overall crisis that this chapter has addressed – of people's doubting politicians' ability to ensure good health, housing, and education systems, now and in future – has its underlying origins in a lack of trust in our politicians and in each other. The four countries in the world where people are most likely to say that a majority of people can be trusted are Denmark, Finland, Norway, and Sweden. Trust is lowest in Greece, Portugal, and Israel among those countries where it is measured in similar ways, and which are also affluent.[58] We can see conspiracies everywhere, if we wish to. Some of the outcomes we complain about are just how things normally operate – but we want better. Where there is greater trust, it is easier to persuade people that if you set out to look after people from the cradle to grave, regardless of any assessment of their usefulness, then they will tend to become more useful people. Then you are more likely to have less secretive governments.

Around the world, crises change minds. Most people do not blame individuals for the state of society, but the governments that have allowed it to deteriorate.[59] But government is supposed to be *of* the people. We are thus left facing a crisis of whether we can be governed. Can we, as a very large group of 8 billion people (soon to be 9 billion), actually organise ourselves well? To begin to answer this, we next turn to what many affluent individuals tend to say is the greatest crisis of all – the climate crisis – and what appears to be our inability, and that of our governments, to address the issue of global warming adequately. Climate is the fifth largest crisis in the eyes of the global middle class. If you wonder why it ranks so low, hopefully the discussion up to this point explains why.

6

Climate Crisis

As the world heats up, willingness to act is falling.
                                          Ipsos, April 2024[1]

The Ipsos April 2024 survey of 24,000 people in thirty-three countries found that after ten consecutive months in which heat records were broken there was less interest than ever in fighting climate change, especially among young men. Moreover, across all age groups, conviction on climate change action was on the wane.[2]

Beliefs, the reports' authors said, lagged behind climate reality. The public in very large numbers in many countries worldwide had become increasingly sceptical about the affordability of transitioning from fossil fuels. In the face of dire predictions, people were turning their backs on the voices of doom. There was enough trouble in the world already. This, in a nutshell, is why climate change is only the fifth most important crisis, even for better-off people; and for poorer people it is even lower down the list of priorities. Worldwide, the view is growing that when politicians say they are doing something to tackle the climate crisis, they are in fact doing something for themselves.

The Intergovernmental Panel on Climate Change (IPCC), the United Nations body that advocates for urgent action on climate change, has begun to try to meet detractors halfway, avoiding the frequent use of the language of catastrophe. The 2023 IPCC report offered a nuanced story in an attempt to regain what the report authors might have believed was a waning consensus. Here are some of their words, from 2023:

> Accelerated climate action can also provide co-benefits. Many mitigation actions would have benefits for health through lower air pollution, active mobility (e.g., walking, cycling), and shifts to sustainable healthy diets. Strong, rapid and sustained reductions in methane emissions can limit near-term warming and improve air quality by reducing global surface ozone. Adaptation can generate multiple additional benefits such as improving agricultural productivity, innovation, health and wellbeing, food security, livelihood, and biodiversity conservation.[3]

New discoveries were being made that could be used to bolster hope. In the year 2020 it was reported that 72 per cent of the carbon captured by a tree is released into the soil rather than being captured simply within the wood of the tree.[4] Thus planting more trees has a far greater impact than previously realised, and as trees grow larger, as they tend to do in air with a greater concentration of carbon dioxide, the amount sequestered in the soil will grow too. But, of course, that would not be enough to outweigh growing pollution caused by our accelerating consumption of fossil fuels.[5]

You might think climate change is the next greatest crisis – both the greatest crisis we face now and the even larger one about to come – but if you do, you are unusual. The climate crisis ranked seventh in the Ipsos December 2023 survey of the greatest worries of people around the world. It had slipped to eighth by June 2024, and then down to ninth by August 2024. It only ranks fifth in this book because I have amalgamated several that rank higher.

Only one person in six worldwide now places the climate in their top three greatest concerns, and that proportion is falling. For people in Australia and the Netherlands it was of the greatest concern in 2022 and 2023, and was the lowest concern of people in Argentina and Peru. By 2024 Singapore and the Netherlands (both low-lying countries) had it as high priorities; in contrast, in

Israel and Argentina it was the lowest of all worries. Concern jumps around by place and time, but also note that hardly any countries in Africa or low-lying Pacific Nations are included in the survey, so this is not the whole global story.

You may think concern about climate change will rise and rise. But it is possible that globally it might instead continue to fall. It is always perceived by the respondents to these global surveys (ever since the surveys began) as less important than the crises that the previous four chapters of this book have summarised. Climate change ranks even lower as a global concern if those others are not grouped together, and relative concern about it has been falling most quickly during 2024 as other crises are currently becoming more important in peoples' minds. The *real* worst crisis, for the large majority, is almost always something else. So, think how the majority react when they are repeatedly told that changing climate is more important by far than any other issue. Think of what most people make of the suggestion that the climate crisis is of paramount importance because of repercussions that they are told have already happened, and how much worse those repercussions are expected to become in future.

Concern about the climate crisis varies by age and social class. It is the peak concern of those who are youngest and most affluent; although as Ipsos pointed out in 2024, this is becoming less and less true of young men. The changing imperative of many younger men as a group became something of an obsession for political commentators in 2024. One report based on a huge number of global surveys claimed that while *young women* around the world were becoming 'the most liberal group in history', *young men* were not: in particular, young men in the US were the only group of any 'actually to have become more conservative since 2014 – or, in the poll's terms, to favour more control rather than freedom'.[6] The report concluded that social media algorithms were magnifying this trend by drawing 'moderately conservative young men towards more extreme and radical conservative male role models and world views'.

Of course, the social media algorithms that govern what we all see on those platforms were all originally owned, and have famously been more recently manipulated, by the new media moguls of today. In some cases there have been obvious alterations to the algorithms due to the takeover of platforms by a few individuals, most notably Elon Musk's purchase of Twitter, which became X. But none of the most used platforms act as a global commons. So why are young women more immune to the climate change-denying mogul-steered social media click-bait than young men? One trite but reasonable answer is that almost all of the software engineers employed to help steer the algorithms to change what we think, are men.[7]

More importantly, younger adults around the world continue to be politically apathetic: they tend not to vote, not to form new political parties, and not to campaign or agitate as much or as vigorously as previous generations. Their parents were also less engaged than their grandparents at the same ages and thus this is all part of a longer-term trend. So rather than asking why more young men are turning to the far right and more young women to the left and to green ideas and parties, we should ask why so many are still not turning to either. Why is apathy rising?

Whose interests are served by keeping young people (especially those most susceptible) in a state of confusion? We know that the richest 10 per cent of people in the world are responsible for a disproportionate amount of the world's carbon emissions – at least two-thirds – owing to ultra-high-consumption lifestyles. Among them (*us* in my case, and probably you too), as Figure 6.1 shows, the richest 1 per cent in the world are far more polluting than the rest of the richest 10 per cent. It is surprising that this is not better known, and that we do not debate this more, and force that group to change their ways – which could be efficiently done by removing some of their riches from them via tax: the riches that finance cruise holidays and second homes, gas-guzzling cars and not having to worry about heating homes or insulation.

The climate crisis is almost entirely a crisis of overconsumption by the undertaxed rich. Historic carbon emissions are also

Figure 6.1: Global emissions of carbon dioxide by income group, in 2019 (tonnes)

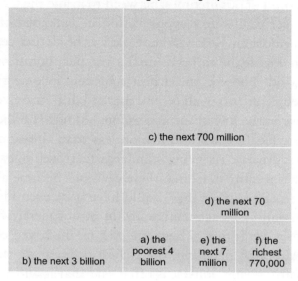

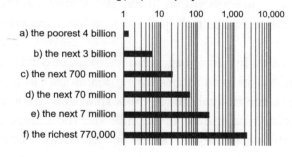

Source: Lucas Chancel, 'Global carbon inequality over 1990–2019', *Nature Sustainability*, Vol. 5, pp.931–938, 29 September 2022.

very much the result of the coal burnt to keep England's wealthy warm, and to create steam power for their mills, and power the trains they travelled on. Up until 1882, one in every two surplus carbon atoms in the atmosphere were 'British carbon'.[8] Almost all of those British emissions are still circulating in the atmosphere; they are older emissions but that does not mean they are not still contributing. There is a group of interests that do not want these issues of retrospective redistribution – also known as reparations – to be addressed.

During most of our lifetimes, between 1990 and 2015, the world's richest 10 per cent were responsible for an estimated 52 per cent of carbon emissions.[9] Alone, the world's richest 1 per cent caused more than double the carbon emissions of the poorest 50 per cent in that period. Those in the richest 1 per cent income group – 77 million people in 2019 – all receive more than US$100,000 a year, while those in the lowest income group – almost 4 billion people in 2019 – typically earn and live on less than US$6,000 a year, or US$10–15 a day. As living standards improved between 1990 and 2019, especially in China, these divisions became a little less acute. A century earlier they would have been even more stark.

Carbon emissions accumulate in the atmosphere, where they can stay for centuries. These are the main driver of climate change. Although people in the richest nations are the biggest cause of carbon emissions, it is often said that it will be those in the poorest nations who will suffer the greatest effects of climate change, as they are already in hotter parts of the world. This is not necessarily true; the rich have most to lose, and not just their wealth.

The rich often live to old age, and so are most affected by heat; the rich tend to live in countries where people are not used to high temperatures; the rich rely much more than most people on business being able to continue as normal; and the rich benefit from political stability, while disruption is one of the likely implications of climate change.

In contrast to the richest people on Earth, the poorest have had to adapt most to change in the recent past: because of a lack of town planning outside of countries like China, many have been forced to live in slums when their grandparents lived in villages; the poor are often forced into itinerant lives, and they make up almost the entire population of refugee camps worldwide. However, I am sceptical about claims that the effects of climate change – both those that have happened and those that are to come – will most harm the poor. Later in this chapter I provide some evidence that (to date) it has been people in richer countries that have suffered most from rising heat, principally because so many in rich countries are old and unprepared for the heatwaves that have already occurred. I suspect the changes to come might most alter the lives of the richest people on Earth and their descendants far more than the poorest. Although that is not necessarily an overall harm, it could be a welcome change. As the climate changes, so can our societies. Adapting to climate change will soon require: 'a quite drastic reduction in income and wealth gaps.'[10]

Climate emergency

Countless missives on the climate emergency describe, in language resembling the Book of Revelation, the dire implications of failing to act now. There are better ways of explaining what needs to be done and why – ways that are less off-putting. The US author Helen Keller made a trenchant and valuable comment in 1912: 'Until the great mass of the people shall be filled with the sense of responsibility for each other's welfare, social justice can never be attained.'[11] The climate emergency might better be framed as a social justice emergency.

Ultimately the climate emergency is about people, although debate often focuses on the planet. The planet will almost certainly be fine: it has known many climates, including warmer than any we are expecting in the near future. Human beings, and how climate affects us, are the subject of this chapter. Implications for the rest of nature, and indirectly for people, is the subject of the next, penultimate chapter.

More nuanced calls to action against climate change tend to play out as follows. The excessive incomes of the richest people spill over and take a significant toll on the quality of life for everyone else; to address this problem, we need to significantly reduce inequality and, in so doing, revive as fast as possible the idea of community and social solidarity. Unless we can live lives that are recognisable and understandable to each other, rather than inhabiting separate economic universes that never connect other than through the poor serving the rich, we will never be able to forge the common purpose that is necessary to build a fairer and more sustainable future.

This kind of message is not wrong, but it is so vague that it is almost pointless. These points are all true, but spelling it out is only the first step. Furthermore, the wordiness and abstraction of messages written in this way may suggest that discourse on climate change is merely an intellectual pursuit.

The direst predictions about the climate are not addressed in this chapter, because I am assuming they are well known to most readers. Instead, I concentrate on how much damage has been caused by climate change to date – by which, in this chapter, I mean damage to people: how numbers of lives lost in natural disasters have increased over time, and are likely to do so again as temperatures continue to rise and as extreme weather events become more frequent. In short, I am addressing the rational basis for the general scepticism that prevails in so many peoples' minds over how bad climate change will be, rather than simply dismissing it as ignorance. Once again, most people are more concerned about how they will get by, what they will do, will there be war, or if they might otherwise suffer crime and violence, and who will care for them and theirs.

Before going further, we should note that when people in countries around the world were asked in August 2020, almost always a tenth and sometimes more than a quarter of respondents believed that climate change was a hoax; Figure 6.2 shows that this included 27 per cent of people in the US.[12] This might help to explain why climate change ranks only fifth in this book as an issue of concern, based on the key present and future fears among the global population.

Of course climate change is not a hoax. It is real, and carbon emissions, along with other pollutants, are the main reason for rising average temperatures. And of course global warming also results in rising sea levels, and rising numbers of extreme weather events. But if you overplay the story, if you cry wolf

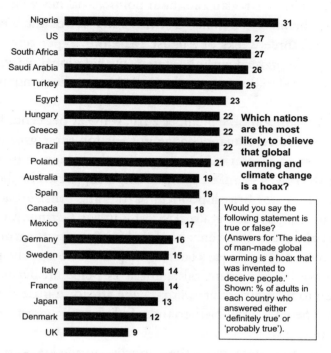

Figure 6.2: Location of people who believe climate change is a hoax, 2020

Source: Poll taken 20 July to 24 August 2020. See: Connor Ibbetson, 'Where do people believe in conspiracy theories?', YouGov, 18 January 2021.

too often and too early, if you downplay the importance of the many other crises that are *more important* in *most people's lives* and in influencing their fears, then you lose sympathy and understanding.

Some surveys undertaken in the US in 2023 and 2024 put updated estimates of how many Americans viewed climate change to be a hoax as a little lower than in 2020, at 15 per cent and 16 per cent, but these used a different methodology to the YouGov survey mentioned at the end of Chapter 5 of this book, and were conducted in ways likely to lower the overall estimate.[13] Ask the question a little differently and you can double that percentage. Give US voters the option to support a climate-change-denying president and you may get an even better idea of their true feelings. In contrast, Figure 6.2 shows it is almost possible to eliminate climate change scepticism if you have the national broadcaster on board (the BBC) and all the main political parties singing from the same hymn sheet. When YouGov interviewed the UK public in the first three weeks of August 2020, only 9 per cent of them said that they agreed with the statement that global warming is a hoax designed to deceive people. Even that number is not insignificant though.

In the Ipsos poll of September 2019, some 25 per cent of people in the UK placed climate change in their top three greatest concerns, almost three times as many as thought it was a hoax. Again, the BBC's steadfast position helps, supported by the agreement of all major British political parties and other broadcasters and newspapers that it is a real threat. Only in Germany, Canada, France, and Australia were a slightly higher proportion of people so concerned. Three years later, by September 2022, the proportion in the UK was identical again at 25 per cent; but now – in addition to the four countries that were already a little more concerned – people in the Netherlands, Italy, and Belgium were also more concerned than those in the UK. By both June and August 2024 (the latest data as I write), concern in the UK had slipped to 20 per cent. There were now ten or eleven countries more concerned than the UK, but in almost all of them this concern had dropped. So even where scepticism is low, there is growing climate crisis fatigue almost everywhere in the world.

What about more widespread scepticism and fatigue than these surveys reveal? Note that even among samples skewed towards the middle class, such as all the ones considered here, there is widespread concern that tackling climate change will not help address other crises. So here we are seeing both fatigue and inaction grow among those typically thought of as being most concerned: those who are more affluent, more engaged online, more urban, and aged under seventy-five.[14]

What did that British sample of 24,290 people polled in early 2024, the one cited above, think about the additional benefits to tackling climate change? Remember, these are the people least likely to believe that climate change is a hoax worldwide.

Nevertheless, only 52 per cent thought that reducing fossil fuel usage might improve air quality, and – amazingly – only 50 per cent of them thought it might help alleviate climate change! A minority of those surveyed (49 per cent) thought that tackling climate change would help the natural environment; only a third (33 per cent) thought energy requirements could be met in future if we do so; and just a quarter thought it would help jobs (25 per cent). Even fewer (23 per cent) thought household energy bills would be reduced, and only one in seven believed that transitioning away from fossil fuels would in any way alleviate the cost-of-living crisis.[15]

Risk assessments

Tackling climate change would help with everything. For some damage that has already been done, there is no going back; but when we talk about risk it is not about what has been done. The irreversible extinctions of countless species are almost all the result of historic and recent human action: the climate had not changed enough by the time most of these extinctions occurred for temperature or sea-level rises to be the cause of those, or other changes to the natural environment resulting from global warming. But it was still us that caused the sixth mass extinction: the hunting to extinction of the last of a few larger mammal species; the much greater effects of deforestation; the spread of monoculture farming; and our usually unwitting introduction of invasive species that crowd out what are in some cases already depleted local species.

Biodiversity loss deserves to be considered in its own right, and we will do so in Chapter 7. But for now, note that the rate of extinction and loss is slowing down. That is just a simple mathematical fact – if it were not the case, then there would be no humans now, or any other large creatures of the kind that the Zoological Society included in its data showing that 70 per cent of the most easily identifiable species existing and known in 1970 are no longer in existence today.[16] The rate of extinction is slowing down even though climate change is still accelerating.[17]

The bulk of scientists who contribute to predictions about the effects of climate change tend to produce fewer extreme scenarios than some of those we'll encounter later in Chapter 7 on wider environmental harms; but they do understandably err towards very bad outcomes, if not the worst that could happen. So, let's begin with the 2014 Intergovernmental Panel on Climate Change (IPCC) report and then look at what was being said more recently.

The IPCC in its 2014 assessment stated: 'It is unlikely that global mean sea level will rise by more than one metre in this century, but the consequence of a greater rise could be so severe that this possibility becomes a significant part of risk assessment.'[18] The report suggested that global sea level had risen by 17 cm between 1901 and 2010, but that this rise had varied greatly worldwide due to changes in ocean currents. As the IPCC stated in 2014: 'Since 1993, the regional rates for the Western Pacific are up to three times larger than the global mean, while those for much of the Eastern Pacific are near zero or negative.' In other words, sea levels may be falling in parts of the eastern Pacific Ocean.

When it came to global population decline, the IPCC made no prediction. That 2014 assessment claimed: 'At present the worldwide burden of human ill-health from climate change is relatively small compared with effects of other stressors and is not well quantified.' It was suggested that mortality among the old had increased during heatwaves, but that there was also reduced mortality from cold due to milder winters. The evidence for those mortality rises came almost entirely from very affluent countries, and it was almost entirely the very old who were reported as having been most badly affected. No claim has been made in any IPCC report that climate change will alter the United Nations predictions for future population growth worldwide. Those UN predictions envision a continuation in the steady slowdown that has occurred since the 1960s, resulting in global population peaking at some point within this century, in its penultimate decade (or possibly earlier if the slowdown is a little faster than currently expected). As stated earlier in this book, but of enough significance to reiterate here, as of July 2024, the UN estimate of peak human population has moved forward to the year 2084 – entirely due to us having fewer children and grandchildren than was expected a few years ago.

The 2014 IPCC report was careful to point out that, to date, despite temperatures already having risen by at least 1°C above normal, the events that might have an impact on mortality were not yet doing so. There was 'low confidence that anthropogenic climate change has affected the frequency and magnitude of fluvial floods on a global scale'; 'low confidence in observed global-scale trends in droughts'; and 'low confidence that long-term changes in tropical cyclone activity are robust [although] it is virtually certain that intense tropical cyclone activity has increased in the North Atlantic since 1970'. The report mentioned that 'limited evidence is available on the impacts of sea-level rise'. Sea levels had definitely risen, but this had not yet had much measurable impact on global human populations. Of course, for people located on a low-lying island in the western or central Pacific, this might have been cold comfort.

One aspect of the 2014 IPCC report that now appears a little odd was that it expressed low confidence about what had happened in the past and was happening in the present, but predicted the future with relative certainty! For example: 'All aspects of food security are potentially affected by climate change, including food production, access, use, and price stability (high confidence).' As far as this refers to a potential outcome, it makes sense, but it is unclear whether the high confidence is about the expected extent of the changes, or whether the effects of climate change are confidently expected to cause food insecurity. An alternative sentence could read: 'It is almost certain that climate change will have a measurable effect on food production, access, use, and price stability.' This would have been a less frightening way of conveying the same information.

Eight years later, the 2022 IPCC assessment mentioned a likelihood of 'increased heat-related human mortality (medium confidence) ... and increased drought-related tree mortality (high confidence)'.[19] The level of expected increase was not given; but it is interesting that the report's authors were more certain about the effects of drought on trees than on people. The IPCC's assessment in 2022 was more strident than the one in 2014, no doubt because there was very little sign of mitigation measures to reduce carbon pollution. As a result of becoming more strident, however, the report also became vaguer about the actual harms already suffered.

The 2022 summary for policymakers was 40 pages long; the technical summary was 85 pages long; and the full report 3,068 pages long. One of the claims made included: 'Increasing weather and climate extreme events have exposed millions of people to acute food insecurity.' It did not say whether food insecurity overall, for all people worldwide and on average, had risen or fallen over time. Occasionally, an overall fall in some measure is first mentioned in passing: 'Although diarrheal diseases have decreased globally, higher temperatures, increased rain and flooding have increased the occurrence of diarrheal diseases, including cholera.' This framing tends to draw attention away from the global trend, which has been for a reduced risk overall for people worldwide. Tellingly, this trend is illustrated by the UN population estimates released in July 2024, which showed that, since the main phase of the pandemic, life expectancy has been continuing to rise remarkably quickly for most people in the world, as diseases, especially those affecting children, continue to diminish.

At times the 2022 report *did* pull back on earlier claims. For example: 'While non-climatic factors are the dominant drivers of existing intrastate violent conflicts, in some assessed regions extreme weather and climate events have had a small, adverse impact on their length, severity or frequency, but the statistical association is weak (medium confidence).' Presumably the medium confidence is being expressed over whether they have a small effect, with the possibility that the effect so far has been negligible? The 2022 report was published after the (largely inter-state) war in Ukraine began, a war which (as yet) few people have attributed to climate change.[20] Nor was the war on Gaza in 2023 and 2024 caused by climate change. There are other wars, in Sudan, Ethiopia, and across the Sahel, where links to recent climate change and growing aridity are more plausible contributors; but even there, economic and political interests from China, the US, and Russia are often mentioned by those involved in attempts to bring about peace. A great deal is said about the effects of aridity lines; much less on how great powers continue to play war games in other peoples' lands which has a far greater effect on violence than the air warming up.

Despite the dominant-drivers rhetoric that characterised the IPCC's stance in 2022, there was no acknowledgement in its reports to the wider public of what makes war possible or almost inevitable in some places and not in others. Of course, without the mass manufacture of arms and continued tolerance of the global arms industry there would be *fewer* wars and they would be *less* deadly. War on the scale it exists today would not be possible without mass kowtowing to politicians who advocate inalienable rights of self-defence for the jigsaw-shaped pieces of land that were mostly only given their borders a century ago (or less). So far there has been very little evidence of climate change increasing the chances of war. War as it is commonly practised today would probably be less popular in a world where more women are in control of politics and the military. But you can blame climate change for war, rather than how we currently run our societies, and few people ask why.

If we are to understand why so many people worldwide do not place climate change higher in their lists of worries, we should look to exaggerated claims that global warming and more erratic weather are the crisis underlying so many other crises. Climate change has been blamed for many other recent disasters: 'The decline of one or more natural resources . . . [has been] cited as a cause of, for example, the ongoing deadly conflicts in Syria starting since 2011, the conflicts and famine in Yemen beginning in 2015, and the economic collapse in Venezuela that began in

2014, to mention a few.'²¹ The 2021 paper I am referring to here also mentions climate refugees, including people crossing the Mediterranean in desperation, but oddly not those crossing into the US from Mexico. So, what does the IPCC say about climate refugees?

The technical summary of the 2022 IPCC report gives more detail: 'Over 20 million people have been internally displaced annually by weather-related extreme events since 2008, with storms and floods the most common drivers (high confidence).'²² What the report does not say is whether this statistic, of one person in four hundred per year, is higher or lower than was the case before 2008, or in 1968, or 1908. Of course, that figure of 20 million people is minuscule in comparison to some of the predictions that have been made of 'climate migrants' for the future. But 2008, 1968, and 1908 were all years of very high migration into countries such as those in Western Europe, due not to climate change but a host of the more usual reasons – wars, oppressive regimes, even pogroms. Furthermore, increased mobility might well be a key reason for why far fewer people die nowadays from disasters involving floods and other climate-related factors than used to be the case.

Similarly, the IPCC has suggested that rising temperatures have slowed the rise in crop yields, and 'decreased sustainable yields of some wild fish populations (high confidence) by 4.1% between 1930 and 2010'. The overall rise in crop yields (in a world with more mouths to feed and where agricultural technology and irrigation keeps on improving) is referred to only in passing, and it is not mentioned that this rise in yields was extremely good news. If that rise had not happened, due to farming technology, the effect would have been devastating for human populations. Relatedly, the main reason for the fall in wild fish populations – overfishing (not changes in ocean chemistry due to climate change) – is not mentioned at the point where the 4.1 per cent figure is given (that just being the change on top of a much larger decline in many fish species). Academic articles on the danger of overfishing rarely mention climate change but do show that the current severe depletions of stocks could have been predicted as long ago as the 1950s, simply from the number of fish being harvested then.²³

Occasionally, over the course of just eight years, the IPCC reports jump from having *low* confidence in a current event causing measurable high harm to *high* confidence, which might make a reader wonder why there were no intermediate periods in which confidence was *medium*, and what might have changed the level of confidence. For example, the 'low confidence in observed global-scale trends in droughts' expressed in the 2014 report shifted in 2022: 'Droughts, floods and rainfall variability have contributed to reduced food availability and increased food prices, threatening food and nutrition security, and the livelihoods of millions globally (high confidence).' Given these sudden changes in levels of certainty, should we be surprised that people are less concerned about climate change than they are about the more immediate threats to their lives and livelihoods from natural disasters? It is not hard to see how others can be terrified by what might actually be crying wolf.

It is possible that the data on droughts affecting food prices changed in the eight years between the two reports, but it is very hard to know if it did. Almost all reports on world food prices rising mention the effects of profiteering and speculation, which caused huge problems during the recent pandemic with global supply chains, and the war in Ukraine. There are no reports of overall reduction in food production worldwide due to an increase in droughts. If anything, humans are now better at producing the food we need than we were a decade ago. Of course, many fears remain that existing farming methods are not sustainable. But they are fears about the future, not evidence that climate change is currently making it harder to feed ourselves, or is reducing total annual food production worldwide.

So, why the high confidence in 2022 that climate change was already leading to high food prices? Was it the conflation of droughts with other events that made it easier to reach a high level of confidence? Perhaps it was that all these factors combined (droughts, floods, and rainfall variability) might now be a more serious threat than were droughts alone? Or perhaps the high confidence is in the perceived increased possibility of a threat, rather than actual increased and measured harm? Droughts are referred to eighty-five times in the 2022 technical report, but at no point does it mention the trend over time. We are not told if more or fewer people over time have been affected by or died in droughts, as compared to the recent past. Again, this ambiguity may help fuel some of the scepticism that exists, not least in the US.

Let's broaden the horizon from the carefully caveated words of the IPCC commissions, to the seven potential outcomes of climate change that other publications have already claimed as catastrophic, but about which the IPCC takes an understandably much more nuanced line: pandemics; resource wars; food, water, and energy security; health impacts; global inflation and stagflation; civil unrest; and refugees and economic migrants.

First, pandemics – they are mentioned often, and more so after some academic and press reports suggested that climate change had contributed to the emergence of the 2019 coronavirus in humans: 'An increase in the number of bat species in a particular region, driven by climate change, may increase the likelihood that a coronavirus harmful to humans is present, transmitted, or evolves there.'[24] In other words, because forty bat species had spread (as a result of climate change) into China's southern Yunnan province over the past hundred years, the chances of experiencing this new disease had risen. Apparently, climate change had also increased the likelihood of the virus jumping from bats, possibly through pangolins, to humans. However, for most of those past hundred years temperatures were much lower than they are now. More importantly, pandemics have been declining in frequency.

There were a huge number of pandemics that impacted disastrously on humans in previous centuries, and many new diseases, such as cholera, broke out in our species. Over the past century in Europe, the disease that has had the greatest effect has been influenza, and the effect has fallen greatly over time (the last well-known deadly pandemics were in 1918, 1957, 1968, and 1977). HIV/AIDS was a new disease, and it caused a huge pandemic, but it is hard to make the case that global warming caused the virus to infect humans: that happened long before there was a significant rise in temperatures.

The overall reduction in the number of new diseases that cause great harm jumping from animals to humans may be because of the huge fall in the number of people farming worldwide. But the key point to note is that there is lack of evidence for an increase in pandemics. We cannot be sure of when previous coronavirus pandemics occurred, because we would have mistaken them for influenza in the past, but the four common cold viruses have all been introduced in the past few centuries, and the last one that might have been associated with a terrible pandemic was 140 years ago (a less terrible one may have arrived between 1949 and 1963, and went largely unnoticed because there were so few older people in the world then).[25] There is evidence that extremely harmful coronavirus epidemics were more frequent and deadly in our distant past.[26] In great contrast, we are not (yet) seeing an increase in the frequency over time in deadly pandemics of any kind. Since it is uncertain when the last coronavirus pandemic that caused many deaths began, prior to the 2019 outbreak, no one can say that the frequency of such events has increased.

Second, climate change has been blamed for an increase in resource wars. The IPCC's 2022 statement rowed back on its previous claims of a weak link between climate change and war frequency. Possibly this was because the invasion of Ukraine offered little opportunity to make such a connection; the IPCC, however, cited new analysis of the previously available data. Their 2014 report had stated: 'Climate change can indirectly increase risks of violent conflict by amplifying well-documented drivers of these conflicts, such as poverty and economic shocks (medium confidence). Multiple lines of evidence relate climate variability to these forms of conflict.' In contrast, the equivalent section of the updated IPCC report, published some six years later, read: 'While non-climatic factors are the dominant drivers of existing intrastate violent conflicts, in some assessed regions extreme weather and climate events have had a small, adverse impact on their length, severity or frequency, but the statistical association is weak (medium confidence).' In simpler words, the IPCC scientists' confidence that climate change has led to more wars is reducing, and their recognition that other factors are far more important has been rising.

Third, climate change is often said to increase food, water, and energy insecurity. As yet, no rise in this has been measured across the globe, except for a few years when other factors – financial speculation and a too-rapid move to biofuels – were blamed. Most recently food insecurity rose; but as a consequence of the war that began in Europe with the Russian invasion of Ukraine in 2022. This was often cited as the key driver for erratic global food price rises at the time. But as I write in 2024 it is rarely mentioned in comparison to the predicted effects of climate change.

In its 2022 report the IPCC stated:

> Although overall agricultural productivity has increased, climate change has slowed this growth over the past 50 years globally (medium confidence), related negative impacts were mainly in mid- and low-latitude regions but positive impacts occurred in some high-latitude regions (high confidence). Ocean warming and ocean acidification have adversely affected food production from shellfish aquaculture and fisheries in some oceanic regions (high confidence). Increasing weather and climate extreme events have exposed millions of people to acute food insecurity.

What the IPCC is less clear about is whether the millions of people now exposed to acute food insecurity represent a fall or an increase in relation to the millions who were so exposed in the past few decades. Similarly, the IPCC is unclear on the proportion of people exposed to energy or water insecurity today, as compared to the past.

Fourth, climate change is said to have had impacts on health. Here is one statement from the 2022 IPCC report that helps illustrate its overall message: 'Although diarrheal diseases have *decreased* globally, higher temperatures, increased rain and flooding have increased the occurrence of diarrheal diseases, including cholera (very high confidence) and other gastrointestinal infections (high confidence)' [emphasis added]. In other words, there has been a *decline* in the incidence of widespread diseases that harm human health, such as those that cause diarrhoea and other leading global causes of infant mortality. That decline is in no way due to climate change, and if it were not for climate change the decline might have been even higher. But there is not a growing global health catastrophe; if anything, the reality is the very opposite when it comes to infant health (and declining deaths due to diarrhoea). Cholera is still extremely rare; it could stay that way if we cared enough. In the nineteenth century, its outbreaks made it the most feared disease in many countries (and those had nothing to do with climate change).

Fifth, climate change has been blamed for global inflation and stagflation, and the rise in the cost of living. We have had, until recently, quite remarkably low rates of inflation worldwide. The Bank of England has a time series on inflation that goes back centuries. Many people suggest that prices will rise as crops fail. So far, as far as I know (and there is a limit to what I can search for), almost no one has pointed to an overall rise in food retail prices of a particular crop and traced it to a specific climate event, or even to overall warming. The only example I have found connects a spring 2024 rise in the price of chocolate Easter eggs to fluctuations in cacao production (see next chapter). Prices said to have risen due to climate change, such as of olive oil, have now fallen as production again rises.[27]

Rises in the price of fish are due almost entirely to overfishing. Shellfish are explicitly mentioned in the IPCC's most recent 2022 and 2023 reports as having been adversely affected.[28] Globally there is no evidence of a decline in the total availability of shellfish or a dramatic rise in its price, however, and claims are often made for the environmental benefits of increasing shellfish aquaculture. These claims are unfortunately likely to be generated by US government–funded environmental organisations, which may have prioritised some commercial US interests over the wide environment.[29]

Sixth, civil unrest is said to rise with climate change. But across the world as a whole it is not rising and, unlike war, is generally low today as compared to past decades (see Chapter 4 in this volume). Climate change has been claimed to be linked to events including the Arab Spring in the early 2010s, the Intifada in Palestine (1987–91), uprisings in South Africa under apartheid, discord in the Soviet Union in the very late 1980s and across Europe and the US in the 1960s. But there are far more obvious and very human reasons for why all these events occurred. Unrest in Chile in 2019 among students is a recent exception to the slowing trend, but it had nothing to do with climate change (despite that likely being a key concern of some of the leading participants). It's hard to construct a data set of civil unrest that people might agree on – would the events of 6 January 2021, when Donald Trump's supporters tried to take over US government buildings, be included? They were hardly caused by climate change, other than a common belief amongst many taking part that it was a hoax.

Those events of 6 January 2021 involved only a few hundreds or thousands of people, and that contested election was not a climate-created event. It could be said that civil unrest is now better contained due to the order being seen in many better organised refugee camps and the nasty authoritarianism of migrant detention centres that have been built in countries neighbouring conflict zones. Perhaps there would be more unrest in the world, more civil unrest, if local police forces today had responded to events more as they cack-handedly did in the recent past, and perhaps civil unrest was higher when there was much less international cooperation over natural disasters as compared to what there is now?

When an extreme weather event occurs today, displacing people, the response is almost always more coordinated than it would have been half a century ago. This is not recognised in the IPCC 2022 report: 'Through displacement and involuntary migration from extreme weather and climate events, climate change has generated and perpetuated vulnerability (medium confidence).' It could also be pointed out that there are now more acts of civil disobedience and protests about climate change and lack of government action, for instance over the matter of insulating homes or failing to do so, flying, or wider pollution, carried out by groups such as Extinction Rebellion, Just Stop Oil, and Insulate Britain.

Seventh, on the matter of refugees and economic migrants, there are many different estimates. One UN body has stated: 'There are no reliable estimates of the number of people on the move today or in the future as a result of environmental factors.'[30] Another claimed in 2022 that 'of 59.1 million people internally displaced in 2021 across the world, most were displaced by climate-related disasters.'[31] A third estimated that in 2021 there were 53.2 million internally displaced people due to conflict and violence in the world, in other words 90 per cent of the 59.1 million.[32] Of course, it is not the precise current number that these commentators are concerned about, but the number of displaced people there might be in future. But were they mainly displaced due to war, or environmental factors?

There will always be predictions of extreme disaster just around the corner. In 2021 a group of researchers, including Paul and Anne Ehrlich – who have been predicting environmental Armageddon since the 1960s – published a paper, titled: 'Underestimating the Challenges of Avoiding a Ghastly Future', which described a future even worse than most climate scientists believed.[33] Among much else, that paper cited 'an estimated 25 million to 1 billion environmental migrants expected by 2050'. These would be mostly people forced to cross borders, rather than those displaced within their own country. The prediction was that between 1 in 320 and 1 in 8 of the Earth's total population will be forced to migrate across a border due to climate change in the next two dozen years or so (and twice that if global population is going to halve, as other apocalyptic forecasts indicate – a scenario described in the next chapter of this book). This fortyfold variation in future estimates certainly does not inspire confidence about what might happen in the next two dozen years.

In the early 2020s it was refugees from war and economic disaster who were among the main concerns in Europe, including those fleeing the war between Ukraine and Russia, and the war in Syria. In the UK it was people forced to travel by small boats across the Channel from France because there was no other way to try to claim asylum. Few claimed that these people were getting in the flimsiest of inflatable boats because of climate change, or that climate change had resulted in the economic collapse of the country from which the largest group arrived that year (Albania in 2022, for example) – or that climate change had made it easier to cross the English Channel because the sea was a little warmer. But there were claims from the World Bank that their programmes in Africa might reduce future potential climate migration from countries there by 60 per cent.[34] There have also been many anecdotal accounts of how climate change has forced people to flee parts of North Africa, such as Chad.[35] But when you read these reports, it is the war and violence that stands out most starkly and you have to ask about the reasons for the wars.[36]

One reaction to such a list of recent events, and to the argument that events linked to global warming have not been as clear or as calamitous as feared, is to dismiss the approach I am taking as far too (to use a neologism) *hopian*. But this argument is not about what will happen, it is about events that are claimed to have happened already. It is not about hope, but about fears we are supposed to have, given the changes that have already occurred. Although of course there should be agreement on what has happened to date in terms of rising temperatures, there is great uncertainty about how much in aggregate those rising temperatures have contributed to other current crises. Over time, the picture of what has occurred to date should become less opaque.

When reflecting on the present and recent past, at least we have evidence, whereas arguing about what will happen is just conjecture, and not dissimilar to holding forth on who will win football's next World Cup.

Natural disasters

One area where there is ample evidence and so less conjecture is the record of natural disasters. If we turn to that issue, we can begin to ask how concerned we should be about rising temperatures, rising sea levels, and extreme weather events – or at least how concerned we should be about the imminent, rather than the medium-term, threats.

UN reports often contain shocking passages:

> UNDRR report published to mark the International Day for Disaster Risk Reduction on October 13, 2020, confirms how extreme weather events have come to dominate the disaster landscape in the 21st century ... There has also been a rise in geophysical events including earthquakes and tsunamis which have killed more people than any of the other natural hazards under review in this report.[37]

So which is it? Have extreme weather events dominated the disaster landscape of the twenty-first century worldwide, or have earthquakes and tsunamis been most dominant in terms of people affected and the number of deaths? At least in the short and medium term, earthquakes and tsunamis do not become more or less common because the atmosphere is heating up. The answer, as that final sentence in the quote above confirms, is that it has not been extreme weather events that have resulted in the greatest number of deaths from natural disasters.

Even if extreme weather events have not yet come to dominate the disaster landscape, surely they are becoming more and more important to it? This is the impression you might get from reading the summary above, and even from reading in detail the report from which the quote above was taken. Unless, that is, you tried to answer the question – by how much and how quickly have things got worse? Do that, when reading the UN publication 'The Human Cost of Disasters: An Overview of the Last 20 Years 2000–2019', and you may quickly become confused.

The UNDRR (United Nations Office for Disaster Risk Reduction) report suggests there has been a near doubling of climate-related disasters in the past twenty years as compared to the previous twenty. Here is the key quote from the report, which is worth reading twice: 'Between 2000 and 2019, there were 510,837 deaths and 3.9 billion people affected by 6,681 climate-related disasters. This compares with 3,656 climate-related events which accounted for 995,330 deaths (47% due to drought/famine) and 3.2 billion affected in the period 1980-1999.'

The number of climate-related disasters reported in the later period – 6,681 – is nearly double that for the previous period, 3,656. And 3.9 billion people is more than 3.2 billion, but it's not much more, and as a proportion of the population of the world (which grew over this period) it represents a reduction. There were 5 billion people on the planet in 1988 and 7 billion by 2011, so per year per person, that is a fall from 1 person in 31 being affected in the 1980s and 1990s, to 1 in 36 in the 2000s and 2010s. But that isn't what is most surprising when you read and reread that paragraph. The near doubling of climate-related disasters has resulted in a near-halving of climate-related disaster deaths. How can that be?

Some 510,837 deaths over twenty years, when the population in the middle of that period was 7 billion people, can be expressed as a rate: 510,837 divided by 7,000 divided by 20, which equals 3.6 deaths per *million* people per year. In the year 2010, in the middle of this period, the crude death rate worldwide was 7.8 per *thousand* per year (over 2,000 times higher). To be precise, for every person who died due to a climate-related disaster, another 2,166 were dying of some other cause, most often a disease the effects of which were brought forward in time because of poverty. How did we come to see climate-related deaths as so important – when they might be among the least likely way anyone around the world now dies?

The data behind 'The Human Cost of Disasters' report is publicly available free of charge for research at the EM-DAT International Disaster database (emdat.be). The organisation that puts it together was established in 1973 and has a very long track record of carefully collecting this data. The data it collects produces those numbers given in the text above and in Table 6.1 shown here. These numbers are taken directly from the published report. It is not hard to replicate exactly the numbers published in the 2020 'The Human Cost of Disasters' report with the numbers from the EM-DAT data.

Table 6.1: People dying due to climate-related disasters per year by decade, 1950–2022

Number per million people	
77	1950s
51	1960s
14	1970s
14	1980s
6	1990s
5	2000s
2	2010s
1	2020s

Source: EM-DAT global data and UN World Population Prospects (November 2022).

So, taking the same data, what do you find if you try to answer the question that the report itself does not ask? Table 6.1 shows what exactly the same data reveals if you calculate the number of people dying in the world each year, for every million people in the world in that year, as a result of a natural disaster, including: drought, extreme temperature, flood, glacial lake outburst impact, insect infestation, landslide, storm, and wildfire. Table 6.1 provides that data by decade. The last decade ends in November 2022, so is just short of three years in length (in the near future that can be updated). In each case, the mid-year data for population has been used to turn these deaths into a number per million people per year. In the 1950s the mid-year population was that for 1955; for the last very short decade it is the global human population in 2021.

Now ask yourself, having seen the data arranged in this way, in terms of mortality, is it true that extreme weather events have come to dominate the disaster landscape? Or are people now seventy-seven times less likely to die from a natural disaster due to an extreme weather event in the 2020s as compared to the 1950s? The correct answer is the latter. We are certainly seeing more extreme weather events; but despite having far more people on the planet than before, often more crowded into river basins and shorelines – and other areas that are more dangerous to live in – we are not seeing more deaths.

The number of people dying in climate-related disasters has fallen because people are now better prepared for disaster, especially the poorest of people of all, who were previously least prepared. Better communications mean that people can be warned and move to safer ground far more easily than before. Safer ground is often not too far away. We have better early-warning systems and weather warnings. We also plan better than we used to and are less likely to place new settlements in areas prone to floods and storms.

Perhaps the best way to understand the issues of attribution and trend is to look at the natural disasters that are not climate-related: the number of deaths per decade due to earthquake, epidemic, mass movement of dry material, and volcanic activity. These have not reduced quite as rapidly as those associated with climate change, but they have reduced substantially. In the 1970s, 11 people out of every million in the world died each year from these, 44 per cent of all deaths from natural disasters. By the 2010s, that number had dropped to 4 people per million by year but had risen to 63 per cent of all deaths. Droughts, heatwaves, and floods are easier to see coming than are earthquakes and tsunamis.

The number of people affected by natural disasters is usually thousands more than the number killed; so far during the 2020s, it has been 14,000 more, as Table 6.2 shows. During the 1950s and 1960s many smaller natural disasters, which did not involve large numbers of people dying, were poorly recorded, so the numbers then were very low. But by the 1970s, once the centre that records them was up and running, it could scan current reports and produce a far more comprehensive list. The next table (Table 6.2) shows that slightly more people have been affected so far by climate-related natural disasters in the 2020s than the 1970s, whereas their chances of dying were more than ten times less in the 2020s (despite the chances of being affected being similar). The peak decade for people being affected was the 1990s.

Table 6.2: People affected by climate-related disasters per year, 1950–2022

Number per thousand people	
1	1950s
6	1960s
13	1970s
25	1980s
35	1990s
34	2000s
23	2010s
14	2020s

Source: EM-DAT global data and UN World population prospects (November 2022).

How did the 'The Human Cost of Disasters' report, published in 2020, deal with this issue? It largely ignored it. It did include a table of the ten deadliest disasters that had occurred between 2000 and 2019 (Table 6.3). None of the top ten occurred after

2010, and most were not climate related. Just above that table, within the main text in the report, is a rather vague statement: 'it is these major events that shape the total figures in a year and a decade, making it a challenge to perceive exact mortality trends over such a relatively short time span.' But even if all the earthquake and tsunami deaths are removed and the table is recreated to show only the number of people dying in climate-related disasters, both the total number and the proportion of people who die as a result of those disasters have declined over time since the early 2000s, and possibly from a few years prior to that.

If, instead of listing the ten deadliest disasters of all kinds, we list the top fifteen that involve a climate-related cause, then the list is *still* dominated by events that occurred in 2010 or before, even if we extend the data through to the end of 2022.

Table 6.3: The ten deadliest natural disasters in the world, 2000–19

Type	Place	Year	Deaths
Earthquake & Tsunami	Indian Ocean	2004	226,408
Earthquake	Haiti	2010	222,570
Storm	Myanmar	2008	138,366
Earthquake	China	2008	87,476
Earthquake	Pakistan	2005	73,338
Heatwave	Europe	2003	72,210
Heatwave	Russia	2010	55,736
Earthquake	Iran	2003	26,716
Earthquake	India	2001	20,005
Drought	Somalia	2010	20,000

Source: Centre for Research on the Epidemiology of Disasters, 'The Human Cost of Disasters: An overview of the last twenty years 2000–2019', Geneva: United Nations Office for Disaster Risk Reduction, 2020.

The first four entries in the Table 6.4 are identical to the four non-earthquake ones in the table above because the data source is identical. The first thing to note from Table 6.4 below is that the first four events occurring in 2010 or earlier account for the very large majority of all climate-related deaths since the year 2000.

The second thing to note is how many of the deaths occurred in Europe and Russia. Had each European country that was affected by the 2003 heatwave been included separately, then five of the top ten disasters would have been in Europe or Russia. The

Table 6.4: Fifteen deadliest climate-associated disasters, 2000–22 (deaths)

1	Storm	Myanmar	2008	138,366
2	Heatwave	Russia	2010	55,736
3	Heatwave	Europe	2003	72,210
4	Drought	Somalia	2010	20,000
5	Storm	The Philippines	2013	7,354
6	Flood	India	2013	6,054
7	Storm	Bangladesh	2007	4,234
8	Heatwave	France	2015	3,275
9	Storm	Haiti	2004	2,754
10	Flood	Haiti	2004	2,665
11	Heatwave	United Kingdom	2020	2,556
12	Drought	Uganda	2022	2,465
13	Heatwave	India	2015	2,248
14	Flood	India	2022	2,035
15	Flood	Pakistan	2010	1,985

Source: EM-DAT global data up to November 2022.

breakdown of the 72,210 deaths attributed to the 2003 heatwave within Europe is given in Table 6.5.

Statements made by academics, politicians, campaigners, and journalists often imply that climate change is already having an effect that is disproportionately concentrated on poorer countries – places that are desperately trying to cope now with the implications of climate change. For example, it is often claimed: 'Most developing countries produce very few greenhouse gases: their economies are just not large or rich enough. What they are desperately trying

Table 6.5: Deaths attributed to the 2003 heatwave in Europe, by country

20,089	Italy
19,490	France
15,090	Spain
9,355	Germany
2,696	Portugal
1,175	Belgium
1,039	Switzerland
965	The Netherlands
788	Croatia
418	The Czech Republic
345	Austria
301	United Kingdom
289	Slovenia
170	Luxembourg
0	Slovakia [included because people were affected]

Source: EM-DAT global data for the year and particular event in 2003.

to do is cope with the climate change they are already experiencing.'[38] While it is certainly true that people in poorer countries contribute far less to greenhouse gas pollution, it is much less clear that, with global temperatures at 1°C above normal, they are coping worse with climate-related disasters than their parents or grandparents did. Europe and Russia have far larger very elderly populations that are most at risk from heatwaves, as does China. Because there were far fewer heatwaves in the past, and perhaps because people in more affluent states are less used to them, the elderly may be much more affected by heatwaves than were their parents or grandparents. Apart from factors such as rising temperatures, their parents and especially their grandparents were less likely ever to become old enough to be at such great risk from a heatwave of the type that hit Europe in 2003.

It is possible that so far in the period since 2010 we have simply been lucky; this cannot be ruled out. However, the number of deaths per year related to climate events over the 2023–29 period will have to be a little more than twice the number that occurred in the first three years of this decade if they are to reach the proportion of the first decade of this century. As I write in the summer of 2024, the tally for 2023 to mid-2024 remains very low. The 2023–29 total would have to be more than seven times higher again than that so far in the 2020s for the death toll to be as bad as that experienced in the 1970s and 1980s – and five times higher yet again to be as bad as in the 1950s, when there was hardly any global warming occurring.

Some people will claim that most deaths due to climate change are not as a result of natural disasters, but we have no rises in mortality in poor countries in the 'all-cause UN mortality data' to suggest an increased impact. The argument then tends to move towards deaths we expect to see in the future. But the question remains: Why are there so few deaths from climate change now, and why are both the deaths and the proportion of people affected by disasters worldwide falling?

One reason is that although extreme weather events have become more common, and worse in duration and intensity, the proportion of people seriously affected has fallen, because on top of early warnings and better communications, the number of people in extreme immiseration has fallen over time. It was people living on just a dollar a day in the 1970s and 1980s who were much more likely to be affected by weather events, and to die. This argument takes us back to near the very start of this book, and the debate about the meaning of Figure 2.1. It is not just that absolute extreme poverty has fallen, however; we have also learnt from the floods and other natural disasters of our recent past and are now better prepared.

Between 14 June 2022 and late October that year, floods in Pakistan killed 1,739 people. That is fewer than those who will have died from COVID-19 there in just a few days during the same period, but the virus was no longer newsworthy by 2022, whereas climate change was. Deaths from the virus are mostly not officially reported in Pakistan, although 145,000 more people died there in 2022 than in 2019. Some 1 per cent of this rise in mortality can be attributed to the floods, and 99 per cent to the ongoing pandemic and its wider effects. Furthermore, those deaths from the floods, out of a population of 225 million people, are about 8 *per million*, so did not alter the worldwide figure of 1 *per million* by more than a decimal place or two.

To put it another way, of everyone who died in Pakistan in 2022 (1,656,000), around 1 in 1,000 died as a result of the climate disaster, 1 in 12 from the pandemic, and as many as 1 in 2 probably died earlier than they otherwise would have due to poverty. The proportion of those dying early due to poverty would have been even higher in the past. The infant mortality rate of Pakistan is thankfully heading downwards, from 1 baby in 10 dying in its first year of life in 1992, to 1 in 12 in 2002, 1 in 15 in 2012, and down to almost 1 in 20 by 2022. But even if the current positive trends continue, then only by 2048 will it be at the same level as the UK in 1950, when poverty was still the main cause of early infant death in the UK – almost 100 years later. Nevertheless, if the climate emergency is making life much harder in Pakistan (and everywhere else where so many are very poor), why does infant mortality continue to reduce?

The same story could be told of the torrential rains that hit Nigeria in October 2022, displacing 1.5 million people and killing 662. The number of those who died was rarely reported in news stories about the event. Instead, it was claimed that these floods had been made eighty times more likely than they otherwise would have been, because temperatures had risen by 1°C.[39] Some might query why there were not eighty times more floods than usual in similar areas in other parts of the world, but they would be labelled sceptics. The more important question is why so few people died from this large event compared to how many were dying in Nigeria from the continued pandemic and how many more from poverty; and what does this suggest for the future, when the number of floods and their intensity will almost certainly rise? Will climate-related deaths in Nigeria ever come, in our lifetimes, to match those from the waning but never-ending pandemic? Can we really imagine a time when the harm caused by climate change rises to be as severe as the harms done to our health, housing, and education by poverty? Some will say that this is the wrong question to be asking, and that climate change will exacerbate poverty – but will it? It is people that cause poverty, especially the rich and greedy.

Perhaps the most damning evidence comes *not* from Nigeria or Pakistan, or from natural disasters, but from how everyday life is being altered, for instance in the now much hotter summers in places as populous as India. Reports from august bodies such as Chatham House bristle with alarming subtitles: 'The risks are compounding, and without immediate action the impacts will be devastating.'[40] This particular report was full of worrying claims, including at least one said to have already occurred: 'In 2019 a potential 302 billion working hours were lost due to temperature increases globally, 52 per cent more than in 2000. To put this in context, COVID-19 resulted in around 580 billion lost working hours globally in 2020; hence temperature increases are already resulting in the equivalent of more than half of COVID-19-induced lost working hours.' I mentioned India above because when you turn to the source for this claim you find that 39 per cent of those hours were lost in India alone.[41]

The idea that India, which lost four years of life expectancy after the pandemic hit (mostly due to the indirect effects of lockdowns, including a reduction in childhood vaccination), was comparably affected by heat in 2019 is risible. The 2022 UN estimates for life expectancy in India were 70.91 years in 2019, the highest ever (despite the high heat that year). The estimate dropped to 70.15 years in 2020 as the pandemic hit; but India was more seriously affected by a huge wave of COVID-19 infections and subsequent lockdowns the year after, in early 2021, when life expectancy fell dramatically to 67.24 years. Nearly four years of life being lost is almost unprecedented and certainly has not occurred in India in any year since the huge death toll as a result of Partition in 1947.

The Chatham House report continues: 'The global food crisis of 2007–08, caused by a conjunction of depleted grain stores, Australian drought and regional crop failures, led to a doubling of global food prices, export bans, food insecurity for importers, social unrest, and mass protests in at least 13 countries, including Cameroon, Egypt, Indonesia, Mexico, Morocco, Nepal, Peru, Senegal and Yemen.'[42] But a UN report put the reasons for the price spike down to 'speculation and diversion of food crops to biofuels'.[43] The phrase 'depleted grain stores' can be read as a euphemism for merchants holding on to what they had as prices rose, partly to ensure prices would rise still further. The growth in biofuels had been largely driven, ironically, by fears of climate change. A *Lancet*-commissioned report on the wider subject argued convincingly that we need to 'reduce the influence of large commercial interests on public policy development'.[44]

Much more could be said, and we should indeed expect more droughts and floods in future, although not every year. There were few floods as large as in earlier years in 2023 or 2024. We should also try to minimise carbon pollution and mitigate its effects. As yet we cannot be sure that people in future will not do what they have clearly been doing up to now, both continuing commercial interests in ways that damage us more with too slow a curtailment, but also adapting to the increased risks and variability. Of course, there are many implications of climate change I have not covered. For example, we should be greatly concerned that land will become contaminated by salt if there is too much leaching due to higher temperatures, and there are at least one thousand and one other possible impacts of climate change that we should worry about. But how will all this affect us in the longer term? Even if food is not running out now, that does not mean we should not be greatly concerned that it might. And finally, what about the unavoidable effects that are already in motion? What about the crisis of our loss of biodiversity that has already occurred, and which is still ongoing? That is where we turn next.

7

Biodiversity

This is the assembly of life that . . . holds the world steady.
Edward O. Wilson[1]

Threats to the environment are a minor concern for the majority of people around the world. Only 9 per cent of those surveyed placed it in their top three greatest concerns in the spring of 2022; in April 2024, it was just 8 per cent. In contrast, among the most progressively engaged members of social and economic elites in the global North, the environment is the greatest concern of all. By this I mean the damage already done to our environment, principally through the acceleration in the rate of extinction of species and the wider fall in biodiversity more generally observed. Biodiversity loss is an even greater concern than climate change to some in this group, and many of them say it will matter even more in future: the great extinction event we have both caused, and are still living through, is what will have the longest-lasting effect. However, continuing to say that the future will be dire has less effect once a part of that future has arrived, and most of the predicted consequences, for humans at least, have not.

In April 2024, let's remember, 34 per cent of people in the world saw inflation as their biggest concern.[2] It was the highest ranked of all the issues listed in the Ipsos survey, and had dropped only 8 percentage points from early 2023, when it was of greatest concern in the history of the survey. By August 2024 some 32 per cent placed it first and inflation was still our greatest collective concern. Poverty and social inequality held steady in the top three concerns (at 30 per cent or 31 per cent) over the first few months of 2024, through to the August; crime and violence was a top three-priority for between 29 per cent to 30 per cent of all people surveyed; and unemployment rose from 27 per cent to 28 per cent. People around the world held fairly fixed views on what concerned them most, with slightly fewer people saying that the cost of living worried them most, as its rise slowed. Concerns over financial and political corruption rose to a top-three concern of 26 per cent in April 2024 but had dropped back to 24 per cent by August, and worries about healthcare held steady at 22 or 23 per cent, rising to 24 per cent in January 2025.

Climate change was seventh in the April 2024 survey as a top-three priority for only 17 per cent of the population surveyed worldwide; had concerns over taxes or immigration control both increased by just a single percentage point, it would have been even less of a priority, falling to eighth or ninth highest ranked. In fact climate change did fall to ninth most important by the August of 2024, a top priority for just 15 per cent by January 2025.

Education worries, fears over military conflict, concerns about moral decline, terrorism, and rises in extremism all trumped threats to the environment as issues that mattered most to the greatest number of people. No wonder only 8 or 9 per cent of people listed the environmental crisis as of greatest concern (7 per cent in January 2025) – which is why it is covered only in this penultimate chapter that you are reading here.

Arguably this chapter should not even be in this book. But although concern for the environment is hardly ever in the top three, it is now always present, a constant threat. So, I include it here because it is not hard to see that it will have long lasting consequences – longer lasting even than climate change. Of course, the world is warming, and the seas are rising; but so far both are doing so not quite as quickly as the most concerned doomsayers predicted. Few people now deny that humans have caused the extinction of a huge number of species, but that rate of extinction has slowed down in recent decades.

So, is the issue of biodiversity loss, coral reef collapse, ocean bleaching, loss of land and rare habitats to the sea, and all the other impacts on the environment that go beyond the immediate habitat change impacts of global warming and more erratic weather, still a contender as the next great crisis that will dominate our children's or grandchildren's lives? Or does the low ranking of concerns about these issues suggest that most people are learning to live with this loss (one that many people in the world are still not even much aware of).

For many environmentalists today, the greatest threat to the planet is still the loss of biodiversity due to human encroachment on land, overfishing of the seas, and the wider effects of pollution, extraction, and capitalism in general. A 2022 sequel to the Club of Rome's famous *The Limits to Growth* (1972) claimed that the original book's outline 'tracked closely with reality', but this is clearly not the case.[3] The suffering envisioned in 1972 has not yet occurred. The new book, *Earth for All*, began with a foreword written by Christiana Figueres, which claims: 'Millions of people around the world are suffering deeply as a result of climate chaos, environmental degradation, and perverse inequality.'[4] While the last of these three – inequality – is true of billions, not millions (as Figueres inaccurately suggests), the first two may be neither as deep nor as widespread as is often assumed, if the way we measure impact is based on conventional measures of human suffering.

Most of the biodiversity loss as a result of our actions has almost certainly already happened; in fact, we may now be seeing a rapid slowdown in the loss of biodiversity, and are probably becoming better at conserving the species that have survived our enormous harms. This is no great claim. It would be hard to have been worse custodians of the planet. But often claims of the damage done are overblown, especially local claims.

I am indigenous to Oxford, in Oxfordshire. In the UK it is common to read statements such as the following about the county I was born in and where I still live: 'Oxfordshire has experienced a massive decline in farmland and woodland biodiversity, many iconic species like hares and turtle doves are under serious threat, at least two butterfly species are extinct, and populations of vital pollinators like bees are crashing, risking the rural economy and heritage at the heart of our way of life.' I don't recognise this idyllic rural scene from my childhood, and I don't know who the 'our' is in this statement. As I say, I am indigenous, so I notice claims about 'our way of life' made about the place I grew up in. I like the idea of otters, but I wonder whether the re-emergence of species such as the otter, which had been very rare in Oxfordshire for many decades, really is increasing the biodiversity of English counties greatly. That biodiversity was more than marginally reduced when we began farming with tractors, but it has never been especially high as compared to other parts of the world.

There are some serious questions to be asked. To what extent are there now places on Earth where biodiversity is being gained rather than lost? For example, in Oxfordshire, water voles are now increasing in numbers along the rivers, as the (Eurasian) otters drive away the American mink.[5] And why would anyone worry about losses of farmland, as in the quote above, when agriculture is and has been the biggest threat to biodiversity? It is well known that farming, especially the intensive tractor-driving farming that became ubiquitous less than a century ago, impacts by far the greatest area of land, much more so than our homes.

Are we starting to farm in more environmentally friendly ways? Or are all those schemes to preserve hedgerows and clean rivers a waste of time? I doubt that they are a waste of time – although we still appear unable to keep our rivers free of human sewage in both Oxfordshire and much of the rest of England. When the river I kayak along becomes polluted, it is almost always because of what has run off the fields and not so much a result of overspill human sewage (I do not kayak on the Thames).

I very much suspect that the future may be more *Wind in the Willows* than the *Lord of the Rings*–style 'Scouring of the Shire' that so many environmentalists currently fear. This means cleaning up our rivers more, and better controlling our own sewage and the effluent from farms. It may require much land in Oxfordshire to be repurposed as solar farms; but this was never land that was a part of 'our way of life' when I was a child.⁶ The Green Party in Oxfordshire is currently split between those who want nothing to change, and those who see the need to reduce our reliance on natural gas for energy by producing more energy locally.

As always, the future will depend a great deal on the choices we make. Our children may not be inheriting ruins, although some adults certainly warn of it. Such warnings are one reason why we still have much of the biodiversity that we currently enjoy – nothing like what existed before we cleared the forest and first farmed, but that we are now, albeit very slowly, reforesting. What environmentalists tend to emphasise, however, are *tipping points*: apparently irreversible scenarios that might occur at any moment – when the bees will no longer come, when the soil will almost all be washed away, and so on. There are hundreds of possible tipping points.⁷

The Biodiversity that ate the storms

Earnest people contact authors like me and urge us to read the thousands of pages of writing in the Millennium Ecosystem Assessment of 2005.⁸ I duly do so, and finally get to page 836 of just the first report to discover: 'Although there is substantial reason to believe that the world in the coming decades can produce sufficient food to feed its growing population, important regional issues exist in the global pattern of cultivated land.'⁹

I had been told to read the report by someone who claimed it had forecast that we were all about to starve. After getting to that page, I told them it did not; they then pointed me to the 2022 IPES-Food report.¹⁰ I read the opening lines of its summary and wondered whether it was a scientific report or the tenets of some New Age religion. Here is how it began: 'Biodiversity loss is increasingly recognized as one of the most pressing challenges of our times as it threatens our own survival. In the words of E. O. Wilson, "This is the assembly of life that took a billion years to evolve. It has eaten the storms – folded them into its genes – and created the world that created us. It holds the world steady."'¹¹

Presumably what Wilson meant was that it was life itself, as it grew in abundance and absorbed carbon from the atmosphere, that cooled down the planet we live on. Extreme weather, including storms, diminished as temperatures fell. The genetic changes that allowed so much plant life to thrive had created the circumstances in which the human species evolved. But the implication is that we may not live much longer in such a welcoming world, because the storms will no longer be metaphorically *eaten* as often. Our weather is about to worsen disastrously.

Such writing suggests a great fall from grace of humankind; it fits well with biblical and many other religious texts. But just as humans lived through floods in the past with enough people surviving, along with their languages, to tell the tale of those devastating events in almost all ancient cultures, so too we may be engaged in much the same thing as we issue great warnings to ourselves – ones that we should act on, but which do not necessarily mean the end, just as those past warnings did not.[12]

It is good to worry about the future. Humans are quite good at worrying. In a book titled *Population 10 Billion*, which I wrote a decade ago, I came up with a list of over forty potential catastrophes that people were worrying about (including killer bee swarms exponentially proliferating and the decline of pollinating insects). In 2017 I updated the list, in *Why Demography Matters*, co-written with Stuart Gietel-Basten; and in 2020 I referred to that list again for a book titled *Slowdown*. Each time I do so, and search out current predictions, a few new potential catastrophes have been added. So I have searched again, but I have also been aided by some of my correspondents.

One paper in the journal *Science* that was sent to me (because a reader of mine thought I was not worrying enough about pollinators) claims there has been 'rapid loss of China's pollinator diversity' – but one that has not yet resulted in the 'crop failures' that might very soon be impeding overall food production in China.[13] I have not been able to find any source of data suggesting a fall in crop production in China. Because China at the end of the 1950s suffered the worst famine in history, in terms of absolute effect on human life, my impression, from searching around the work of fellow geographers in China, is that vigilance and worry on this issue are especially high there.

A second report (also sent by a correspondent because I was not worrying as much as they were) claimed: 'After an 18% increase in 2022, the World Bank's food price index is forecast to decline by 6% in 2023 and stabilise in 2024.'[14] The report identified many threats, but it did not claim that the 18 per cent increase was due to ecological collapse or climate change. No doubt I will be sent more reports about impending environmental collapse as a result of writing these words. There are literally millions of such warnings published. So many, in fact, that I worry there is a danger that we have now cried wolf so often that we may not spot what we should be most concerned about when, or if, it eventually does happen. Could it be, that hidden within all these academic and other papers, is the real and most urgent warning we need to heed, but it is hidden by so many other claims that the end is nigh?

A third report dated October 2022 (also recommended to me to improve my understanding of these issues) included a prediction of the arrival of 'Hell on Earth' the following year. This prediction was made from someone who had claimed four years earlier that 'only' 80 million people a year around the world were headed towards starvation.[15] This someone was the United Nations' World Food Programme executive director, David Beasley, so hard not to take seriously. Again, the 2022–23 spike in food prices was caused neither by ecological collapse nor climate change; but here was another report suggesting it was. War and speculators were the true curse and cause. Hell on Earth arrived in 2023, the result of atrocities committed by one group of humans bombing the homes of others whom they do not see as human. People starve when we do not care enough about them. They die of starvation if we prevent aid agencies from bringing in food, and in extreme cases they die far quicker when we deny those UN agencies the right to supply water to adults and children.[16]

It would be quite remarkable if we don't see an event in the next few years involving crop failure in part of the world due to extreme weather events exacerbated by climate change. For me, the key question is whether it will be accompanied by a rise in hunger. And that will depend on how food is distributed around the globe, and whether a few people are permitted to profit greatly from that potential disaster. If we do allow such profiteering, that will ensure it is an actual disaster, just as when we permit war or defend people's right to wage war. When I say there is enough food – and that it is us who cause starvation through the evils we tolerate – one response I often hear is that eventually the impact of our numbers, our technology, and our affluence will be too much. I am told that we will not be able to save others in faraway places, or others will not be able to save us when drought, or storm damage, or great floods, hit us.

Many of my correspondents on population matters mention the equation I = PAT. This is the old ecologist's model that people's impact (I) on overall sustainability can be calculated by multiplying the number of people on the planet (P) by the average level of affluence in the world (A), multiplied again by some technological constant (T). When I was young, I = PAT was a model favoured by some geography schoolteachers. It is easy to see why so many people have found it convincing, but its popularity has declined since its flaw became widely apparent. There is a Wikipedia page on I = PAT which explains some of the problems, but it is unclear about the most basic problem of all.

According to Wikipedia: 'Environmental impact is a function of human numbers, affluence (that is, resources consumed per capita) and technology.'[17] In other words, I = P x A x T is the same as I = P x R/P x T, where R is total resources consumed.

I = P x R/P x T can be rewritten as I = R x T; and this helps explain how human population numbers do not influence I (impact) at all – they simply drop out of the equation when population is not included twice (as it is in the original formulation).

It is a little like that old numbers trick: think of a number, say, population to the nearest billion (8). Now double it, add 20 (for global resource use measured in some mega units), halve the result (technology effect) and take away the number you first thought of (8). The answer will always be 10 mega-units no matter what number you first think of. The equation I = PAT works in the same way: it's just as convincing to the uninitiated, and it has taken some time and effort to explain to others, even teachers, the chicanery of its formulation.

The key point here is that total human numbers are not the issue with our impact on the planet. As mentioned above, I = PAT was once popular among geography teachers, and taught in quite a few UK university geography departments in the 1980s and 1990s. Today, of course, that is far rarer. At one point I used to show trainee geography teachers how you could substitute G for P, where G is the number of pet gerbils in the world and A becomes total resources consumed worldwide divided by gerbils.

Of course, it is more sensible to substitute internal combustion engines, or aeroplanes, or heating boilers, or even cows for P (rather than pet gerbils), but the point is the same. If it were not the case that a few humans have huge carbon footprints and most have tiny ones, then the gerbil example would not work. It works because the example uses pets (not wild gerbils), and most pet gerbils live in countries with high carbon footprints, so the distribution of pet gerbils is a better match than people to the distribution of pollution.

I really don't expect to change the minds of those people who send me angry letters and emails in response to my books. I expect them to read paragraphs such as the ones above and be incredulous. It once took me an hour to explain to a geography teacher (who was older and wiser than me, but not quite as numerate) why I = PAT is a chimera. He had been wedded to the idea and had taught it to his students at various schools for decades. Of course, there is a great deal that we were taught at school that turns out not to be true. In the 1980s I was taught that an Ice Age was about to start, one which was, even then apparently, a little overdue. I was taught that the world was about to cool rapidly.

I received many angry letters following one 2022 article that annoyed quite a few *Guardian* readers, mainly because of the title: 'Don't Panic about the Birth of Baby 8 Billion. Before He's 65, Our Numbers Will Be in Reverse'.[18] My correspondents pointed me to articles and BBC news reports, highlighting quotes such as 'I have this deep grief and anger around not having a second child amidst the climate crisis.'[19] I fully acknowledge that there are many people in the world who see both the current climate crisis and the wider crisis of collapsing biodiversity as the existential issues of our times, and that there are a few who do not have children because of this. Others notice just how little attention the political right afford to these issues. One reviewer recently noted when commenting on several recently published geopolitics books written by more reactionary authors:

> Global warming is scrambling the landscape, threatening to drown islands, make deserts of grasslands and turn rivers to dust. It's bizarre how little geopolitical treatises make of this. 'Any reader will have noticed that I do not deal with the question,' admits George Friedman at the end of his book *The Next 100 Years*. Save for minor comments and asides, the same could be said of Ian Morris's *Geography Is Destiny*, Tim Marshall's *Prisoners of Geography*, Robert D. Kaplan's *The Revenge of Geography* and Peter Zeihan's *The Accidental Superpower*.[20]

What these men tend to write about is the decline of Western powers and the threats they perceive as coming from China or Russia. Given the ranking of issues in this book according to their actual impact, such perceived threats from the countries that are so often said to not share our politics may turn out to be among the least of our future problems.

In autumn 2022, the great and good of the environmental and economic world were asked to produce quotes in support of a new environmental book, *Earth for All: A Survival Guide for Humanity*.[21] Ban Ki-moon, eighth Secretary-General of the United Nations and deputy chair of the Elders, wrote that the book would help us 'ensure well-being for all – in any country – on our finite planet. Together, we can build a world that is genuinely equitable.' Thomas Piketty, author of *Capital in the Twenty-First Century*, wrote: '*Earth For All* conclusively shows that humanity's future on a liveable planet depends on drastically reducing socio-economic inequality and a more equitable distribution of wealth and power. Essential reading on our long journey toward an "Earth for All" society.'

Vanessa Nakate, climate activist and founder of the Africa-based Rise Up Movement, wrote, 'we [must] start putting people before profit. And we need the rich and the polluters to pay their share for the loss and damage that the climate crisis is already unleashing on poor, vulnerable communities around the globe.' Not all the quotes mention greater equality. Some were more interested in 'balance' or, as one endorser's review promised: 'Collapse is still avoidable. Here's how. If we'd paid attention to *The Limits to Growth* in 1972, we wouldn't be in the fix we're in today; as the modelling in this book makes clear, what's left of this decade may be our last best hope to get it at least partly right.' There was something of a clear break between those who emphasised economic inequality and those who worried more about environmental 'limits'. This may be the crux of the issue. The 'biodiversity that ate the storms' viewpoint tends to be held mostly by people who are better off, and more worried about the storms they imagine are to come than they appear to be concerned over the economic, political, and social ones the majority of the world's human inhabitants are currently weathering.

It is not just old men, and a smaller number of women, who write about our cataclysmic future from their better-than-averagely-upholstered armchairs. Younger and often equally privileged converts join in too.[22] I am only labouring this point because there is currently a crisis of environmental crisis amplification. This amplification appeared to accelerate with a shift in the years leading up to 2019, when some commentators began to feel a growing concern with intangible losses that, they said: 'cannot and perhaps should not be quantified'.[23]

The shift coincided with an increasing clarity that quantifiable losses – such as mortality, population displacement, war, or economic losses – were showing little evidence that suffering over time has been connected with climate and environmental change.[24] To reiterate: continuing to say that the future will be dire has less effect once that future has arrived, and the predicted consequences have not.

The intangible losses that are listed in a 2022 'Carbon Brief Report' include dire effects on culture, traditions and heritage, dignity, identity, ways of knowing, emotional well-being, a sense of order in the world, self-determination and influence, a sense of place, social fabric, sovereignty, and territory.[25] The briefing also implied, rather improbably, that mortality is intangible, and so cannot be quantified. It quoted a professor of environmental geography: 'We've got a category of things that are economic – and then we've got a category of things that we should really care about. Economics looks pretty unimportant if there's a risk you're going to lose your life.'[26] But what is the actual risk that you are going to lose your life? That surely is possible to calculate?

I suspect that in the near future there will be less discussion about the risk of loss of life due to how we harm the environment and more about the even more intangible of the supposedly intangible harms. Of course, it is true that billions of people are now living in fear of the possible effects of climate and wider environmental change. But how much of that fear has been caused by changes to date, as opposed to speculation about changes yet to come or amplified messaging from groups that are constantly spreading alarm that time has almost run out?

One threat is that younger people become demoralised and apathetic as a result of some of the cataclysmic predictions that so far do not hold water, at least not in the extreme ways they are described, namely that we are literally approaching a cataclysm (a sudden violent upheaval).[27] Some young people think that it is futile to try to live more sustainably because it already seems too late. There is ample evidence that a very large number of young people in the most affluent countries, as well as affluent youngsters in poorer countries, have already become incredibly disheartened and disillusioned. The mindless pursuit of growth has been a disaster for us and our planet; but anything that promotes nihilism could be just as harmful in future. The fear is certainly enormous.

Among 10,000 people aged between ages sixteen and twenty-five who completed a survey in ten rich, middle-income, and poor countries in 2021, 45 per cent said that fear of climate change was affecting how they functioned, and 59 per cent were either extremely worried or very worried about its implications.[28] The fear was highest among young people in India and the Philippines, and lowest in France and Finland.[29] This could be because it is projected that the effects of climate and wider environmental change will be greater in the former two countries, although to date France has suffered more *quantified* climate-related deaths than India, despite its much smaller population. Alternatively, it could be because young people with access to the internet and time to engage in surveys such as this in the former two countries (India and the Philippines) tend to be from much better-off backgrounds in contrast to most people in those two countries.

Across the whole 10,000-person sample of young people, 39 per cent said they would hesitate to have children because of the environmental crisis – suggesting that they are an unusual sample, given how many people in many of the countries surveyed have already had children by age twenty-five. Bearing that in mind, it is worth noting that across all countries, two-thirds of young adults reported feeling sad and afraid about climate change, and a majority felt angry, helpless, powerless, guilty, and anxious, while only 31 per cent were optimistic, and 29 per cent were indifferent. Some 56 per cent agreed with the statement: 'Humanity is doomed.'

Meanwhile, some of their parents' generation are looking for ways to soothe these fears. Comments on the findings of widespread doom by other researchers suggest that:

> The best chance of increasing optimism and hope in the eco-anxious young and old is to ensure they have access to the best and

most reliable information on climate mitigation and adaptation. Especially important is information on how they could connect more strongly with nature, contribute to greener choices at an individual level, and join forces with like-minded communities and groups. Spending time in nature as a family is one of many actions suggested by the Royal College of Psychiatrists to manage 'eco-distress' in children and young people.[30]

Spending time with likeminded people who believe that humanity is doomed, however, might not have the desired effect. Would it not also help if they had some sense of the actual level of harm caused to date, as well as what in the world is currently causing most suffering to humanity, how harms in the past have been mitigated, and also what is causing the greatest joy and happiness?

This is not a book about joy and happiness (my editor has told me that the text is already too long), but it may help to put in context the various crises we face, and give some perspective on our rational worries over what the next greatest crisis will be. In case you think I am being too blasé, here is a long but worthwhile quotation from some people who really do worry about the environmental crisis. It is a statement on what is possible:

> To avoid catastrophic ecological collapse, it is clear that drastic and challenging societal transformations must occur at all levels, from the individual to institutional, and from supply through to demand. From an energy-use perspective, the current work suggests that meeting these challenges does not, in theory, preclude extending decent living standards, universally, to a population of ~10 billion. Decent living is of course a subjective concept in public discourse. However, the current work offers a response to the clichéd populist objection that environmentalists are proposing that we return to living in caves. With tongue firmly in cheek, the response roughly goes 'Yes, perhaps, but these caves have highly-efficient facilities for cooking, storing food and washing clothes; low-energy lighting throughout; 50L of clean water supplied per day per person, with 15L heated to a comfortable bathing

temperature; they maintain an air temperature of around 20°C throughout the year, irrespective of geography; have a computer with access to global ICT networks; are linked to extensive transport networks providing ~5000–15,000 km of mobility per person each year via various modes; and are also served by substantially larger caves where universal healthcare is available and others that provide education for everyone between 5 and 19 years old.' And at the same time, it is possible that the amount of people's lives that must be spent working would be substantially reduced.[31]

Tipping points

Some environmental campaigners argue that decoupling growth from land use and therefore from biodiversity loss, and decoupling growth from ocean exploitation, are much harder problems than dealing with the implications of climate change, and that these issues have been underrepresented in debates. They suggest that environmental sustainability requires that a whole range of environmental indicators be maintained below potential tipping points and thus above key thresholds – not just a single overriding threshold such as 1.5, 2.0, or 2.5°C for temperature. They point out that climate is not everything – the wider environment matters just as much, including biodiversity loss – and they have a very valid point. They do also tend to present a model of the world in which so much could suddenly go wrong when various thresholds are passed, or even when an apparent tipping point is reached, giving the impression of a very small chance that catastrophe can be averted.

We appear to pass tipping points quite often, but little actually tips, very little changes. This is why I say so earnestly that there is a danger of crying wolf. As with the last chapter, I'll assume that many of the nightmare scenarios are known to anyone reading this book – but also that by now you are aware that loss of biodiversity is often the greatest fear of those who have least to fear in other ways. Often the writers of books and reports on these issues discuss the need to get 'biodiversity back up to the levels that existed seventy years ago'. This is impossible, as species that have become extinct cannot be recreated in some *Jurassic Park*–type fantasy. They insist that maximum mitigation is essential, often meaning that there is an urgent need for there to be far fewer humans on the planet in the very near future. That drop in human numbers will not begin to happen until the end of this century unless there is a far greater crisis than any of those described in this book (which would be an account which read as science fiction) – and also a much greater crisis than those all our ancestors had ever lived though. A sudden *worldwide* drop in the number of humans has never happened. Previous enormous disasters have been largely local to particular continents.

We should try to preserve and increase as much of the biodiversity that still exists as we can, and we should be aware that climate change may even accelerate the development of new species – although that would still be a slow process. It is important to be aware that the desire to see the human population fall has a shadowy history, with advocates proposing ways to engineer a supposedly optimum population level.[32] It tends to be older environmentalists who call for population curbs, while their younger counterparts tend to want people's behaviour, especially that of older, wealthy people, to be curbed instead. But it is good that some of the population-control suggestions made in the past, including mass sterilisation, or adding contraceptives to cities' water supply, are now being made far less frequently, and are rarely taken seriously today.[33]

Despite the ridiculing of past suggestions on curbing human population, some of those who are most concerned about biodiversity still think there are simply too many people on the planet and that current human land use is too extensive. Some believe that a faster worldwide adoption of vegetarian or vegan diets could help greatly (which is definitely true, as we need to eat less meat), while others are less sure that this alone will be enough. Some suggest that technological breakthroughs, such as growing proteins in labs, or effective carbon capture and storage, might be part of the solution. However, our solutions to past great dilemmas have rarely been purely technological; they were always, when successful, ultimately social innovations too.

Birth control is one technology that was transformational. UK births peaked nine months after the trial of Annie Besant and Charles Bradlaugh in 1877 for disseminating information about contraception. The trial was effectively the best possible form of publicity for condoms. Birth rates from then on fell consistently, not just in the UK but across Europe. Those rates then collapsed once the pill became widely available less than a century later. Not all technologies are overhyped. Sometimes the simplest of technologies are the most effective.

As some conservation scientists are now arguing:

> We can choose to adequately and equitably feed a population of 10 billion by 2050 – even as we reduce or eliminate global greenhouse gas emissions and staunch biodiversity loss . . . [But] low- or middle-income countries are most often called on to tackle overpopulation. And the people calling for action tend to be from high-income, high-consumption countries. But people from lower income countries reject these calls. Pakistani academic Adil Najam has observed these countries are 'weary of international population policy in the name of the environment'. Overall, the world's wealthiest 1% account for 15% of the world's carbon emissions. That's more than double the emissions of the poorest 50% of the planet – who are the most vulnerable to climate change. Prince William, for instance, has linked African [human] population growth to wildlife loss – even though he has three children and comes from a family with a carbon footprint almost 1,600 times higher than the average Nigerian family . . . Again, a mirror may be useful here. It turns out demand from rich countries is the single largest driver of biodiversity loss globally.[34]

Meanwhile, other commentators, often much older people, still focus on the idea of there being too many people in poorer countries. John Vidal, the *Guardian*'s environment editor for three decades, who retired in 2017, wrote in 2022, shortly before he died:

Until now, the orthodox western intellectual argument has been that the number of people does not matter as much as how people use resources. Consumption and inequality are the problem, not population size. True, the wealthiest 10% consume about 20 times more energy overall than the bottom 10%. So of course the rich must change their behaviour. But making climate breakdown all about consumption has become an excuse for countries to do nowhere near enough to reduce their populations.[35]

The population of the world is set to fall within the lifetimes of today's children – when the largest global baby boom of all, of which John and I are both a part, has died out. Before we get to that point, the affluent among us are very *unlikely* to run out of food. Why do I say that? Because the latest, 2019, Intergovernmental Science-Policy Platform on Biodiversity and Ecosystem Services (IPBES) report says so.[36]

To reiterate, the precursor to the 2019 IPBES report, the Millennium Ecosystem Assessment of 2005, concluded: 'Although there is substantial reason to believe that the world in the coming decades can produce sufficient food to feed its growing [human] population, important regional issues exist in the global pattern of cultivated land.' Very often these reports do not see food production as a great problem, and only very rarely do any of them now mention a concern with population levels. But that does not stop a significant number of people who are concerned about overpopulation citing these huge international reports as evidence, as if they did. This irks me, which is why I stress this again here. One of the reasons I have read all these reports is that I have been repeatedly told that they prove there are too many people on Earth.

In the 1,148 pages of the 2019 IPBES report, 'family planning' is referred to only four times, and once in connection to 'women's empowerment and their access to family planning'. Population growth is usually mentioned in relation to its being low, for example:

> Scenarios and pathways that explore the effects of low-to-moderate population growth, and transformative changes in the production

and consumption of energy, food, feed, fibre and water, sustainable use, equitable sharing of the benefits arising from use and nature-friendly climate adaptation and mitigation will better support the achievement of future societal and environmental objectives.

In other words, population growth is described in a positive light.

One reason the IPBES scientists' conclusion about our human numbers is positive is that the UN is currently forecasting low-to-moderate population growth, which has been expected for many decades now. In fact, the projections have recently been becoming even lower with each two-year period that passes. The question now is not whether the human population of the planet is set to stabilise and decline slightly, but instead when during the next seventy years the decline will begin. As a result, reports where this is known simply do not support the idea that growing populations are leading humanity to apocalypse. That does not mean we should not be greatly concerned about species loss, however.[37]

In case you are in any doubt that there are renewed claims that we are at an environmental tipping point due to too many people, consider this example. On 20 May 2021 Christopher Bystroff published a paper in the peer-reviewed academic journal *PLoS One*, titled 'Footprints to Singularity: A Global Population Model Explains Late 20th Century Slow-Down and Predicts Peak within Ten Years'.[38] Bystroff is a professor in both the Department of Biological Sciences and the Department of Computer Science, at Rensselaer Polytechnic Institute, in the city of Troy, New York. According to his academic website he works on the folding and design of proteins, enzymes, vaccine antigens, and biosensors. His lab is also involved in 'a collaborative effort to develop a contraceptive vaccine. The vaccine will produce temporary and reversible infertility. Instead of having to take an action to be protected, you will be protected by default, and you would need to take an action to be temporarily fertile again.'[39]

Bystroff's paper was widely shared by environmental campaigners. In particular, one graph in the paper received special attention (reproduced here as Figure 7.1). It suggests that, if business as usual continues, then there will be a rapid decline in the worldwide human population to 4 billion people by the year 2040, due to half the population of the world dying. That number would then halve and almost halve again within the next twenty years to stand at just over a billion.

To put it another way, a disaster greater than any other in all of human history and prehistory is predicted by models such as Bystroff's to occur over the course of the next dozen or so years. So at one political extreme, a concern about biodiversity is also a concern about the supposed need to reduce the diversity and volume of human life itself in the future. This ties in with a belief that there will be much less human life very soon regardless of what we do, and so we should start planning now to reduce our numbers enormously. Such assertions would not be so troubling if it were a wish confined to a few on the green fringes; but, as revealed through their statements about not having children themselves, some of these ideas have come to permeate and now pervade the thinking and beliefs of many young adults in affluent countries.

You may wonder why Bystroff's paper was so widely shared by advocates, since his model was flawed even when it was published. The fourth illustration in his paper (Figure 7.1 here) suggests that a population peak had already occurred, with falls thereafter. But this did not happen; instead, global population has continued to rise, albeit more slowly than before, to 8 billion people. Bar devastating nuclear war, or a large asteroid colliding with our planet, Bystroff's scenario is extremely unlikely to happen. Furthermore, whenever there have been population falls in the course of world history, it has been due to a sudden regional event such as famine, a new disease, or war. Global human population has never before fallen greatly overall, in aggregate.[40]

Bystroff's study was shared widely by environmental campaigners between themselves, and to others including me, because it resonated with those who thought the end was nigh and were looking to convince others about the need for urgent action. The

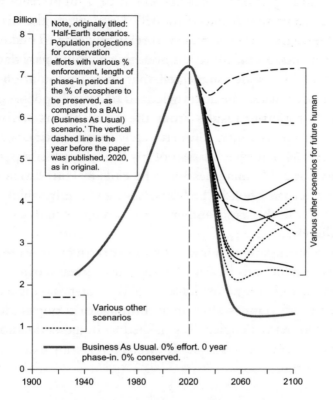

Figure 7.1: Cataclysmic scenarios for human population, 2020–2100

Note, originally titled: 'Half-Earth scenarios. Population projections for conservation efforts with various % enforcement, length of phase-in period and the % of ecosphere to be preserved, as compared to a BAU (Business As Usual) scenario.' The vertical dashed line is the year before the paper was published, 2020, as in original.

Source: Christopher Bystroff, 'Footprints to singularity: A global population model explains late 20th century slow-down and predicts peak within ten years', *PLoS One*, Vol. 16, No. 5, e0247214, pp.1–20, 2021.

response from Bystroff's academic peers, however, has been muted. As I write, only one academic paper – published in the *Journal of Fungi* – has cited it.[41]

What Bystroff had done was to treat humans as what is known as a K-selected species, because he claimed: 'To treat humans differently from all other K-selected species would be a form of "human exceptionalism", which is not scientific.' K-selected species are those, like elephants and bison, that give birth to few offspring that each have a high chance of survival, and that have relatively stable populations depending on the availability of food.

Bystroff had fitted a series of curves to the population record of the world between the year 1500 and 1970, to produce what he called a 'hyper-exponential model'. Unsurprisingly, his model fitted the past record, because it is relatively easy to make a wide variety of models fit the very smoothly changing past data. One version of his model suggested that world population would peak in 2016, which he acknowledged had not happened, but he added: 'Upcoming results from the 2020 census will greatly resolve this uncertainty.' Unfortunately for this claim, there is no world census. Another version of his model set his hypothetical peak at 2022. He imagines what he calls a 'Half-Earth world', named after the book by E. O. Wilson: a world in which human pressures on the environment are somehow halved, almost immediately.

One repercussion of a few extremely driven environmentalists' emphasis on humans having already caused great harm – without explaining which humans have done this, or how – is to spread worries that even a stable or declining world population may still be too many people. This has led to suggestions about how to make it decline faster in future. Here is an example from another author:

> Let us assume, however, that population does stabilise around 10 billion or perhaps declines thereafter. Would this be a good enough reason for dismissing population growth anxieties, as sceptics do? Might environmentalists not still wonder whether such levels are sustainable or desirable, especially when coupled with aspirations for global economic development and equity and in light of current ecological challenges?[42]

Here the assumption is that if the global population were to fall earlier and faster than is currently predicted, all surviving people might become better off (economic development would occur with fewer mouths to feed), more equal (with fewer of us around we would apparently share better), and there would be fewer ecological challenges overall.

But – because the ecological challenges we face are caused almost entirely by a small proportion of people who pollute the most, who expand agricultural ranges most thoughtlessly, who share least, and whose actions and governments do least to promote sustainable economic development – the reverse could well be the case; unless, that is, the fall in population were among the richest people in the rich world. That relatively modest proviso is hardly ever included in such proposals, which tend to assume, without thinking carefully about it, that it is the billions of poorer people whose numbers would fall. This is despite the fact that numbers of the rich could be made to fall simply through taxation making them less rich, as opposed to the use of enforced mass sterilisation, or worse.

Most of the current rise in global population is due to people living longer, not because of a greater number of babies being born. Because so few people involved in the more extreme side of the ecological debate realise this, papers such as Bystroff's end with remarkable fantasies that could actually result in a *higher population*. Higher because his fantasy would result in more births than are currently predicted as so many people in the world are now so old. To explain, Bystroff concludes his paper as follows:

> To build a mental picture of a society that has achieved balance with nature, imagine a people with a strong religious prohibition against growth, so engrained that no policing is required. A woman of child-bearing age in the Half-Earth world is permitted to have another child only if she is 'blessed' by an elderly person, who, on his deathbed, bequeaths to her his one and only 'blessing' – the right to procreate. The one-to-one matching of deaths to births would guarantee population stability.

The UN Population Division's 2022 prediction for the year when births worldwide will equal deaths is 2086 – when the children born in 2022 are aged sixty-four. It is not very long to wait, and that year may come earlier, as in recent years each new UN projection has brought it forward because fewer babies are being born than were expected (in fact, the 2024 projection brought the date forward to 2084). So we are not heading for stability but for falling population, unless we were to adopt Bystroff's 'blessings' and have more children than we currently are heading towards.

Try to imagine the year 2086 (or 2084, the updated UN prediction, let's not split hairs). There are possibly 10 billion people on Earth, but only 119 million babies are born that year, so just 1.2 per cent of the population are babies – in contrast with 1.7 per cent in 2022. Life expectancy in 2086 was projected (in 2022) to be 80.8 years worldwide, only a few more than it is today. The median age in 2086 is 40, and rising; in 2022 it was only 30. By 2086, the majority of people in the world are projected to be aged over 40; half of those would be aged over 60 – and the world is waiting for the old to die so that it has less of a top-heavy population pyramid. Too many babies is already *not our problem* in the 2020s; soon we may be worrying more about too few young adults in many parts (in fact the majority) of the world, where women have been having fewer than two children each for quite some time.

For some years to come we may have to tolerate unhelpful articles being published on population because so many folks have not caught up with what is happening. A section of the *Guardian* paid for by the Bill and Melinda Gates Foundation in 2022 published an article on Tanzania, one of the tiny number of countries now predicted to contribute most to population growth in future. The article was illustrated by images of crowded cities reminiscent of the introduction to the Ehrlichs' 1968 book *The Population Bomb*, which described standing in the centre of a crowd in a large city in the poor world and foretelling the end of times. The article pointed out that in Tanzania: 'The population has increased by 37% over the past decade to almost 63 million according to the latest UN figures, and, projections suggest, is expected to grow between 2% and 3% a year until 2050.'[43] What it didn't say was that this was the rate at which the entire world's population had been growing back in 1968; it also didn't say that what the UN was predicting is actually a dramatic decline in births for Tanzania, based on what had already been happening in that country: a decline that had accelerated over the past twenty years and was projected to decline at twice that rate again over the next twenty years. The projected 2–3 per cent annual growth in Tanzania's population is not due to the declining birth rate, but the rapidly declining mortality rate.

In fact, the *rate of growth* in population is already rapidly falling in Tanzania, from 2.9 per cent in 2022, to an expected 2.5 per cent in 2035, 2.0 per cent in 2049, 1.5 per cent in 2065, 1.0 per cent in 2085, and 0.8 per cent in 2094. It is not projected to stop falling. One day, of course, it will, as is inevitable.

What the article on Tanzania did say is that it would be good if more efforts were made to help people access contraceptives and better education, and that as regards birth control there had been a dwindling of 'donor resources'. Of course, that is all true. But it also reported that the government in Tanzania has pledged to increase the share of its scarce resources that it spends on these things. What it could have also said is that governments elsewhere in the better-off world have been trying to make it harder for people to access sex education and contraceptives, and especially to have access to abortion clinics. Some of those same people have been trying to prevent contraceptives being included in overseas aid.

In Poland, severe restrictions on abortion were further tightened in January 2021. The US followed suit the following year. In November 2021, Iran passed a law to curb access to abortion, eliminate free provision of contraception, prohibit voluntary sterilisation, restrict prenatal screening, and broaden state surveillance on those accessing contraception. In 2022, China introduced measures to 'reduce abortions that are not medically necessary'. In addition, Belarus, Japan, South Korea, Hungary, Turkey, and Russia have introduced policies to cajole women into having large families in ways known to be ineffective and to cause misery and fear; such policies try to manipulate women, but are never successful.[44] With all this going on elsewhere, why criticise people or politicians in Tanzania?

The majority of people today live in countries where the birth rate is fewer than two children per woman. In 2022 it was less than 1.5 in 46 countries, and in South Korea much less than one child per woman (0.81 in 2021, and still falling as I write). These rates almost all lowered again when updated by the UN on 11 July 2024. The fear of population growth is a hangover from the 1960s and 1970s.[45] Paul Ehrlich, among other ecologists of that era, prophesied that the oceans would be dead in less than a decade from overfishing due to population growth, that the US would be rationing water by 1974 and food by 1980, that there would be famines worldwide, and that the population would have to be sterilised by putting agents in their food and water.[46] More than fifty-five years later, undeterred by evidence or events, Paul Ehrlich and a few of his surviving colleagues continue to suggest that the future will be ghastly, and that we are all still underestimating just how dire the next few years will be.[47]

Bystroff is clearly not alone. In a paper published in a very eminent academic collection in 2023, William Rees wrote: 'In short, the continuity of civilisation requires a cooperative, planned major contraction of both the material economy and human populations. The overall goal must be to establish and maintain the necessary conditions for a smaller human family (one to two billion people) to enjoy both economic and ecological security through "one-planet living".'[48] Rees is an emeritus professor at the University of British Columbia. He draws graphs such as the one below (reproduced as Figure 7.2).[49]

You might think that I am being selective in quoting from the reports of academics with extreme views, and they are indeed unusual people. But they also reflect more widely held views about the imminent loss of habitat for humans, disseminated by much less unusual people who warn that any problems today are the start of something much larger to come. However, we need to realise that these doom scenarios tend to have a limited impact beyond, at worst, fuelling conspiracy theories that climate change science is a hoax to try to achieve terrible outcomes, in service of

Figure 7.2: More cataclysmic scenarios for human population, 2020–2100

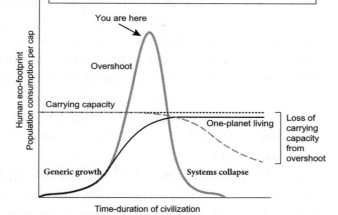

Source: William Rees, 'The human eco-predicament: Overshoot and the population conundrum', *Vienna Yearbook of Population Research*, Vol. 21, pp. 1–19, 2023.

world domination, by some shadowy elite group. However, the reality is more mess-up than conspiracy.

So to try to better understand why so few people worldwide see environmental issues as the greatest of threats, let's turn to sea-level rise, and in particular – via a number of other examples – a very misguided plan for a tiny coastal village in Wales that people have been living in for only just over one hundred years and that you almost certainly have never heard of. My parents live nearby. It is a place that is mostly used for retirement, where houses were cheap to begin with, and then became unsaleable due to the fear of rising sea levels because of climate change. But we'll start with Manila and then the coast of Africa, and briefly hop over to New York, before turning to Wales and the Cardigan Bay coastline of Gwynedd, near the home of Bronwen and David Dorling.

Sea-level rise

Major disasters are now routinely presented as if they were the product of climate change, due to sea-level rise, an increase in tropical storms, or both. The 2009 flooding of Manila in the Philippines is now a case study of how climate change can be offered as the sole reason for a disaster, despite this being inaccurate. As a sceptical report explained: 'In retrospective pieces published on anniversaries of the disaster, the possibility of climate change being a factor had hardened into certainty . . . the relationship between [tropical storm] Ondoy and climate change was resolved through editorial practices rather than through scientific method.'[50] It was simply assumed that the storm was due to climate change.

In 2022, a study reported that a fifth of all outstanding heritage sites on the coastline of Africa were at risk from a once-in-a-hundred-year extreme event such a huge storm surge followed by flooding. The study did not mention tsunamis, which are not caused by climate change and always remain a threat.[51] The study did suggest that sea-level rise and more extreme weather events would increase the current overall threat threefold by 2050. We cannot know what will actually unfold, although we should expect ancient heritage sites situated on coastlines to be some of the most vulnerable structures.

Even New York's famous skyscrapers are threatened by sea-level rise, as they are currently sinking under their own weight at a rate of 1–2 millimetres a year. Couple that with 22 centimetres of sea-level rises on that coast since 1950 (and still rising) and worsening storms, and there may be a problem, although the experts are not sure if the greatest danger is from flooding or falling buildings, claiming that New York and other coastal cities 'have to get planning for this. If you get repeated exposure to seawater, you can corrode steel and destabilize buildings, which you clearly don't want. Flooding also kills people, too, which is probably the greatest concern.'[52]

In the UK, the first village officially lost to sea-level rise was Fairbourne, in Gwynedd, Wales. In recent years it became very hard to sell property in the village because of what was claimed to be the threat of sea-level rise – but there is another story behind this headline.[53] In the Welsh Shoreline Management Plan 2 (SMP2), dated 2011, it was stated that Fairbourne's property owners and businesses would have to be relocated within the next fifty years, with managing the realignment of the coast to begin shortly after 2025. That sounds simple, but it is not.

Fairbourne lies south of the mouth of the River Mawddach and is protected from the sea by a spit. The valley of the Mawddach Estuary was created by the effects of glaciation in the last ice age. It is a typical U-shaped valley. At the end of the ice age, the ice cap over North Wales and its associated glaciers melted. At that time, sea levels were much lower than they are today and much of the Cardigan Bay area was then above sea level. A forest developed in this area, the remains of which, with shifting sands, periodically becomes visible off the coast of Fairbourne. It is likely that at this time the Mawddach River was not tidal where it crossed the present coastline. Subsequently, the sea level rose; the forest in Cardigan Bay was completely flooded and destroyed; and the coastline of Cardigan Bay settled, apart from dune areas, roughly to where it is today. With the rise in sea level, the Mawddach River became tidal.

One worry concerning Fairbourne was that global warming might cause more violent storms and potentially higher storm surges. But this is the UK Met Office prediction at the time the SMP2 report was written:

> Around the UK the size of surge expected to occur on average about once in 50 years is projected to increase by less than 0.9 mm/year (not including relative mean sea level change) over the 21st

century. In most locations this trend cannot be clearly distinguished from natural variability. Thus our assessment suggests that this component of extreme sea level will be much less important than was implied by UKCIP02, where corresponding values exceeded 5 mm/year in places.'[54]

By 2022, the UK Met Office was even more cautious: 'However, the UKCP18 model results suggest a relatively small contribution from storm surge changes and we don't yet know whether storm surges will become more severe, less severe or remain the same.'[55]

Sometimes it helps to observe very local phenomena, rather than thinking globally. There has been a single instance of flooding from the sea coming over the spit in recent years, affecting the conservatory of one property. It needs to be pointed out that this was not simply a natural phenomenon. First, there is a car park on top of the spit: a large area is paved and an even larger area has been impacted by vehicles. As a result, it was no longer a loose, free-draining area of shingle with water running through it and back to the beach, waves splashing onto it in a storm that caused extensive flooding of other towns and villages. In the car park in Fairbourne this resulted in a small lake developing. This lake then drained through a gap in the low bank on the landward side that had been cut together with a flight of steps, for easier beach access. I have stood at the first point of sea-level rise assumed to lead to inundation of a UK settlement many times and watched the trickle of water and pondered. It is likely that no planning permission had been sought for the steps, and this would not have been given. However, that was a warning not to interfere further with the free draining of the top of the spit. It was human action and not the rise in the sea that mattered here.

It is easy to understand how someone could look at the environment agency's flood map of Fairbourne and think that it was defended on the seaward side by a 2-mile long artificial sea wall. This had been built to the necessary height for defence against current sea levels and it is easy to imagine that sea-level rise could be managed by raising the wall along its whole length. Given that it is a natural spit and erosion was happening at the southern end, it would make sense to think it was becoming damaged by natural processes. In 2021 the authorities decided to repair the damage done to the spit, and they stated: 'We are committed to maintaining Fairbourne's flood defences until 2054.'[56]

But what about the possibility of Fairbourne being flooded from the Mawddach Estuary? There have been detailed assessments in various Fairbourne flood risk management schemes published over the years, which have suggested that the better and much lower-cost option was to strengthen the existing inland defences at their current height, rather than work on the spit. Of course, coastline erosion does occur, and it has been occurring for centuries on the east coast of England, but not as a result of sea-level rise. In contrast, in 2013, the coastal authority in Wales stated: 'In Fairbourne, we will hold the line until 2025, and then move to a position of managing the realignment of the coast, and then move to a position of no active intervention in 2105.'[57]

Deciding in 2013 what you are going to decide in 2025 is very strange, considering the uncertainty about the speed of sea-level rise. One complete unknown is how much sea-level rises will affect the extents of high and low tides. If the tidal range were to fall at twice the rate of sea-level rise, the highest high tides would be exactly the same height as now. The next date mentioned – 'no active intervention in 2105' – is equally puzzling. That is forty-two years after they had planned to have relocated everyone. In the years after 2013, both the local Gwynedd council and the Welsh government authorities appeared to backtrack on their direst warnings about the fate awaiting Fairbourne.

Examples like this show why it is possible for people to be so sceptical of the imminent threat of sea-level rise: such rises are slow and don't necessarily result in inundation, even of the most low-lying village in the UK.

Food, water, and energy

What of the much greater fear – not of losing settlements on some coastlines, but of running out of food and water due to environmental changes caused mainly by humankind?

In the 1972 book *The Limits to Growth*, a report prepared for the Club of Rome just a few years after it was founded, a group of researchers claimed that their model showed: 'If the present growth trends in world population, industrialization, pollution, food production, and resource depletion continue unchanged, the limits to growth on this planet will be reached sometime within the next one hundred years. The most probable result will be a rather sudden and uncontrollable decline in both population and industrial capacity.'[58]

To date, despite the ongoing trend towards population-growth slowdown, and despite huge increases in industrialisation, pollution, food production, and resource depletion, no sudden (let alone uncontrollable) decline in either the world's population or industrial capacity has occurred.

There is no doubt that great damage has been done, and half of those researchers' hundred-year forecasting period remains. But the direst predictions have yet to occur. Catastrophic events such as the Great Chinese Famine (1959–61) have not been repeated, and fewer people have died in famines in each decade since that one.

The original authors of *The Limits to Growth* have gone on to do very different things. One of the four authors of the 1972 book, Jørgen Randers, is now listed as a former member of the Environmental Sustainability Council at AstraZeneca UK amongst much else on the Club of Rome's Wikipedia page.[59] Hopefully, researchers in future will look back at this period more critically and look more carefully into the authors' thinking, and ask why their claims, and the youthful exuberance of the early environmental modellers, were not better questioned earlier.

Despite the dire predictions not having come to pass, the ideas that first began to be widely propagated through that report to the Club of Rome have grown; today, its successors warn about

Figure 7.3: Going hungry is caused by poverty and inequality – not by droughts

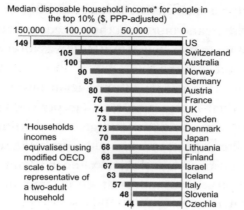

A country of extremes: the wealthiest Americans are the richest people in the developed world, but America's poorest are also the most likely to go hungry (2023 or most recent data).

Source: John Burn-Murdoch, 'It is inequality not overall prosperity, that causes hunger', Twitter/X, Tweet of 6:14pm, 8 December 2023. Reporting on his *Financial Times* article based on the Luxembourg Income Study.

new tipping points and limits to growth that should concern us. There is tipping point fatigue among many people who are now becoming inured to the repeated warnings.

Food becomes scarce when a country becomes poor or when a group within a country becomes poorer (Figure 7.3). In the country where I am writing these words, in the eighteen months to May 2023, food prices rose by 25 per cent. A typical British household spent a seventh of their income on food by then, so the rise in food prices mattered far more than the increase in energy prices, which represented only a twentieth of their annual income. The food-price shock was far bigger than the energy-price shock; this was the case for a majority of households, but especially those with more children and more mouths to feed. It doesn't cost more to heat a room no matter how many children are in it. It does cost more to feed more mouths.[60]

Estimates are that people in poor countries spend a greater proportion of their incomes on food (40 per cent) than those in rich countries (17 per cent), on average.[61] But within those poorer nations the difference is enormous. In sub-Saharan Africa, the range is 60 per cent to less than 10 per cent. Poor people in the US spend over three times more of their incomes on food than do rich people in Africa.[62]

From the *Financial Times* we learnt in late 2023 that worldwide:

> The number of people facing hunger surged to more than 735 million by 2022, up by 20 per cent compared with 2019, according to the UN, with Africa the worst affected region. Across the globe the cost of essentials, such as milk and eggs, shot up, prompting governments to impose price controls. Food price inflation has since started to come down in most rich countries but remains sticky in many parts of the world. Agricultural commodity markets over the past three years have been 'mayhem' ... prices of wheat – a staple for billions, especially in developing countries – could be volatile as the world enters a fifth year of deficit in global supplies of the grain.[63]

These fluctuations are not about bad harvests, poor weather, or environmental decline. They are about wars, commercial financial speculation and profiteering.

So food-price fluctuations are hardly ever the result of environmental factors. The same is very often the case for water. A country that receives as much rain as the UK does and can still run out of drinkable water if it is just badly managed. Two years before the financial crash of 2008, it was reported that the UK's largest water company, Thames Water, was to be sold by its private owner to another private owner. According to the magazine *Private Eye*, the company had not been properly investing in infrastructure and did not plan to do so, so it had missed every target to stop leaks; the magazine noted that the deal would allow executives to pocket millions, and would make shareholders £3.5 billion in profit (in 2006 prices).

In 2023, the collapse of Thames Water, by then £14 billion in debt, was still not widely seen as part of the failure of the privatisation introduced by a past UK government. It is possible that the executives running the company had not been expecting interest rates to rise when they did. Like so many of their kind, they had probably hoped that the party and then the after-party could roll on a little longer. But the construction of such a huge debt pile had been deliberate.

Macquarie, the bank that owned Thames Water at the time, claimed most of the debt had been added via loans to invest in repairing pipes, improving water storage, and cleaning. But what little money had actually been spent on such things had in fact been almost entirely financed from customer payments, almost every year, so only a small portion of the borrowed money was ever used for system investments, while most of it was used to pay internal dividends.[64]

By 2023, many private UK water companies claimed they had not been paying dividends for the past five years. But so-called *internal* shareholders did receive dividends, and then went on to pay regular shareholders. As the Equality Trust commented at the time: 'This is exactly what privatised utilities are designed to do: extract profit from services and pay dividends to shareholders.'[65] In summer 2023 government ministers began to talk of taking Thames Water into 'temporary public ownership'.[66]

Shareholders and economic power seem to be what matters most. The global trade networks shift as manufacturing moves.[67] This is as true of food, and in some cases water, as it is of other goods. But it makes us uncomfortable to think about things essential to life being traded in the same way as any other product. A decent country tries to keep the supply of water out of the clutches of profiteers, at least. The UK is very unusual among European states in having privatised its water supplies. But despite that, the British rarely now consider this fact, and other examples like it, as being unusual. They had been taught that private was good; that a freely traded commodity would always be well supplied. But just as water becomes threatened if people are permitted to profit from it, so too with energy supplies.

Like concerns over food and water, issues of energy were not directly addressed in the 2022 Ipsos survey that has been used to order the chapters of this book according to the priorities of people worldwide; but they feature indirectly in concerns over the environment, climate change, inflation, and inequality.[68] In the equivalent survey for China, issues of environmental pollution, much of it caused by energy and transport, rank as the ninth most pressing for all survey respondents, and the eighth most important for people aged under thirty-five – hardly any higher than elsewhere in the world, and as important for women as for men (the surveys in China interestingly divide concerns between the sexes).

How swiftly are we converting our sources of energy to renewables? China may well be in the lead here, but it is also a highly polluting country. In a world with many more elderly people, will we find keeping warm in winter easier in future? If so, by when, and at what cost? In terms of energy used to allow travel, there have been huge changes: the shift from the bicycle to the automobile in China, for example.

Are our cities becoming better planned or not? And now that the pandemic is mostly over, apart from its longer-term effects, are we likely to see air travel increase again at the enormous rates it was rising in the years before the pandemic hit? As of early 2024 it had not quite recovered: 'Globally, full year 2023 traffic was at 94.1% of pre-pandemic (2019) levels. December 2023 total traffic rose 25.3% compared to December 2022 and reached 97.5% of the

December 2019 level. Fourth quarter traffic was at 98.2% of 2019, reflecting the strong recovery towards the end of the year.'[69]

It is not good that by early 2024, air travel was almost back to where it had been in 2019, but it is perhaps telling that it took so long to recover. Even though there were far more people in the world in 2024 than in 2019, and especially more adults, fewer were flying. Similar to the wasteful airlines, oil companies have a reputation for being uncaring, but when there is an oil spill at a production facility today, the behaviour of owners and senior management is now more closely scrutinised.[70]

Let's end with a more positive story of where we may be heading. How much money is spent in different parts of the world trying to address the falls in biodiversity? The answer, it would appear, is that it depends not only on how rich a country is, but also, crucially, on its level of economic equality.

The country leading the world spending on biodiversity improvements is Norway, which spends twice as much, per capita, as do Sweden, France, and Germany. These three countries spend more than twice as much as the UK, which is also far more economically unequal. If we want to halt the decline of biodiversity as rapidly as possible, we need to increase economic equality wherever we live.[71]

Colleagues of mine working in the Leverhulme Centre for Anthropocene Biodiversity at the University of York conducted a review of studies of income inequality and biodiversity. The majority of studies that they found suggested that more unequal regions had lower levels of biodiversity.[72] They pointed out that the Overseas Development Institute has estimated the 'fair share' that all countries should be paying to contribute to nature restoration in low- and middle-income countries. To date, only two countries pay that fair share – Norway and Sweden – with Norway paying far more than its fair share. Meanwhile, many rich countries, including the UK, Canada, New Zealand, Italy, and Spain, pay less than half of what they should to compensate for biodiversity loss. It is the more economically unequal countries that pay the least.[73]

If you are concerned about our continued losses of biodiversity then you need to understand the crisis that the majority of people in the world rank highest – those costs of living, and see how inflation, poverty, and social and economic inequality interact to influence what is socially sustainable and determine what can be environmentally possible.

Conclusion

Doomsday Clock stays at 90 seconds to midnight.
News headline, Tuesday, 23 January 2024[1]

The Doomsday Clock was created in 1947, set then at seven minutes to midnight. Just two years later, when the Soviet Union first tested a nuclear bomb, it was moved forward by four minutes. Four years later in 1953, when the United States first tested a hydrogen bomb, the clock was moved forward another minute, to two minutes to midnight. The furthest back in time it has ever been placed was seventeen minutes to midnight, and then only briefly, in 1991, at what was assumed to be the end of the Cold War.

Albert Einstein established the *Bulletin of the Atomic Scientists* shortly after the end of the Second World War, with Robert Oppenheimer as its first chair.[2] These scientists and their successors have moved the minute hand forwards and backwards in time depending on their impression of the current risk of global catastrophe. By 2015 it had returned to its place in 1949, at three minutes to midnight: climate change had been added to its remit. Then, with the advent of superpower war again in Europe, over the soil of Ukraine, the clock's minute hand moved forwards to its closest to midnight since the height of the Cold War – just ninety seconds from Doomsday. We are still at that point as I write these words in late 2024. Troops from Ukraine are now in Russia itself, Israel is in Lebanon and Syria, and there is no sign of improvement on the immediate horizon.

THE NEXT CRISIS

We are ever more rapidly running out of time. But, at some point, one day, this ticking forwards towards midnight will stop, and the threat will be lifted. The second hand, and then the minute hand, and perhaps (can we dream?) even the hour hand will reverse. The time's arrow of the Doomsday Clock can reverse. The crucial question is: What crises will have been avoided – or not – before we reach this new and better time?

The next really big crisis will very likely be something that we are hardly concerned about right now – not climate, nor artificial intelligence, nor the chauvinist authoritarians being elected on a surge of populist far-right votes around the world.

The next crisis is always (or for centuries has been) something that comes out of the blue – it can be quite different from our fears. A crisis can be both bad things that happen and the fear of bad things that might happen. Often the fear is based on a bad thing having begun, and the threat of it becoming worse. It is not hard to see that almost all the greatest crises in recent centuries were hardly imagined, or were not imagined at all, just a century before they became reality.

A few people fear the almost completely unknown – a black hole appearing between here and the moon, for example, and sucking us in. If that were to occur, it would all be over very quickly. Others fear an alien invasion from outer space, on which nothing has been said in this book and nothing will be, other than in one endnote[3] and – in case it reassures you – the probability of alien arrival has to be higher than a black hole appearing between here and the moon, but lower than anything we consider seriously.

The next crisis might be something like a new disease, or our development of a very new type of weapon, or – as it was in ancient times (and possibly again) – a great flood. You might think a great flood unlikely, but what if an asteroid hit the planet and caused a tsunami? That is many millions of times more likely than a black hole forming nearby, and many thousands of times more likely than alien life arriving. We know that simply because of how often large asteroids have hit the Earth in the past.

Conclusion

New life only began on Earth once. But just because the chance of an asteroid striking Earth is millions of times more likely than a black hole appearing between us and the moon, that does not mean that we should live in great fear of the hypothetical asteroid. Asteroid strikes of great magnitude are also extremely rare. Our worst crises, within the past couple of centuries, have almost always been homegrown (terrestrial).

Often a crisis seems to well up out of nowhere. That is why the atomic scientists have now added climate change, disruptive technologies, and biosecurity to their *Bulletin*'s headline banner of great concerns.[4] Perhaps it is because they are scientists, rather than social scientists, that they do not include the greatest concern of most people on the planet, and the issue that most concerns so many social scientists today: how to get by, the cost of living, inequality, and poverty.

The current upsurge in research into inequality worldwide is partly due to a movement within the elite. In October 2023, under the title 'Rising Interest', Turgut Keskintürk, a PhD student at Duke University, wrote: 'A few months ago Beth Popp Berman [a professor of sociology at the University of Michigan] posted a tweet, saying "I love you, sociologists, but do all of us have to work on inequality?"'[5] Berman had posted a graph (reproduced here as Figure 8.1) with the comment: 'It is fair to say that something happened in sociology over these last few decades.'

The data in Figure 8.1 imply that nearly four out of five articles published in the *American Sociological Review* (*ASR*) now mention inequality in one form or another. If we make a (perhaps dubious) assumption that the *ASR* represents the core output of the discipline, this means that the overwhelming majority of sociologists talk about inequality.

Elite academic journals and universities are a part of the elite. In a way, there is already a revolution under way within the elite, something much greater than a debate – a change in our understanding, if not yet in our actions. Next, what we should really want to know is: Will it make a difference for the better that more sociologists are focusing so much on inequality? It may do, as changes to how we thought almost certainly did before, when inequality fell in every rich nation in the world from 1918 until the 1970s. The rise of ideas about socialism played a large part in that, although little of that thinking occurred then in universities. Today, universities do not exist exclusively for cosmetic purposes, as temples to past truths, and to award students with degrees. What is studied within them also, almost always, has a

Figure 8.1: Frequency of mentions of inequality, *American Sociological Review*, 1936–2019

Inequality in Sociology: the % of articles using the word 'inequality' or 'inequalities' in the *American Sociological Review*, 1936–2019

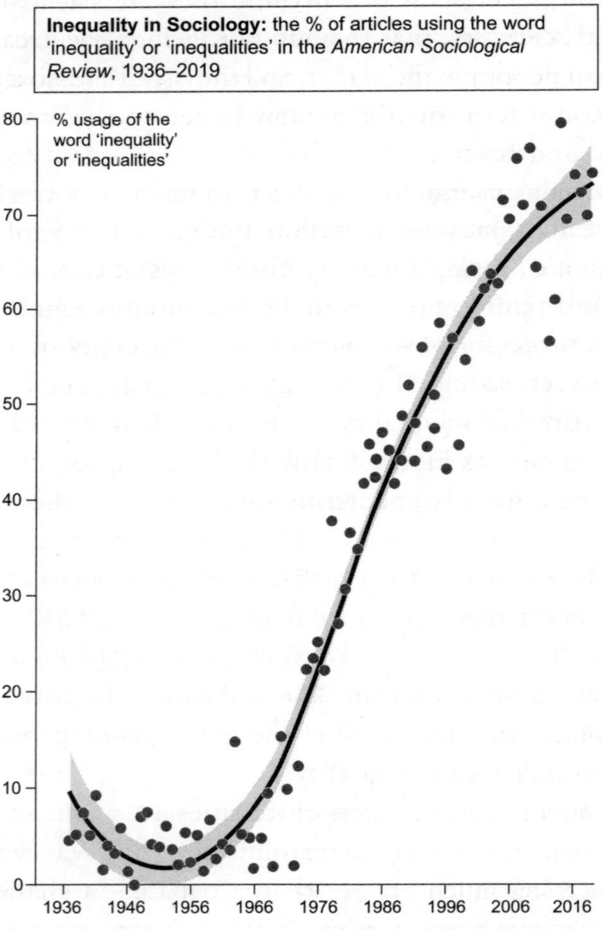

Source: Turgut Keskintürk, 'Sociology's Inequality Problem', Blog, 10 October 2023, tkeskinturk.github.io/blog/inequality/.

lasting impact on the societies they are a part of. Sometimes this is direct, but usually it is through very indirect means.

Figure 8.1 very simply illustrates what has increasingly concerned the majority of sociologists writing in one of the major sociology journals since 1936. It reveals something that every social scientist and especially every sociologist may have imagined was the case but might be surprised to see confirmed so clearly. Inequality and its consequences and corollaries have come to dominate our concerns, not just internationally in public surveys, but also across the social sciences.

Inequality is now the underlying issue of most importance in social policy studies, politics, human geography, education studies, human development, and sociology; and it is also the greatest current concern of the more enlightened economists – and now even many of the much less enlightened, more mainstream, more conventional ones.[6] Inequality is an issue that has spread into the studies undertaken by historians and across anthropology. It appears increasingly frequently in the debates of academic theologians and philosophers. No course in English, film studies, or even classics or art history is now complete without at least one module on this aspect of the human condition and how it has impacted the field.

Occasionally there is a complaint from within the social science community at the dominance of studies into the harmful effects of economic inequality. The graph above was produced as a result of one such complaint. Here, more fully now, is the more detailed text that accompanied it:

> A few months ago Beth Popp Berman posted a tweet, saying 'I love you, sociologists, but do all of us have to work on inequality?' This generated a plethora of responses from sociologists, some arguing that inequality defines the subject-matter of sociology (much like 'markets' in economics), while others emphasizing a pervasive feeling that inequality per se has become the topic of sociology, broadly construed. Going forward, one particularly interesting response stated that 'a prof once told me that if I

want to publish in a top sociology journal, I need to emphasize how a social process I've identified in my research perpetuates or exacerbates inequality.' I wondered if this was indeed the case and compiled all articles published in the American Sociological Review between 1936 and 2019 from the Constellate, and counted the number of articles that include the words 'inequality' or 'inequalities' anywhere in the manuscript.[7]

One general truism is that whatever the greatest crisis is today, it will not be the greatest crisis in the medium term. The great crisis of economic inequality should soon begin, albeit slightly at first, to abate. Economic inequality should fall, both because we have identified it as such an important issue and will do something about it, but also because it will have reached such heights in so many places due to factors which are not perennial but are contingent on our times. If it does fall, the cause of that fall may itself come to be seen by richer people as the next great crisis. However, across most of Europe in recent years income inequalities have already been gently falling.[8]

In the near future, a fall in economic inequality is not just entirely possible, but probable.[9] No crisis disappears entirely, but crises can abate very quickly if the circumstances are right. They have to abate, or we would be living waist-high in a sea of crises. Some abate largely by themselves, such as a huge forest fire burning itself out. Others abate because we take effective action to tackle the crisis. Often it is a combination of the two. The implementation of the required solution is what I think might be seen as the next crisis, especially as events never run smoothly.

Sometimes, widespread fears disappear almost entirely as issues to be taken seriously. Think of the widely perceived greatest crisis of a century ago that preoccupied the minds of so many apparently great thinkers in the West – that the working class was breeding idiots. No one talks proudly today about their great-grandmother or grandfather as a pioneer of the eugenics movement. Yet even when a non-crisis, such as the fear of an ever expanding residuum disappears in a puff of smoke, something else – something unexpected – always arrives to take its place. There is always a next crisis. Often the next crisis is the reason why an existing fear abates. The Second World War–era Nazis have sealed the coffin of eugenics, at least for a while.

Crises come and crises go. The advent of the First World War and its unexpected continuation for many years swept aside what we had most worried about in Europe prior to the conflagration. We no longer even commonly know about most of those key pre-1914 issues of wider public concern. Similarly, a century after that war ended, when the pandemic arrived in 2019, we suddenly worried much less about other issues. Too many people flying around the globe emitting carbon was of almost no concern when almost all the planes were grounded. Now that is a growing concern again.

What will the seventh crisis be?

The list of crises we have looked at in this book includes one that is very familiar. It is the first and still the most important: poverty caused by inequality. The second great crisis is one that arose as an abiding, widespread fear just over a century ago: the fear of not being needed, of there being too little work. It can be traced back to concerns over the sharing of work between human and horse power, later partially replaced by steam power, and to a moment when most of us no longer needed to work in the fields. Unemployment continues to preoccupy the minds of multitudes, right through to today's fears that artificial intelligence will put them out of a job.

The third great crisis of our times is ancient – older than mass poverty, because poverty has not always been with us.[10] That third crisis now manifests very differently than it did a century or five millennia ago: it is the crisis of violence and war. This is a crisis we have confronted so many times before in our history that we even have religious commandments about not killing each other. We don't have ancient religious advice about more recent crises, such as a commandment to ensure that our brothers and sisters have something useful to occupy their time, because until very recent times it was never a problem.

The fourth great crisis is much more recent than the first three, not least because state health care and mass education are so recent. We always worried about these issues in other ways, but not so systematically as we do now. Only recently have we moved away from models in which there was charity health provision for the lucky, private physicians only for the very rich, and organised education only for the rich too. Across the world, there were very few schools for poor boys until just over a century ago; education for girls mostly came a little later, alongside more widespread health care for all, more systematic concerns about how we are all housed, and how our sewage is removed and our clean water supplied. The fourth great crisis of cradle-to-grave protection came about not only as our total numbers rose greatly and our societies became more complex, but also as we began to have fewer children and could rely progressively less on our own families for help – there was once a much more obvious and functional kin-based society.

The fifth great crisis is one that a century ago we did not even suspect could be an issue: climate change. Although it is only fair to point out that a few people will claim it had been understood shortly before then, by some far-sighted individuals who turned out to be right. Someone might even try to claim that there was an edict in an old religious book about worrying over what you put into the skies. But let's be clear-headed on this: for the vast majority of people, concerns that we, ourselves, might be altering our own climate with potentially dire consequences simply did not exist in the childhoods of older adults alive today. Our actions have probably been altering the climate for millennia, perhaps since we first flooded fields to grow rice, and we further reduced carbon sequestration by weeding. But any initial effects were tiny compared to those of industrialisation, the effects of which were not measurable until centuries after the first serious extraction of coal.[11]

Conclusion

The sixth great crisis of our times dates back to the arguments put forward by Malthus in Europe and almost certainly also made by others in other continents and earlier contexts that I, and most of you reading this book, do not know of. It is the crisis that has transformed over time from there being too many people for the amount of land, to too many people doing too much harm to nature. It is said by some to be the worst crisis of all, because it led to an ongoing mass extinction. It is our loss of biodiversity, initially due to our growing numbers and later accelerating because our greed has been growing even faster than our numbers, especially the greed of a very few.

Here is the list again:

1. Poverty, inequality, and those costs of living.
2. Sharing the work, immigration, and unemployment.
3. Violence, crime, terror, war, and a safe home.
4. Health care, education, social care, and corruption.
5. Climate change, food, water, energy, and travel.
6. Biodiversity and human population control.

In conclusion, this book's title should lead us to ask the following questions: What will, at first, become number seven, the crisis that is not yet on the list? What crisis will emerge, probably as a minor concern at first, and then rise up the ranks, eventually to become the greatest crisis of all – possibly even to supplant number one, possibly in the lifetimes of those who are younger than average? Or what might come out of nowhere to surpass the others immediately? What will be the next crisis?

We cannot, unfortunately, find a clue in global surveys about our greatest concerns. The list of six above, which map onto Chapters 2–7 of this book, include in one way or another all the current crises that are mentioned in those global surveys. We can, of course, scour the literature for new candidates to the list, but that is not a particularly reliable method. There are always people announcing the end is nigh for one obscure reason or another – sometimes carrying signs or emblazoning their fears across their clothing.[12]

Given how fast great crises have arisen in the past, if there is no new one in our lifetimes, then the next might well occur in our children's lifetimes. But the fact that there will be a new great crisis is not necessarily a terrible thing; especially if the crisis is partly about implementing a solution. If poverty caused by inequality is knocked off the top spot, it would very likely be as a result of significant progress in reducing economic inequality, perhaps made during the remainder of our lives – unless, of course, it is because there is a new crisis that is much worse than any we currently worry about, and our collective compound of concerns is worsening overall.

Here is one possibility, although I do not believe it will be the next crisis. What if the problem is not that transitioning to renewables is too expensive, but that saving the planet is not sufficiently profitable? Or, as a famous *New Yorker* cartoon put it: 'Yes, the planet got destroyed. But for a beautiful moment in time we created a lot of value for shareholders.'[13] What if *we* are unable to adapt in time? What if numbers five and six in the list above are what rise within our children's lifetimes, or ours if we are young, into first place, as has been widely predicted? And what if they are the last of the great crises? The ones that end it all and also end our ability to tally up crises, to measure how many minutes are left to midnight? What then?

The argument that follows the *New Yorker* cartoon example continues:

> Liberal ideology has tended to duck the problem of capitalism altogether, opting instead to imagine that [the myth of] 'economic life' (i.e. competitive egalitarian markets) still rules the roost. This myopia is manifest in the economics curricula of major universities, which despite the best efforts of various campaigns and Institutes for New Economic Thinking have continued to exclude theories that emphasise power, uncertainty, monopoly and instability, and cling to an orthodoxy in which economic activity is chiefly determined by prices and incentives. Politicians, meanwhile, cleave to liberal fairy tales about making work pay, social mobility

and ownership for all, which are increasingly divorced from a reality of in-work poverty, unearned wealth and spiralling rents. And financial services masquerade as just another 'sector' among many, selling their wares in a marketplace like humble shopkeepers.

William Davies, the academic speculating about this, concludes that to avert an apocalypse: 'The priority, as it has been now for decades, is *to go as big and as soon as possible* [emphasis added].'[14] In other words, either the species shrinks and also regresses in its (our) ability or organise and coordinate – and what we call civilisation and think of as culture does too – or we end capitalism, now, big time. A nice simple choice, you might assume, almost as if there were a God giving us an easy choice: tick box A or B; take the blue pill and continue to oblivion believing mistakenly that all will be OK in the end, or take the red pill and open your eyes.

Unfortunately, it is never that easy. Often when we are told that 'it is easier to imagine an end to the world than an end to capitalism', we are being called to rediscover our collective imaginations.[15] In fact, we have been imagining an end to capitalism for a very long time. I will draw this conclusion to an end with an example that was taught to thousands of children over a century ago in Socialist Sunday Schools. But first, we must address the doomsayers one final time.

In his essay, which I have quoted from at some length, Davies is reviewing a book by Brett Christophers, in which the story of the discovery of electricity for human use serves as a warning about the limits of human ability. The suggestion is that as a commodity, electricity 'was and is not a suitable object for marketisation and profit generation in the first place': 'Ecologically speaking, neoliberalism could scarcely have come at a worse time.' But this is to imagine that something else had been possible.

The next crisis is very rarely the last crisis made bigger. It is also almost never something that is a current, widely held fear. I could be wrong, but the precedent suggests that the next big crisis is generally (but not always) something new.

After all, electricity, it could easily be argued, is one route out of carbon pollution. If we can generate enough electricity without using fossil fuels to do so, then in colder countries we can keep our homes warm in non-polluting ways, and in countries that are already hot (and often getting ever hotter) we can cool down where we live, work, and play while trying to work out how to clean up the mess we have created.

What would we do without electricity? We easily forget that it was discovered less than three hundred years ago, with the turbo-generators that make it a possible widespread power source having been available for less than half that time. National grids such as that in the UK have existed only since 1926; many people were not even connected to the mains in rural Oxfordshire when I was a child.

Before speculating further about the next crisis, it is worth considering briefly what would make it a crisis. It will only rise high up the ranks if its effect (or potential effect) is really terrible. What is also necessary for a new crisis to emerge, normally, is that other current crises abate in importance. There will always be crises. Many people want to claim that the ones they are most interested in are worst: the use of pesticides, for example, or lack of access to organic foods. But unless something can be shown to be causing damage on a par with the current worst crises in the world, it has little chance of becoming a contender.

If we are ingenious enough to partially solve some of our greatest crises, then the scope for others to become the next largest one rises. Should you believe humans cannot solve problems, think about just one group of the greatest crises of the century before last: cholera, bubonic plague, smallpox, measles, yellow fever, and tuberculosis. Most of these diseases still kill and harm many people worldwide, but much fewer than they did in the past – because we intervened.

When death (particularly child mortality due to diseases) was more common around the world, we intervened. Had anyone suggested that progress on such a wide scale was possible before germ theory had been established, they might well have been ridiculed. Similarly, today, the accepted wisdom is that poverty has always been with us, but that does not mean that it need be in future. Especially as it has not, in fact, been with most of us for most of human history.

Many current (although underreported) studies show that inequality is falling across most of the world in terms of income, if not yet wealth.[16] Poverty can be severely reduced – at times almost eliminated – but only when inequalities are reduced. What might motivate us to prioritise this today? We would have to understand that the claim that inequality harms us all is not just theoretical. In the UK today the average five-year-old is shorter than one born five years earlier, who in turn is shorter than one born five years earlier again. Our children have been shrinking ever since the cohort who were in the womb in the years 2005–10. The primary reason is almost certainly poor nutrition, now worsening.[17] We are often starting from a low base.

Just as we find it hard to imagine that at some time, very likely in the lifetime of some of those alive now, the simple issue of how to get by in the world will not be the greatest crisis of our times, so too we might struggle to imagine the second greatest crisis in the world no longer being a top priority. The number of younger people in the world has been rapidly falling for decades now. It is hard to imagine a future in which we will not find enough things for all of them to do. Similarly, fear of immigrants is manufactured rather than innate; the idea that we will not have understood how to share the work, or that we might fail to welcome arriving migrants in a future where there are far fewer young people, is almost laughable.

The third great crisis of violence, crime, and terror could get worse. Alternatively, given that the position of women has improved more in the past century than in several previous millennia, perhaps we are on the cusp of a far more peaceful world? We just can't see it yet. Just as we cannot clearly see the next crisis to come, so we fail to see how current ones may diminish. We need to be a bit less paranoid and a bit more pronoid – to believe more often in the good will of others and the general pervasiveness of serendipity.[18] Pronoia is something we humans in recent years could have practised more often. It is what underlies socialism, but it is easier to be paranoid. As Joseph Heller put it so well in *Catch 22*: 'Just because you're paranoid doesn't mean they aren't after you.'[19]

Our ideas about the largest current crises and what the next largest crisis might be are greatly skewed by whose voices are currently the loudest. Only a few people with the luxury of thinking big dominate global discourse on this subject. Only a tiny minority of us live lives where we have the luxury to be able to write articles like the one that imagines: 'In 27 years' time, society as we know it will have collapsed. Food will be extremely limited. Lawlessness will have taken over the land. Gangs will roam the countryside scavenging for resources like food, water and fuel. This breakdown won't be sudden. It will happen over a period of months. It might even have already begun.' Those words may sound like the beginning of a clichéd gothic-dystopian fantasy, but Bill McGuire, a professor of geophysical and climate hazards at University College London (UCL) and author of *Hothouse Earth: An Inhabitant's Guide*, doesn't think so. He is expecting, and preparing for, widespread riots by 2050. The riots will begin, he says, 'as they have throughout history, when we run out of food'.[20] That particular article continues by suggesting there is a threshold after which food production falls: 'Researchers have since reported there is now a 66 per cent chance that Earth will surpass this warming threshold anytime between 2023 and 2027.' He is so precise – 66 (not 65 or 67) per cent; 2027 (not 2026 or 2028) – as to seem hyperbolic.

Then there is the opposite view. Books are appearing with titles such as this one by Hannah Ritchie: *Not the End of the World: How We Can Be the First Generation to Build a Sustainable Planet*. She is a respected colleague of mine at the university where I work. Soon after its January 2024 publication, Ritchie complained that she was only being asked about her climate chapter. She posted on X at the start of 2024 to garner interest in her book, and made these points (even though her comments were specific to the UK, they can be read as applying far more widely):

> While most journalists have only asked me climate questions about my forthcoming book, that is only one chapter of it . . . Climate is not the only problem!
> Chapter by chapter I cover air pollution, climate, deforestation, food, biodiversity loss, ocean plastics, and overfishing.
> In fact, climate is not even the biggest problem for human well-being right now (although that could change).
> Air pollution kills millions every year.
> The good news is that many of the solutions we need thread across multiple problems.
> Why low-carbon technologies need to be affordable.
> People care about the environment but it ranks below the economy in UK polls (whether we like it or not).
> Install renewables to reduce energy bills, insulate homes, make public transport & EVs [electric vehicles] cheaper, & people will adopt them.
> Top issues facing the country [UK], first poll of 2024
> Economy: 53% (-9 vs first poll of 2023)
> Health: 45% (-5)
> Immigration: 39% (+7)
> Housing: 25% (+8)
> Environment: 22% (-1)
> Crime: 17% (+1)
> Brexit: 14% (-3)
> Education: 11% (±0)
> Tax: 10% (-1)
> Defence: 9% (±0)
> Welfare: 8% (-2)
> Family/childcare: 7% (±0)
> Pensions: 6% (-1)
> Transport: 5% (±0).[21]

Geography as the study of crisis

The academic discipline of geography is, in many ways, the study of crises as they affect people and the Earth. Human geographers are fascinated by the first four of the great current crises. The geographies of poverty and inequality and how the world is divided by wealth and development are core to my discipline. Issues of how we share out the work and manage immigration are all both geographical and very relevant; these are often mentioned in school geography syllabuses around the world. War, geopolitics, and crime also feature highly; as do the fourth great set of issues ranging from topics about the unequal provision of health care (both globally and locally) to how education is geographically determined and often deterministic too. It would be fair to say that we geographers concern ourselves with issues such as social care or corruption a little less. We don't have a monopoly on the topics of crisis. But we do have a greater claim to a greater stake than any other academic discipline by a country mile.

Climate change is within the purview of physical geographers, and by implication how this might impact food, water, energy, and travel – as well as biodiversity. A few physical geographers complain how dominant climate change has become within academic geography, especially those with an abiding interest in volcanoes, rivers, and oxbow lakes. Although many geographers manage to find obscure preoccupations, our students prefer to know about the big issues of the day. Crises are what makes geography most interesting, from the effects of flooding and understanding tsunamis, to why people riot. But like other academics, we have our insecurities about how to connect with the general public, how relevant we might be, and whether we are capable of responding to the growth in public anxiety.[22]

Geographers are far from alone in having an interest in crisis. On the cost of living and climate, for example, based on 27,000 observations taken from across 121 countries, a physicist and three analysts working at the German Central Bank recently argued: 'Higher temperatures increase food and headline inflation persistently over 12 months in both higher- and lower-income countries.'[23] Furthermore, as explained by the World Weather Attribution group of scientists, many of whom are based in geography and environment university departments, the effects we are seeing, linking prices to climate, are real. As yet, most of the examples they gave were not devastating. For instance, and as touched on earlier in this book, in spring 2024, some people noticed that their chocolate Easter egg was smaller and more expensive; they were told that climate change hitting crop production in West Africa was a significant part of the reason. It is not just crop growth that is affected, but also people's ability to harvest it when working in the heat: 'Roughly half of the west African population also lives in informal housing, rendering millions of people highly vulnerable to extreme heat.'[24] It was other academic researchers, some of whom were associated with the World Weather Attribution group, who produced the research behind those Easter egg headlines.

We can survive without chocolate eggs, and the eggs may not be as small in future Easters (would it be a bad thing if they were?). But there will always be something else that will make a shocking headline. What matters most is not the newspaper story of today, but the underlying issues and how crises connect. As a 2021 committee made up of a remarkable number of Nobel laureates explained: 'More equal societies tend to score highly on metrics of well-being and happiness. Reducing inequality raises social capital. There is a greater sense of community and more trust in government. These factors make it easier to make collective, long-term decisions. Humanity's future depends on the ability to make long-term, collective decisions to navigate the Anthropocene.'[25] In other words, if we were better able to control the greedy, we would almost certainly do better in terms of ensuring a more reliable distribution of chocolate in future (along with more important things).

What would be required to stop climate change rising up the ranks of the crises that we, collectively, most worry about? Below is just one take, which argues that if you really wish to tackle climate change you also have to simultaneously address the half-dozen worse crises of our times. All the other crises contribute greatly to climate change being so apparently intractable. Many people have explained, in many different ways, what has to be done. These are increasingly described as wicked problems: social, cultural, political, and environmental problems that appear very difficult or even impossible to solve because of their complex and interconnected nature. What is hardest, however, is collating and assessing the endless list of solutions being offered to our problem of wickedness. Here is an example of the multitude that are presented, in this case by two senior lecturers in political economy and geography, both working at the University of Sydney:

> This would entail a rebalancing of the current private sector dominated positions on climate finance, and a reorientation of states away from their current focus on least-cost and de-risking logics towards a willingness to direct private capital and expand public wealth for climate ends. It would also require a reworking of state institutions, such as central banks or state-owned enterprises, to enable democratic engagement and public deliberation, especially from workers and affected and marginalized communities. Perhaps most importantly, this position expands the social, temporal and spatial horizons of climate finance to recognize historical and geographical responsibilities and obligations. This means paying climate debts as reparations incurred through the intersections of rapacious, extractive colonialisms, racial-capitalist formations and the uneven impacts of the resulting climate change.[26]

That quotation may appear radical, utopian, or simply wordy. If so, here is another example of much the same thing being said in another way by another set of academics. This next group are based in Paris, working for the pan-national Organisation for Economic Co-operation and Development (OECD). It reports that the super-rich could be relieved of some of their riches through a climate tax on wealth, which could be used to fund adaptation to climate change.[27] In short, their model proposed raising US$295 billion a year through a 1.5 per cent tax on any personal wealth in excess of US$10 million held by the richest people on Earth. That would more than cover the US$202 billion annual estimated planet-wide cost of adaptation to climate change and dwarf the current US$29 billion being spent a year in the 2020s. Some 73 per cent of the revenue would come from high-income countries and all the rest from upper-middle-income countries, while most (51 per cent) of the spending would be within countries from which no funds had been raised, and a further 11 per cent spent in the very lowest-income countries.

There is a slow revolution taking place today. It is in how huge groups of people think – especially academics, but also in the beliefs of growing numbers of the policymakers they work with. Academics, for all their unwieldy methods and apparent unworldliness, are often ahead of the curve when it comes to new ways of thinking. The predictable calls to reorientate, rework, re-enable, and rethink are often, almost repetitively, reiterated; but there are also much smaller but just as effective acts, which are also becoming routine. As Oxford-based geographer Chris Lizotte put it recently, we need to 'revalorize small, maybe even utterly banal, acts of kindness'.[28]

Move on a few years and you will soon find such calls for more direct action becoming louder and more frequent, with many of the newer voices calling for more love and kindness. I have lost count of all the book proposals I was sent in 2024 to review, as an academic, which had the word *love* in their titles. Many of those books will be in print shortly after this one is published.

The slow revolution that is currently under way, one we do not easily recognise because it is so slow, is not just taking place among academics in the obscure journals where they tend to publish. It also features increasingly in what a growing number of very affluent people are now saying publicly, and which a few have been saying for over a decade consistently. In 2013, Warren Buffett's son Peter, the chairman of a charity, wrote about some of the problems with charity in general:

> This just keeps the existing structure of inequality in place. The rich sleep better at night, while others get just enough to keep the pot from boiling over. Nearly every time someone feels better by doing good, on the other side of the world (or street), someone else is further locked into a system that will not allow the true flourishing of his or her nature or the opportunity to live a joyful and fulfilled life . . . Often I hear people say, 'if only they had what we have' (clean water, access to health products and free markets, better education, safer living conditions). Yes, these are all important. But no 'charitable' (I hate that word) intervention can solve any of these issues. It can only kick the can down the road.[29]

Perhaps the next crisis will be the widespread realisation that we are playing a rigged game of Monopoly, as a report from David Brancaccio and Rose Conlon of Minnesota Public Radio's *Marketplace Morning Report* put it in 2021:

> It turns out that having more money doesn't necessarily make a person more inclined to share their money with others – in fact, research suggests the opposite is true . . . the experiment reveals a fundamental bias that most humans share . . . When something good happens to you, we think about the things that we did that contributed to that success.[30]

As money at the very top became more concentrated, the super-rich grew surer of themselves, the middle was squeezed and more of the poor went hungry. The next crisis could be the outcome of a dawning realisation that we have no omniscient gods ruling over us, just super-rich adults who behave like spoilt children, and who have increasingly come to think they know it all. In 2024 it was revealed that every single new young *billionaire* in the world without exception, in a list including all those aged thirty or under, had inherited their wealth. The youngest was a nineteen-year-old university student.[31]

How will the extremely wealthy get so much wealthier in future, given all the crises we currently face, and could their growing avarice be the next crisis? Recent research from Switzerland, one of the favourite European enclaves of the ultra-rich, has shown that a quarter (25 per cent) of the increased wealth of the country's top 0.1 per cent since the 1970s has been due to the reduction of taxes on their wealth. For the best-off 1 per cent, who have also taken an increasingly greater share of wealth there, a smaller but still significant proportion of their higher take (18 per cent) is the result of that group also being taxed less in recent years.[32]

The world's super-rich have become more and more adept at securing advantages for their offspring in other ways, including terms of entry to elite academic institutions. In the US, for example, it was revealed in 2023 that if two students with identical academic credentials applied to the same elite private university in that country, the student from a family in the richest 1 per cent was twice as likely as a middle-class student to be offered a place. These findings flew in the face of claims that such universities had needs-blind academic criteria as their main entry requirements. Interestingly, the same pattern was not found in the intake to the most elite of the US public universities, such as Berkeley or Michigan. The much-vaunted openness of institutions such as Columbia, Harvard, MIT, Princeton, Stanford, the University of Pennsylvania, and Yale was exposed to be, at least collectively, a publicity stunt.[33]

This particular story was based on a study by Raj Chetty, a tenured economist at Harvard, who explains: 'Whether intentionally or not – we currently have a system that appears to have affirmative action for kids from the richest families, the top 1% in particular, which gives them a substantial leg up in admissions relative to other kids.'[34]

It is not impossible to imagine that the next crisis will emerge around merit and fairness. As I write in August 2024, the prime minister of Bangladesh has just resigned and fled her country due to protests that began as a result of corruption in civil service appointments. Five years earlier, on the other side of the world, there had been an uprising by Chile's school and university students over living conditions and unfairness. But there are many other issues that vie to be the next potential crises.

From AI to China to women

One common theme in the early 2020s was an oft-repeated claim that the next crisis would be linked to technology and a renewed fascination with AI (artificial intelligence). By the time you read these words, however, it is likely that the current AI bubble will have deflated. They always do. Each is based on the premise that most people find computers almost impossible to understand. Too little knowledge can be a dangerous thing.

Soon we will no longer be typing into keyboards unless we choose to (by soon, I mean within less than half a dozen years). We will simply talk to devices, and they will turn our words into text. Those of us who are lazy will also ask AI to give our message a particular slant: polite, authoritative, friendly, loving, whatever. There is nothing surprising about any of this. It was more surprising when number plates could first be recognised from photographs – a huge breakthrough that relied on the most advanced AI of those times (and much the same neural network technology as used today) – or when automatic translation began a little later, by training the machine using European Union documents that had carefully been translated by humans. Those were more pronounced advances than the final refinements of speech recognition soon to come. Arguably, we should have been most surprised by the advent of AI in the late 1960s, not by its subsequent more incremental achievements.

In a previous era, people gazed with incredulity upon mechanical looms, or with wonder over the ingenuity behind the invention of the so-called governor that kept steam engine oscillations steady. The first creation of writing, the invention of Archimedes' screw, and the discovery that there was a simple and beautiful relationship in mathematics between the constants e, i, and π were all wonders to those who questioned how all this could work and queried who first worked these things out. Dozens of centuries separated such discoveries. In truth, there is rarely a sudden shout of 'Eureka!'. Just as, in truth, we stumbled our way into designing and refining spoken languages, and then cuneiform script, alphabets, poetry, prose, plays, and politics.

The mechanical keyboard was a device whose layout – such as Latin-language keyboards' QWERTY and similar variants – was originally designed to slow down how quickly we typed so that the keys would not jam. Electrical keyboards adopted the same design and became widely used less than fifty years ago; it was an inefficient design, but we were used to it. It is often when there is a jump from an inbuilt inefficiency to something new that we are most awed (if you are old enough, think back to phones you had to use by rotating a dial).

That we are so awed by science and technology says more about us than it does about the wonders of science. It is because discovery is collective that we wonder how it can happen. No individual alone could invent these things.

Policymakers and government advisers are wary of giving technology credit for driving events, but they are also often in awe. As Geoff Mulgan, former adviser to Tony Blair, explained in 2023 about those who raised warnings of crises in the past: 'In retrospect, they were wrong about population as the key aspect of this and wrong about "peak oil". Indeed, the wicked problems of the time – including population growth and endemic inflation – were solved more by politics and social organization than by technology (though fertilizers, new agricultural methods and contraceptives all played their part). Could they have known? And what should have been done?'[35] Mulgan's remedy was to 'weave science and politics together', which is laudable, but perhaps rather misses out people, especially the people with less power.[36] A great many of our current crises are the product of politicians not caring enough about other people.

In the US, Mulgan's equivalent, the economist Joseph Stiglitz, argues for a global future with

> governance architecture, based on the minimal set of rules necessary to make our global system work. We need narrow agreements to advance shared goals and to ensure some semblance of a level

playing field. Advanced economies should be allowed to provide subsidies only for narrowly defined objectives, like the green transition, and only if they commit to transfer technology and provide a commensurate amount of funding to developing countries.[37]

Stiglitz's and Mulgan's answer to 'what comes after neoliberalism?', it appears, is more neoliberalism, but somehow a softer, kinder version. As Stiglitz comments in the same text: 'Whether we want to admit it or not, we are also competing with authoritarian governments to win their hearts and minds. With our current playbook, we've been losing.' However, when many people from other parts of the world look at how the UK and US behave, they see two authoritarian governments in command of disproportionately oversized militaries and harbouring self-perceptions of having a god-given right to lead the world and to arm despots. We rarely see ourselves as others see us.

So will the next crisis involve China becoming the world's dominant economic power, displacing the US? China's ascent certainly shows no sign of halting. This is hard for some to accept; but many more people across the world might welcome a less militaristic bully at the top, especially one that does not lay claim to so many atolls in so many oceans so very far away from its land. Imagine if the UK and US had only territorial ambitions on a par with China's to islands in the South China Sea. The fact that many will criticise this comment helps to illustrate that the transition will be harder for Europeans to take than the move of power from the United Provinces to England in one century, and from England to the Americas in another. In another way, however, it is a similar shift of the locus of power in the world, again westwards, but this time right across the Pacific Ocean: halfway around the globe rather than baby steps across the North Sea or a childhood stride over the Atlantic.

What is moving most obviously of all is the money. It is capital that flowed west from Amsterdam to London, and then to Liverpool, to New York, to Los Angeles, to Shanghai and Beijing: money moving relentlessly westwards; its global geographical centre of gravity shifting to where it has the greatest opportunity of concentration over the course of the last half-millennium. It could keep moving westwards again, towards the current (and also interestingly the ancient) human population centre of the planet, which is within India. But if we simply carry on doing what we have been doing for more than four hundred years, then it is likely to result in more and ever greater crises. States acting in their national interest eventually becomes a recipe for disaster.

Maybe China will be different as it becomes a more dominant world power. What makes China most like its European and North American precursors is that its politburo is currently almost entirely dominated by men. What happens when that ends? It *will* end, for many reasons – not least that the majority of older families in China have only one adult child, and in roughly half of all cases, she is a woman.

Recent research comparing Norway and the US has demonstrated what happens when women are no longer held back: 'In Norway, the gender-gap has virtually disappeared over time, a development that appears to be attributable to the increasing share of women in parliament. In the US, the gap has remained remarkably stable over time.'[38] What that study found is that what is happening in one place, Norway, is something that could be repeated everywhere. In Norway over the five most recent decades compared by the researchers, the gender bias in public policies has disappeared. In fact, in the measures made by these researchers, the coefficient of discrimination for women in Norway even changed sign over these decades, moving from 0.47 to -0.12. Being female stopped being a great disadvantage and became a slight advantage.

This is also the case when controlling for differences across income groups. There is a supposition in this work that we should aim for .00 and not -0.12 – although there is a reparations argument to be made that it would only be fair if women held a majority of political positions in future, if only for a few decades. One academic has suggested that the ideal short-term future would be a parliament where 55 per cent of the politicians were women and

45 per cent men, and also argues that gender relations are quickly changing, with far-reaching implications.[39]

Turning back to the first study, which public policies are of more interest to women than men? The paper focuses on women's expressed policy preferences in surveys. This approach, it is claimed,

> avoids the problems of having to define what constitutes women's interests and takes into account that women have myriads of policy views arising from a range of different identities that go beyond their gender. It also allows for a more comprehensive assessment of the effectiveness of descriptive representation, as it considers a wide range of issues rather than merely focusing on a select few that women in parliament may prioritize.

The study is cautious in its conclusions, stating: 'An important feature of the economic inequality that exists in most societies today between men and women is that it gets more dramatic as one moves up the income scale.' So even if there is a power rebalancing going on in Norway, and in many similar places, especially in cities, if just a few people at the top have the most power, the women among them are likely to have less influence than the men because of the corrupting effect of income inequality and of women to behave more like men in such scenarios.[40] Power may corrupt, and absolute power may corrupt absolutely, but money and the inequitable allocation of it is a clear measure of corruption as it is happening.

In 2021, Megan MacKenzie and Nicole Wegner presented a series of papers by over a dozen other writers making an even stronger argument that patriarchal capitalism is a major driving force behind war in our current era, and suggesting that we end war with feminism.[41] Studies such as theirs, implying that the nation-state is closely linked to patriarchy and reproduces it, now greatly outnumber masculinist visions.[42] It may be that this emerging rejection of macho conceptions of the nation-state may become something much bigger in the near future. The next big thing will already have started to grow somewhere. If you are interested in a model of what is possible consider the Left Alliance of Finland, where it has been women who in recent years have held most of the key party positions.

Last words

Where are we heading now? In 2020 the World Bank predicted that the pandemic that began in late 2019 would, *by the measures they used*, cause the first increase in global poverty in at least twenty-five years and reverse decades of what the Bank had reported as global poverty reduction.[43] The kind of measure they used – those living on $1.90 a day – had been criticised as unfit for purpose over a century earlier, by those who studied poverty most closely in the richer parts of the world. Nevertheless, we had a great collective shock in 2020, and we may not yet have realised what the full implications of the recent global pandemic will be.

For progressive thinkers on poverty, for over a century and a half now, being able to partake in the norms of society is what matters most. This, it now transpires has been true from the stone age to the 2020s – and the proportion who are poor was far greater by that measure than these absolute poverty lines would suggest (and much less in the past and especially in the distant past). All the same, let's persevere with the World Bank measure. It predicted a return to poverty levels of 2017 in 2020, and then a small fall in the extreme poverty rate in 2021, globally.

It is still questionable whether this occurred – whether there was a halt or reversal in decades of reduction of poverty based on an obsolete measure. More importantly, people worldwide learnt in 2020 that you could stop doing what you normally did and the world did not end. This meant that many of us no longer had to commute every day, in order to be able to work, although much of the most important work – cleaning, caring, health care – could not be conducted remotely.

In 2022, the World Bank released a new report in which it used the term 'nowcast', to mean *guessing*. Figure 8.2 combines the data from both reports. The new report included survey data for only twenty countries in 2020 and a variety of much less reliable information to forecast the 2022 point. Yet its researchers felt confident enough to report: 'Based on the additional data collected over the last two years, it is now clearer that the COVID-19 pandemic has indeed triggered the most pronounced setback in the fight against global poverty since 1990, and most likely since World War II.'[44] If we take this statement seriously, we have just lived through the next crisis.

In 2023, the tense of the sentence changed when Oxfam reported: 'The World Bank says we are likely seeing the biggest increase in global inequality and poverty since WW2.'[45] In other words, an event thought to have occurred in 2020 was described as ongoing in 2023. But what had actually happened in 2020, and what was really occurring in 2023? The next crisis could have begun in late 2019, as the graph in Figure 8.2 implies. We did not know until we were knee-deep in it that so much had begun to change. Four months later, in May 2023, the World Bank issued a new report suggesting that its estimates had become more chaotic.[46] By June 2024, the graph was no longer included in its annual update.[47] So the more that time passes, the less we know about what we were apparently so certain of in 2022 and 2023. Data for India was missing. More importantly, mortality was still above the expected levels, long after the pandemic was said to have ended. But we did not really know why, as deaths due to COVID-19 were recorded as falling.[48]

Only with analysis at the national and international level can we understand trends such as recent changes to poverty and inequality or the impact of diseases – folklore and supposition do not work. But we need the state to provide this data, and as the 2024 World Bank report confirmed, the data for India is still unreliable. We need the state to be capable and caring enough, not just for sewer systems and infrastructure, but also for data; and we also need it to ensure freedom, to allow the kinds of anarchy that we thrive on in everyday life and interactions.

Figure 8.2: World Bank's 2020 'nowcast' of global poverty rates, 2015–22

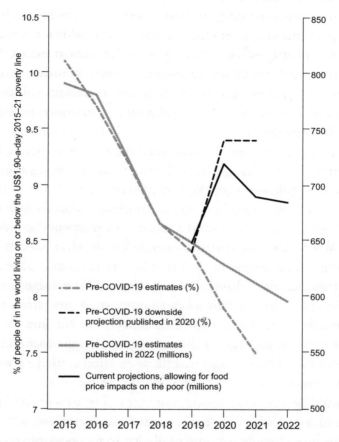

Sources: World Bank, 'Poverty and Shared Prosperity 2020: Reversals of Fortune', Washington, DC: World Bank, 2020, doi.org/10.1596/978-1-4648-1602-4 (shown with dashed lines) and World Bank, 'Poverty and Shared Prosperity 2022: Correcting Course', Washington, DC: World Bank, 2022, worldbank.org.

Most day-to-day transactions are not entirely determined by hierarchy. We don't use the market to arrange our lives or rule our social interactions. But we cannot rely on our natural proclivity for cooperation to understand the medium- and long-term implications of current trends, from a financial meltdown to a pandemic disease we have not encountered before. We need the state.

It is still mothers, in the main, who bring up children. They don't charge for it. All transactions, for a long period of time, were performed without a hierarchy organising them, and even when there is a hierarchy, it is often very thin. This is the case for most of us. In Al-Andalus in Iberia, under Moorish rule (711 CE onwards, for seven centuries), the average subsistence farmer got on with daily life, unconcerned with what authority was in power. When the Catholic Church returned to power, little changed in what is now present-day Spain, although there was the shock of the civil war in the 1930s and of the modern democratic era after 1970. Nothing lasts forever, but life is very similar for most people most of the time, despite the great crises swirling around their governments, the changes to their churches, and the fundamental beliefs, the philosophy, of those in charge.

So, at last, the time has come to confess. What do I think the next crisis will be, given what I think I know about the unknown unknowns? If we look at the present crises, they are all things that affect livelihoods in one way or another, and all have an impact on health. I think the next crisis will be something that directly affects our health more than most of our current woes. One possibility is that it will be us collectively realising that how we live today is bad for our health, especially our mental health, but before settling on one most likely possibility there are a final few to consider.

It could be a crisis of ageing, but that is a crisis we have because we are lucky enough to live in a time of low births and good medicine for more people – a time of plenty, in fact possibly too much plenty. But if the young refuse to behave as the old wish them to – refuse to get into debt, refuse (more often than expected) to start a family, refuse to wait into midlife and beyond for an inheritance but live more for today – then ageing could be the next crisis.

At the start of writing this book I asked you what your top three concerns were, so it is only fair if I now tell you my top three worries from the list of eighteen that this book began with (see page 10), many of which are not huge worries – but they are concerning enough. Here is my list, which differs from that of most people who were presented with the longer list:

1. Coronavirus (COVID-19).
2. Maintaining social programmes.
3. Military conflict between nations in future.

Why do I still worry about a pandemic that is thought to have ended? Because as yet we do not know the effects of repeated reinfection from a novel coronavirus – and the pandemic has not yet ended. We are showered with stories about the effects of the virus on mental health.[49] But I worry more about the physical effects of repeated infections on others. I do worry that we may still be in period of relief, where we think that crisis is over, without realising that it is not. I worry that the old, and especially old men, may not live as long as they did before 2019. If this worry of mine is valid, it should be becoming evident not too long after this book is published. A new disease presents an additional health burden if it has become endemic.

We know that we are not going to vaccinate most people on the planet. We know that almost everyone has acquired immunity because most of us have caught the new disease at least once. But because we know that this particular immunity wanes, we know that almost all of us will catch it again and again – most likely for the rest of our lives. I don't so much worry about us oldies – including myself.[50] I do worry about the young.

I worry that we may fail to properly support social programmes because the greedy will spend enough of their money trying to convince us not to. I am not sanguine about how hard it will be to achieve the distribution of resources required for this in future. That is why this is my second greatest fear for the future.

On my third greatest fear, to be honest, the great crisis of my teenage years four decades ago – the threat of nuclear war – will probably always be my subconscious first concern, even though it was not explicitly listed in those eighteen questions. It is why I rank war as my third fear, because the nuclear threat has abated a little. The ranking of crises probably changes so slowly because some are mostly in our minds, and our collective mind can only truly change with our deaths.

Finally, what should we do? Personally, I am in favour of what Thomas Piketty terms 'a participatory, democratic, and ecological socialism', similar to that of Finland's Left Alliance, because the next crisis is most probably already here and so are its solutions.[51] For me, the next crisis is the combination of all the great crises we are already living with. The solutions have been around for a long time. Just because we are still working on how to implement them, does not mean that they have failed. We live with great crises because a few people have been so resistant to the solutions and because crises often benefit the powerful. But the solutions have been a long time in the planning. For example, I have always liked the fourth Socialist Sunday School commandment: 'Honour the good, be courteous to all, bow down to none.'[52] Why do I like socialists' Sunday school lessons? It is not just because of the hopeful illuminated and illuminating banners (Figure 8.3), but because they are the product of tens (if not hundreds) of thousands of people over several centuries trying to think of how we might live a better life and avert future crises.

But now I have told you the fourth commandment, you will want to know what the other nine are.[53] So here are the alternatives to the much older religious edicts to live by. Here are the solutions to the next crisis, the realisation that it is already here – it is what we are living with and continue to tolerate. When reading them, you might want to think about which of these might be worth promoting most strongly today; and how it is that people collectively learn to behave better.

1. Love your schoolfellows, they will become your fellow workers and companions in life.
2. Love learning, which is the food of the mind; be as grateful to your teacher as to your parents.
3. Make every day holy by good and useful deeds and kindly actions.
4. Honour good people, be courteous and respect all, bow down to none.

5. Do not hate or offend anyone. Do not seek revenge, but stand up for your rights and resist tyranny.
6. Be not cowardly, protect the feeble and love justice.
7. Remember that all good things of the Earth are the result of labour. Whoever enjoys them without working for them is stealing the bread of the worker.
8. Observe and think in order to discover the truth. Do not believe what is contrary to reason and never deceive yourself or others.
9. Do not think that he who loves his own country must hate and despise other nations, or wish for war, which is a remnant of barbarism.
10. Help to bring about the day when all nations shall live fraternally together in peace and prosperity.

People have spent a very long time developing ways of dealing with crises, ways of avoiding a new crisis, and better ways to live through an era of repeated crisis. The ten commandments above concern issues such as solidarity and striking for workers' rights, widening access to education, living through eras of war, and achieving lasting peace.

The fourth Socialist Sunday School commandment appeared on the reverse of a famous banner which pictured two fruit trees representing knowledge and truth (Figure 8.3). The banner showed fields of corn to symbolise abundance and plenty, and the poppy flower whose 'ability to grow in disturbed soil signifies beauty emerging from disturbance'.[54] The poppy was the flower of crisis – hope growing out of the disturbed land. It stood for this idea long before the outbreak of the First World War, which is why it became the symbol of hope for peace after that war.

The banner I am describing was made by a local city councillor, almost exactly a hundred and ten years before I typed these words. Bradford councillor Fred Liles made it for the East Bradford Socialist Sunday School and presented it to them in early 1914. I very much suspect he had some help!

THE NEXT CRISIS

As an online description explains: 'Liles made the banner in 1914 before the flower was adopted as a symbol of remembrance. The rising sun in the background is a common occurrence in visual political communication, and represents the possibilities of a better life beyond the present one.'[55]

We, in nations that are not at war, have lived through times of worse inequality than today – worse poverty, worse fear, worse violence. There has been much worse inequality in Europe; people rose up in 1848 as a result, although the uprisings mostly failed. Also in 1848, the hymn 'All Things Bright and Beautiful' was published.[56] So ask yourself this: What is the third verse about? I had to sing this song very often in my first and second primary schools when I was a very young child. Here are its words:

Figure 8.3: Banner of the East Bradford Socialist Sunday School, Fred Liles, 1914

Source: Danny Dorling, Figure 4.4 from *Peak Injustice: Solving Britain's Inequality Crisis*, Bristol: Policy Press, 2024

Conclusion

> The rich man in his castle,
> The poor man at his gate,
> God made them, high or lowly,
> And ordered their estate.

In April 1848, Queen Victoria left London for the Isle of Wight under threat of civil unrest.[57] *The Communist Manifesto* had been published by Friedrich Engels and Karl Marx a few weeks earlier. There were crises everywhere that year, and the world became a better place for it, even though none of the uprisings succeeded in the short term. Despite that, as a child I had to sing that God had made people the class they were, that he ordered them from high to low, implying that everything should stay as it is. Not that much had changed between 1848 and 1968 in what we taught children to think about. A lot has changed since.

What you think depends on what you believe to be true, on what you have experienced or can imagine, and how you come to be convinced of one particular tale over another – of what you are made to sing as a child and how you respond. In recent years we have learned so much more about our origins from the work of thousands of archaeologists who are getting better at understanding what their millions of finds can tell us about our inherent nature. According to one recent summary:

> The short story is that early humans were puny primates. To survive, they had to learn to share meat and vegetables, to share childcare and to share sexual joy. To do this, they had to discipline would-be bullies and transcend the dominance hierarchies of their primate ancestors. And for at least 200,000 years, they lived in egalitarian societies where men and women were equal too.[58]

What if more of us had grown up knowing that this was the case – that human pre-history has not been one long story of war, bloodshed, competition, greed, and battles for dominance? That the next crisis will most likely simply be a part of a series of connected crises that are no more than a couple of centuries old – they do not reflect some dire natural order of human life, they instead show how we are slowly and unsteadily reordering how we live. God does not order our estate.

I leave the last words to the wonderful James Butler:

> People are good. Not always, everywhere, all the time, but really very often and without personal advantage. And if you want a model for love of place, community or country, it will be in the people rebuilding and repairing rather than those who destroy without thought.[59]

Notes

1. Crisis

1. The title of a radio show transcript which begins: 'I think 2023 will be a very interesting ride and I'm not sure people are sufficiently aware of the risks, of the uncertainty, because we're confronted with something we haven't seen before.' Peter Giger, Group Chief Risk Officer at Zurich Insurance Group, from: 'World Economic Forum, Welcome to the Age of the Polycrisis: the Global Risks Report 2023', Radio Davos, 11 January 2023.
2. Adversity, complications, tribulations, and dire straits – none of these words were any longer sufficient to take the place of the stronger term by the middle of the century just past. See Mark Greif, *The Age of the Crisis of Man: Thought and Fiction in America, 1933–1973*, New Jersey: Princeton University Press, 2015.
3. As I finished writing this draft, in January 2025, Norway's press had been ranked highest in the international rankings for the seventh year running. See Reporters Without Borders, '2023 World Press Freedom Index – Journalism Threatened by Fake Content Industry', rsf.org, 24 June 2024.
4. David Graeber, *The Ultimate Hidden Truth of the World*, London: Allen Lane, 2024.
5. Sophie Heading and Saadia Zahidi, 'Global Risks Report 2023', World Economic Forum, 11 January 2023.

6. Mark Gregory, 'Massive Global IT Outage Hits Banks, Airports, Supermarkets – and a Single Software Update Is Likely To Blame', The Conversation, 19 July 2024.
7. Only a minority of chief risk officers are happy for their faces to appear online, or so it would appear from their webpages titled 'Chief Risk Officers Community', weforum.org (last viewed 9 August 2024).
8. Jarrett Walker, 'The Dangers of Elite Projection', kottke.org, 16 December 2022.
9. Jo Helme, 'Enrique Peñalosa: An Advanced City Is One Where the Rich Take Public Transport', citychangers.org, 12 April 2021.
10. Michael Roberts, 'Polycrisis and Depression in the 21st Century', Committee for the Abolition of Illegitimate Debt, cadtm.org, 6 January 2023.
11. Kelly Beaver, 'The UK: The Calm Before the Storm?', Ipsos press release, 6 December 2023.
12. Apparently the expression 'by a long chalk' arose in English pubs in the early 1800s, for tallying scores in games with chalk. I mention this to include some trivia in these endnotes, but also to point out that even in times and places of great upheaval, most people find time to play and be happy as well.
13. A technical note explains that the Ipsos global country average has not been adjusted to the population size of each country, so as not to pretend any accuracy in representing the whole world. Nevertheless, by August 2023 the monthly sample consisted of 'approximately 1000+ individuals in each of Australia, Belgium, Brazil, Canada, France, Germany, Great Britain, Italy, Israel (excluding Palestine), Japan, Mexico, Spain, Sweden, and the US, and approximately 500+ individuals in each of Argentina, Chile, Colombia, Hungary, India, Indonesia, Malaysia, the Netherlands, Peru, Poland, Singapore, South Africa, South Korea, Thailand and Turkey. The samples in Argentina, Australia, Belgium, Canada, France, Germany, Great Britain, Hungary, Italy, Japan, the Netherlands, Poland, South Korea, Spain, Sweden, and the US can be taken as representative of these countries' general adult

population under the age of 75. The samples in Brazil, Chile, Colombia, India, Indonesia, Malaysia, Mexico, Peru, Singapore, South Africa, Thailand and Turkey are more urban, more educated, and/or more affluent than the general population. The survey results for these markets [to use the wording of the surveyors] should be viewed as reflecting the views of the more "connected" segment of these populations.' Ipsos, 'What Worries the World – August 2023', ipsos.com, 29 August 2023.

14. April 2022 is used as representative, but it differs little from June 2024 (see following endnotes).
15. Ipsos, 'What Worries the World – August 2023', ipsos.com, 29 August 2023.
16. Ipsos, 'What Worries the World – June 2024', ipsos.com, 1 June 2024.
17. Ipsos, 'What Worries the World – April 2022', ipsos.com, 29 April 2022.
18. Moral decline and the rise of extremism and terrorism, but more usually more minor crimes, are included here most often by respondents, along with an abiding worry over possible military conflict between nations.
19. Concerns over coronavirus (COVID-19) are included here, as well as issues concerning maintaining social programmes, and access to credit.

2. Those Costs of Living

1. Albena Azmanova, 'How Far-Right Parties Seduced Young Voters Across Europe', *Guardian*, 14 June 2024. Azmanova, professor of political and at City St George's, University of London, is also the author of *Capitalism on Edge: How Fighting Precarity Can Achieve Radical Change Without Crisis or Utopia*, New York: Columbia University Press, 2020.
2. Michael Clemence and Harriet Fowler, *Ipsos Views: What Worries the World*, London: Ipsos Knowledge Centre, 19 June 2017.
3. By July 2024, unemployment still ranked both below inflation and also below poverty and inequality (separately) as a global

concern. Unemployment was by then the greatest concern of people living in South Africa, Columbia, and Argentina. It can suddenly rise, often more quickly than those costs of living.
4. In the poorest countries in the world, if you cannot farm or find paid employment, you starve. This means there is no, or very little, unemployment in these countries.
5. Lu Hiam and Danny Dorling, 'The UK Government Has Failed To Act on Extreme Poverty', *British Medical Journal*, Vol. 383, 14 November 2023, p. 2638.
6. Nick Romeo, *The Alternative: How to Build a Just Economy*, London: John Murray, 2024.
7. Angus Hanton, *Vassal State: How America Runs Britain*, London: Swift Press, 2024.
8. François Bourguignon and Christian Morrisson, 'Inequality Among World Citizens: 1820–1992', *American Economic Review*, Vol. 92, No. 4, September 2002, pp. 727–44.
9. Danny Dorling, 'Eugenics and the Fear of Too Many People', *Peak Injustice*, Bristol: Policy Press, 2024, pp. 245–300.
10. See data in Figure 32, at dannydorling.org/books/SLOWDOWN/Data.html.
11. Danny Dorling, 'World Population Projections: Just Little Bits of History Repeating?', *Significance Magazine*, Vol. 20, No. 4, 2023, pp. 22–7.
12. Andreas Backhaus, 'Pregnancies and Contraceptive Use in Four African Countries during the COVID-19 Pandemic', *Vienna Yearbook of Population Research*, Vol. 20, 2022, pp. 459–76.
13. Rachel Shin, 'The World's Top Inequality Researcher Breaks Down his Surprising Findings that We Really Are All Becoming More Equal', *Fortune*, 16 June 2023.
14. Marco Cozzani, Peter Fallesen, Giampiero Passaretta, Juho Härkönen, and Fabrizio Bernardi, 'The Consequences of the COVID-19 Pandemic for Fertility and Birth Outcomes: Evidence from Spanish Birth Registers', *Population and Development Review*, Vol. 50, No. S1, 16 July 2024, pp. 153–76.
15. 'A Left-Wing Coalition Called New Popular Front Is On Course for a Surprise Victory in France's Snap Parliamentary Election',

and 'Jubilation and Stunned Silence: France Reacts To Exit Polls', BBC News, 8 July 2024.
16. Julien Rousselon and Mathilde Viennot, 'Inégalités primaires, redistribution: comment la France se situe en Europe', *France Stratégie*, Premier ministre, 2 December 2020.
17. Ibid.
18. Oxfam, 'Etats des lieux de la pauvreté en France', Oxfam France, 2 November 2022.
19. Angelique Christafis, '"People Feel Suffocated": Cost of Living Tops French Concerns Before Election', *Guardian*, 22 March 2022.
20. Laurent Jeanneau, 'Les Français ont une vision biaisée des inégalités', *Alternatives Economiques*, 10 August 2022.
21. Danny Dorling, *Seven Children: Inequality and Britain's Next Generation*, London: Hurst, 2024.
22. As of 18 August 2024, the latest version is dated 28 November 2023: wider.unu.edu/data.
23. Lucas Chancel, Twitter/X, 11 April 2023: x.com/lucas_chancel/status/1645749634843770882.
24. Fred Skulthorp, 'The Blue Wall Is Crumbling: A Sense of Decline Suffuses the Home Counties', UnHerd, 25 April 2023.
25. Hannah Paylor and Amy Baker, 'The Long Shadow of the Cost of Living Emergency', *Carnegie UK*, 27 April 2023.
26. See Danny Dorling, 'Prof. Danny Dorling Looks at Our Cost of Living Research', *Carnegie UK*, 23 May 2023.
27. Will Snell, 'Eight in 10 Brits Are Concerned that the Wealthy Don't Contribute their Fair Share of Taxes', Fairness Foundation Report, 18 May 2023.
28. 'China: Foreign investment', Santander: Trade Markets (santandertrade.com), accessed 8 August 2024.
29. Tim Harford, *Understand: The Economy*, BBC Radio 4, 2 December 2022.
30. Stewart Lansley, *The Richer, the Poorer: How Britain Enriched the Few and Failed the Poor, a 200-Year History*, Bristol University Press, 2021.
31. Alister Doyle and Alistair Scrutton, 'Privacy, What Privacy? Many Nordic Tax Records Are a Phone Call Away', Reuters, 12 April 2016.

32. Anu Kantola and Hanna Kuusela, 'Vanguard Fantasies: The Wealthy Upper Classes as Politically Spirited Wealth Elite Establishment', *Sociological Review*, 29 November 2023.
33. Jan Drewnowski, 'The Affluence Line', *Social Indicators Research*, Vol. 5, 1978, pp. 263–78.
34. Maureen Ramsey, 'A Modest Proposal: the Case for a Maximum Wage', *Contemporary Politics*, Vol. 11, No. 4, 2005, pp. 201–15.
35. Ingrid Robeyns, 'Having Too Much', in J. Knight and M. Schwartzberg (eds), *NOMOS LVI: Wealth* (Yearbook of the American Society for Political and Legal Philosophy), New York University Press, 2017.
36. Pierre Concialdi, 'What Does It Mean To Be Rich? Some Conceptual and Empirical Issues', *European Journal of Social Security*, Vol. 20, No. 1, 2018, pp. 3–20.
37. Marcelo Medeiros, 'The Rich and the Poor: The Construction of an Affluence Line from the Poverty Line', *Social Indicators Research*, Vol. 78, No. 1, 2006, pp. 1–18.
38. Ingrid Robeyns, Vincent Buskens, Arnout van de Rijt, Nina Vergeldt, and Tanja van der Lippe, 'How Rich is Too Rich? Measuring the Riches Line', *Social Indicators Research*, Vol. 154, 2021, pp. 115–43.
39. Ibid., Section 4.1.
40. Julian Baggini, 'Should We Ban Billionaires? A Philosopher Investigates: There Is No Fundamental Right to Unlimited Wealth', *Prospect Magazine*, 5 April 2023.
41. Philipp Heimberger, Twitter/X, 15 April 2023, twitter.com/heimbergecon/status/1647105794045878274.
42. Will Snell, 'Eight in 10 Britons Think Early Years Workers' Pay Is Too Low', Fairness Foundation, 12 March 2023.
43. Tom Wall, 'Staff and Bosses at Royal Society of Arts Accuse Each Other of Threats and Lies in Pay Row', *Guardian*, 6 April 2024.
44. Daniel Chandler, *Free and Equal: What Would a Fair Society Look Like?*, London: Allen Lane, 2023, pp. 238–9.
45. Danny Dorling, 'Are Things About To Get Better?' *Prospect Magazine*, May 2023, pp. 38–41.

46. Andrew Speke, 'What We Learnt from this Year's Tax List: The Latest Annual Report Only Highlights Government Failure To Properly Tax the Super Rich', *Red Pepper*, 18 February 2023. See also BBC, 'What does non-dom mean and how are the rules changing?', BBC News, 27 September 2024, which stated: '74,000 people claimed non-dom status in 2022-23'.

3. Sharing the Work

1. One of many similar messages I received from university colleagues around the world in 2023 and 2024.
2. Ipsos, 'What Worries the World – July 2024', ipsos.com, 29 July 2024.
3. Acting seems to be a popular career for those now educated there; see 'List of People Educated at Haileybury and Imperial Service College', wikipedia.org.
4. Danny Dorling, *Population 10 Billion*, London: Constable, 2013, p. 113.
5. For more on artificial intelligence, see the section at the end of this chapter, and the conclusion of this book. It is currently not a widespread fear, although it is one that tends to preoccupy some better-off people, especially book editors and others working high up in publishing.
6. Richard Easterlin and Kelsey O'Connor, 'The Easterlin Paradox', IZA Discussion Paper No. 13923, December 2020.
7. Fred Pampel and Elizabeth Peters, 'The Easterlin Effect', *Annual Review of Sociology*, Vol. 21, 1995, pp. 163–94.
8. Michael Savage, 'ITV News Is More Trusted than BBC after Lineker Row and Sharp Controversy', *Observer*, 19 March 2023.
9. The least-popular use of government money was the mistreatment of refugees (ibid., which cites a March 2023 Optimum Survey of 2,000 British adults, weighted to be politically and nationally representative with the data given here: https://opinium.com/wp-content/uploads/2023/03/VI-2023-03-15-Observer-Tables-v2-3.xlsx).
10. Ted Van Green, '6 Facts about Americans' Views of Government Spending and the Deficit', Pew Research Centre Report, 24 May 2023.

11. Ibid.
12. Aaron Spray, 'Abandoned Detroit: What the Great Rust Belt City Is Like Today', *Travel*, 23 September 2023.
13. John Burn-Murdoch, 'The Tories Have Become Unmoored from the British People', *Financial Times*, 30 September 2022. Some of the arguments that follow originally appeared in: Danny Dorling, *Brexit: A Failed Project in a Failing State*, London: Friedrich Ebert Stiftung, 2023.
14. The words UK, *British*, *English*, and *county* all appear in this paragraph. I apologise for the apparent ambiguity and inconsistency, but each has a precise meaning. The counties in question, by the way, are not the same as the counties used for administrative purposes in the UK, but those used for cricketing, and not at all like a US county.
15. Although a few of the older grandparents had been young adults in the north or Wales in the early 1930s.
16. Vincent Keter, 'Government Policy on "British Jobs for British Workers"', House of Commons Library, Standard Note SN/BT/4501, 16 September 2009.
17. The well-off pay very low taxes in the UK too: those earning four times average incomes pay the least in Europe when compared to their contemporaries earning four times average pay on the mainland. See Adam Corlett, Felica Odamtten, and Lalitha Try, 'The Living Standards Audit 2022', Resolution Foundation, 4 July 2022, Figure 24.
18. Jon Henley, 'Crises Have Split European Voters into Five "Tribes"', *Guardian*, 12 February 2024.
19. Long-term issues such as the decline of the British Empire, the Cold War, and industrial unrest might have mattered more in earlier decades. To see how much these issues can change over time, consider how they have varied in the USA since 1945. Christopher Wlezien, 'On the Salience of Political Issues', Nuffield College Politics Working Paper, 2003-W10, 2003.
20. YouGov, 'The Most Important Issues Facing the Country', 2 June 2023.

21. Danny Dorling and Sally Tomlinson, *Rule Britannia: Brexit and the End of Empire*, London: Biteback, 2019.
22. Geoff Tily, 'Budget 2023 – Was That It?', TUC blog, 14 March 2023.
23. Becky Morton, 'UK Pledges £84m To Stop Illegal Migration "At Source"', BBC News, 18 July 2024.
24. See Danny Dorling, *Seven Children*, London: Hurst, 2024; Danny Dorling, *Peak Injustice*, Bristol: Policy Press, 2024.
25. Jonathan Portes, 'Immigration and the UK Economy after Brexit', *Oxford Review of Economic Policy*, Vol. 38, No. 1, 25 January 2022, pp. 82–96.
26. Danny Dorling, 'Migration: A Long-Run Perspective', IPPR, 23 April 2009.
27. Trading Economics, 'GDP Per Capita PPP: Europe', tradingeconomics.com, 4 June 2023.
28. Hanna Ziady, 'Elon Musk Says "Civil War Is Inevitable" as UK Rocked by Far-Right Riots. He's Part of the Problem', CNN, 6 August 2024.
29. Dorling, 'Migration', see note 26 above.
30. It was also a net beneficiary of more immigrants than emigrants for people born in the early 1770s and around the year 1800 (both times of low births). Net migration is calculated by adding up how many people died in a place who were born in a particular year and subtracting the number of births from that. If the number is positive, then more people (net) have arrived than were born there. If it is negative, then more of those born in that particular year have left, than entered.
31. Adam Tooze, 'The Climate Emergency Really Is a New Type of Crisis – Consider the "Triple Inequality" at the Heart of It, *Guardian*, 23 November 2023.
32. Thomas Malthus, 'An Essay on the Principle of Population', London: J. Johnson, 1798.
33. Fareid Atta, 'Cambridge Is the "Chinese Capital" of the UK: The Number of Chinese Nationals Who Call Cambridge Home Has Risen by 66% since the Last Census', *Cambridge News*, 13 November 2022.

34. James Bridle, 'The stupidity of AI: Artificial Intelligence in its Current Form Is Based on the Wholesale Appropriation of Existing Culture, and the Notion that It Is Actually Intelligent Could Be Actively Dangerous', *Guardian*, 16 March 2023.
35. John Maynard Keynes, *Economic Possibilities for Our Grandchildren*, New York: W. W. Norton & Co., 1963 (1930), pp. 358–73; Elizabeth Kolbert, 'No Time', *New Yorker*, 19 May 2014.
36. John Maynard Keynes, *How to Pay for the War*, London: Macmillan, 1940, p. 74.
37. David Murray, 'Scottish Child Payment Reduces Food Bank Uptake', Bylines Scotland, 8 February 2024.
38. Charlotte Miles, 'Emergency Food Parcel Distribution in Scotland April – September 2023', Trussell Trust, 30 September 2023, p. 3.

4. War and a Home

1. This speech began: 'They'll soon have us losing World War III. We won't even be in World War III, we'll be losing World War III with weapons the likes of which nobody has ever seen before.' Jennifer Shutt, 'In CPAC Speech, Trump Predicts "Losing World War III" if He Is Not Elected', *Kansas Reflector*, 24 February 2024.
2. Tamás Dávid-Barrett, *Gendered Species*, 2024, available at genderedspecies.com.
3. Nancy Lindisfarne and Jonathan Neale, *Why Men? A Human History of Violence and Inequality*, London: Hurst, 2023.
4. Viktor Sunnemark, 'How Gang Violence Took Hold of Sweden – in Five Charts', *Guardian*, 30 November 2023.
5. Richard Wilkinson and Kate Pickett, 'Why the World Cannot Afford the Rich: Equality Is Essential for Sustainability. The Science Is Clear – People in More-Equal Societies are More Trusting and More Likely to Protect the Environment than Are Those in Unequal, Consumer-Driven Ones', *Nature*, 12 March 2024.
6. Nancy Lindisfarne and Jonathan Neale, 'The Meaning of Ceasefire: Gaza, Genocide, Resistance and Climate Change', Anne

Bonny (a blog concerning Gender, Class, Politics, Resistance and Climate Change), 7 February 2024.
7. According to the global head of trends and foresight at Ipsos Strategy Global Trends, author of 'A New World Disorder? Navigating a Polycrisis'. See Billie Ing, 'Global Trends 2023', Ipsos, February 2023.
8. Ipsos, 'Ipsos Releases an Update to Global Trends 2023: Polarisation, Pessimism and Positivity', 21 November 2023.
9. The report also noted: 'Tackling climate change is still important, with an average of 75% of people agreeing that we are headed for disaster unless we change our habits quickly. However, people are becoming more cautious in their attitudes towards climate change, as they are also facing rising cost-of-living pressures. Across the comparable 26 countries who were included in the last update and this one, agreement has slipped in 22 of them.'
10. Shannon Watts, Twitter/X, 30 April 2023, twitter.com/shannonrwatts/status/1652773442377388034. For the source of the data wrapped up in a particularly American response, see Erin Douglas and Alex Ford, 'Deaths From Firearms Keep Climbing in Texas, Decades after Lawmakers Began Weakening Gun Regulations', *Texas Tribune*, 10 May 2023.
11. CDC, *Firearm Mortality by State*, National Centre for Health Statistics of the Centre for Disease Control, last accessed 24 July 2024.
12. John Gramlich, 'What the Data Says about Gun Deaths in the US', Pew Research Centre Report, 26 April 2023.
13. Sofia Quaglia, 'How a Medieval Murder Map Helped Solve a 700-Year-Old London Cold Case', Atlas Obscura, 25 January 2024.
14. 'Unlocking the Truth for 40 Years', Inquest (online), accessed 9 March 2024.
15. Connor Brooks and Sean Goodison, 'Federal Deaths in Custody and During Arrest, 2020 – Statistical Tables', Bureau of Justice Statistics, Office of Justice Programs, US Department of Justice, July 2023.

16. Jaclyn Diaz, 'Deaths in Custody Are a Crisis, and Data on Them is a Black Hole, a New Report Says', NPR, 28 February 2023.
17. Niki Papadogiannaki and Vicky Yiagopoulou, 'The Normalization of Political Violence and the 2023 Legislative Elections in Greece', The Armed Conflict Location and Event Data Project (ACLED) Report, acleddata.com, 18 May 2023 (graphics by Ana Marco).
18. See Richard Wilkinson and Kate Pickett, 'The Spirit Level at 15', Equality Trust, 2024, Figure 14, equalitytrust.org.
19. World Bank, 'Pathways for Peace: Inclusive Approaches to Preventing Violent Conflict', International Bank for Reconstruction and Development, 2018.
20. 'Multi-National Force – Iraq (MNF-I)', wikipedia.org.
21. 'American-led Intervention in the Syrian Civil War', wikipedia.org.
22. World Bank, 'Pathways for Peace', p. 15, Figure 1.3.
23. Sarah Cheikhali, 'The Spatial Antecedents for Drone Governance in Afghanistan', *Human Geography*, Vol. 16, No. 2, 2023, pp. 117–29.
24. Jonathan Neale, 'Climate Dispatch from Afghanistan', *Ecologist*, 8 March 2024.
25. 'U.S. Troop Withdrawal from Afghanistan', wikipedia.org.
26. Sophia Jones, Gerry Simpson, Alexx Perepölov, et al., 'Beneath the Rubble: Documenting Devastation and Loss in Mariupol: A Human Rights Watch and Situ Research and Truth Hounds Investigation', hrw.org, 8 February 2024.
27. Senay Boztas, '"Stop Inciting Foreigner Hatred": UN Housing Rapporteur', DutchNews, 6 March 2024.
28. Annie Lowrey, 'The U.S. Needs More Housing than Almost Anyone Can Imagine', *Atlantic*, 21 November 2022.
29. Chang-Tai Hsieh and Enrico Moretti, 'Housing Constraints and Spatial Misallocation', *American Economic Journal: Macroeconomics*, Vol. 11, No. 2, 2019, pp. 1–39.
30. Youqin Huang, Shenjing He, and Li Gan, 'Introduction to SI: Homeownership and Housing Divide in China', *Cities*, Vol. 108, 2021, p. 102967.
31. Danny Dorling, 'A Letter from Helsinki', *Public Sector Focus*, July/August 2022, pp. 12–15.

32. Ben Ansell, 'A Puzzling Inheritance: Why, in a World Where Wealth Matters More Than Ever, We Want To Tax It Less', benansell.substack, 27 January 2023.
33. Ingrid Robeyns, *Limitarianism: The Case Against Extreme Wealth*, London: Allen Lane, 2024.
34. Tax Justice UK, 'Brits Back an Annual Tax on the Super-Rich To Help Rebuild the NHS and Public Services', taxjustice.uk/blog, 13 March 2023.
35. Patriotic Millionaires, 'Wealthiest 6 per cent of Brits Support a Wealth Tax', patrioticmillionaires.uk, 13 March 2023.
36. Ingvild Almås, Alexander Cappelen, and Bertil Tungodden, 'Cutthroat Capitalism Versus Cuddly Socialism: Are Americans More Meritocratic and Efficiency-Seeking Than Scandinavians?', *Journal of Political Economy*, Vol. 128, No. 5, 2020, pp. 1753–88.
37. Elizabeth Suhay, Marko Klasnja, and Gonzalo Rivero, 'Ideology of Affluence: Explanations for Inequality and Economic Policy Preferences among Rich Americans', *Journal of Politics*, Vol. 83, No. 1, 2021, pp. 367–80.
38. The word 'weird' became a buzzword in the summer of 2024 following a comment about Republicans: 'Because they don't see it, they've given Democrats an opportunity to do what Nixon did: to make their party the party of the silent majority and to define Republicans as one of the worst things a party can be in modern American politics. Weird.' Jamelle Bouie, 'The Reason Trump and Vance Really Hate Being Called "Weird"', *New York Times*, 9 August 2024.
39. Paul Piff, 'Does Money Make You Mean?', TED, 20 December 2013.
40. Alex Yeandle, Jane Green, and Tiphaine Le Corre, 'People Are Becoming Poorer – Does This Mean There Is More Public Demand for Redistribution?', Nuffield Politics Research Centre Report, April 2023.
41. Rupert Neate, '"From Another Galaxy": Hunt Makes Few Friends in Surrey Town with £100k Remarks', *Guardian*, 30 March 2024.
42. Anoosh Chakelian, 'Sixty per cent of Brits Earning £80,000–£100,000 Say They're "About Average"', *New Statesman*, 4 July 2022.

43. Wars almost always result in more men dying, sometimes altering the global balance of the sexes, as after 1950, and resulting in fewer boys being born for a time: population.un.org/wpp. For an extreme example, see Mostafa Saadat, 'Declined Sex Ratio at Birth in Fallujah (Iraq) during Iraq War with Iran', *Experimental and Clinical Science Journal*, 28 June 2011, Vol. 10, pp. 97–100; Tom Eley, 'Cancer Rate in Fallujah Worse than Hiroshima', World Socialist (online), 23 July 2010.
44. Despite older men usually dying earlier than older women. Sharon Moalem, *The Better Half: On the Genetic Superiority of Women*, New York: Farrar, Straus and Giroux, 2020.
45. Dávid-Barrett, *Gendered Species*, p. 175.
46. Arun Advani, George Bangham, and Jack Leslie, 'The UK's Wealth Distribution and Characteristics of High Wealth Households', Resolution Foundation, December 2020.
47. John Burn-Murdoch, 'The Anglosphere Needs To Learn To Love Apartment Living. Housebuilding Rates in English-Speaking States Have Fallen behind the Rest of the Developed World', *Financial Times*, 17 March 2023.
48. Jean-Benoit Pilet, Lior Sheffer, Luzia Helfer, Frederic Varone, Rens Vliegenthart, and Stefaan Walgrave, 'Do Politicians Outside the United States Also Think Voters Are More Conservative than They Really Are?', *American Political Science Review*, Vol. 118, No. 2, 14 June 2023, pp. 1037–45.
49. Miguel Pereira, 'Understanding and Reducing Biases in Elite Beliefs About the Electorate', *American Political Science Review*, Vol. 115, No.4, 2021, pp. 1308–24.
50. Chris Lizotte and Kirsi Paulina Kallio, 'Youth Far-Right Politics in Finland as a Form of Lived Citizenship', *Space and Polity*, 9 March 2023.
51. Edward Shils and Michael Young, 'The Meaning of the Coronation', *Sociological Review*, Vol. 1, No. 2, December 1953, pp. 63–81.
52. Erik Angner, 'How Economics Can Save the World', New Forum Network blog, OECD, 28 April 2023.
53. Erik has a Clark Kent-styled photo accompanying his piece, looking a little like Superman (without the cape).

54. 'Piketty 10 Years On: Attitudes to Wealth Inequality in Britain Today', All Party Parliamentary Group and Policy Institute at King's College (London), 22 May 2023.
55. John Burn-Murdoch, 'Britain's Winter of Discontent Is the Inevitable Result of Austerity: A Decade of Tory Spending Cuts Left the Country Vulnerable to the External Shocks of the Past Two Years, *Financial Times,* 23 December 2022.
56. 'The impacts have been stark, from ballooning waiting lists and worsening A&E performance, to a rise in avoidable deaths and stalling life expectancy'. Ibid. The graphs can also be found at twitter.com/sebkraemer/status/1653159234555527169.

5. Cradle to Grave

1. Kim Guillon, 'Global Report: 45% of People Have Not Felt True Happiness for More Than Two Years', oracle.com, 15 June 2022.
2. John Helliwell, Haifang Huang, Max Norton, Leonard Goff, and Shun Wang, 'World Happiness, Trust, and Social Connections in Times of Crisis', in World Happiness Report 2023, UN Sustainable Development Solutions Network, Kuala Lumpur, Malaysia, 2023.
3. Similarly, the Dutch successfully reopened schools in June 2020, February 2021, and January 2022 very shortly after the first three peaks in infections there. 'Dutch Schools, Cafes and Museums To Reopen in June', Reuters, 20 May 2020, and 'Dutch Primary Schools To Reopen in First Easing of Corona Measures in Months', Reuters, 31 January 2021 (the schools had been shut from mid-December, for six weeks), and 'Dutch To Reopen Schools Despite High Infection Rates', Reuters, 3 January 2022.
4. Branko Milanović, Twitter/X, 21 March 2023.
5. Danny Dorling, 'Review of Branco Milanović's Global Inequality: A New Approach for the Age of Globalization', *Journal of Critical Social Policy*, Vol. 38, No. 2, 23 March 2018, pp. 444–6, and 'A Review of Branko Milanović's Capitalism and Global Income Inequality', *Catalyst: A Journal of Theory and Strategy*, 30 August 2022.

6. Culture and language may matter, although they should have less influence on changes over time. French premier Charles de Gaulle famously, if only reportedly, suggested that 'Happy people are idiots' many decades ago. Gretchen Rubin, 'Happiness Myth No. 1: Happy People Are Annoying and Stupid', *Slate*, 2 March 2009.
7. See the comprehensive survey of social conditions in China, a 'nationwide large-scale continuous sample survey project initiated by the Institute of Sociology of the Chinese Academy of Social Sciences in 2005 . . . The sample covers 30 provinces and cities nationwide and 596 villages. By the end of December [2017], a total of 9,718 questionnaires were collected.' Chinese Social Sciences (CSS) Comprehensive Survey, Chinese Institute of Social Sciences, 15 April 2019, isss.pku.edu.cn/english/data/other/1301184.htm.
8. Derek Thompson, 'America Fails the Civilization Test', *Atlantic*, 21 April 2023.
9. 'Years of painstaking investigations in multiple countries into the appalling treatment of patients in private hospitals', Max Lawson, '75 Years Ago This Week a Miracle Happened in My Country', Equals blog, 7 July 2023.
10. John Burn-Murdoch, 'Why Are Americans Dying So Young?', *Financial Times*, 31 March 2023.
11. Lu Hiam, Danny Dorling, and Martin McKee, 'Falling Down the Global Ranks: Life Expectancy in the UK 1950–2021', *Journal of the Royal Society of Medicine*, Vol. 166, No. 3, 16 March 2023, pp. 89–92.
12. Sarah Toy, 'U.S. Maternal Mortality Hits Highest Level Since 1965: Black Mothers Are the Most Affected, 2021 Data Show', *Wall Street Journal*, 16 March 2023.
13. First reported to be occurring in the UK in November 2022. Danny Dorling, *Shattered Nation: Inequality and the Geography of a Failing State*, London: Verso, 2023, p. 241.
14. Céline Mouzon, 'Pourquoi Le Système de santé français va mal', *Alternatives Economiques*, 1 February 2020.
15. Bernard Jomier and Catherine Deroche, 'La Situation de l'hôpital et le système de santé en France', Le Rapport de la commission

d'enquête, 29 March 2020, senat.fr/rap/r21-587-1/r21-587-1-syn.pdf.
16. Béatrice Madeline, 'Le Vieillissement de la population, un défi qui dépasse de loin le problème des retraites', *Le Monde*, 5 March 2023.
17. Petits Frères des Pauvres, Twitter/X, 23 May 2023.
18. Victor Vasseur, '"Les Fossoyeurs". Un livre-enquête révèle les graves dérives dans les Ehpad du groupe Orpea', Radio France, 25 January 2022.
19. 'Communiqué de presse: La PPL bien vieillir', Fondation Hospitalière de France, 18 April 2023.
20. 'Happiest Countries in the World 2024 (and 2023 and 2022)', World Population Review (online), accessed 29 March 2024.
21. John Burn-Murdoch, 'What We Get Wrong When We Talk about Global Warming: We Emphasise the Wrong Numbers in What Is a Present Reality, Not a Future Threat', *Financial Times*, 21 July 2023.
22. For example, English university fees are now higher than those in the US, on average. 'Education at a Glance 2022', OECD. 'Most countries in the OECD charge no fees at all for a first degree. England charges by far the highest of all': Socialist Economics, Twitter/X, 3 May 2023. The OECD did a follow-up in 2019: 'Skills Matter: Additional Results from the Survey of Adult Skills', OECD Skills Studies, updated 10 December 2024, at oecd.org.
23. In 2017, some 16,406 adults in England and Wales were prosecuted for their children's truancy. As the authors of the report that provided these figures conclude: 'It is clear that women are disproportionately pursued for this offence.' Rona Epstein, Geraldine Brown, and Sarah O'Flynn, 'Prosecuting Parents for Truancy: Who Pays the Price?', Centre for Crime and Justice Studies, London, 4 February 2019.
24. One example of the crisis can be found in the Los Angeles suburb that was home in the 1940s to a young President George H. W. Bush, but later came to be seen as an impoverished ghetto: Compton is an area where families are taking their children out of

state-funded schools in favour of home schooling, in many cases because (they say) they want a Christian education. Benjamin Herold, *Disillusioned: Five Families and the Unraveling of America's Suburbs*, London: Penguin Press, 2024; and Brooke Masters, 'Why are America's Suburbs Failing?', *Financial Times*, 1 February 2024.

25. Matthew Fischer-Post, Nicolas Hérault, and Roger Wilkins, 'Distributional National Accounts for Australia, 1991–2018', IZA Discussion Paper 15651, October 2022, https://docs.iza.org/dp15651.pdf.

26. John Hills, *Good Times, Bad Times: The Welfare Myth of Them and Us*, Bristol: Policy Press, 2015.

27. Roger Wilkins, Matthew Fischer-Post, and Nicolas Herault, 'Unequal? Our Analysis Suggests Australia Is a More Equal Society than Has Been Thought', The Conversation, 13 April 2023.

28. 'Seniors', Department of Social Services, Australian Government, dss.gov.au/seniors/benefits-payments/age-pension.

29. 'L'état de la France. Présidentielle 2022: quelle note donner au système scolaire français?', *Courrier International*, 3 April 2022.

30. 'L'Éducation nationale en chiffres en 2021', Ministère de l'éducation nationale et de la recherche, education.gouv.fr/l-education-nationale-en-chiffres-2021-324545#.

31. Romain Imbach and Violaine Morin, 'Entre école publique et école privée, les chiffres de la fracture sociale', *Le Monde*, 8 November 2022.

32. Valérie Albouy and Thomas Wanecq, 'Les Inégalités sociales d'accès aux grandes écoles', Institut national de la statistique et des études économiques, 1 June 2003, insee.fr/fr/statistiques/1375870.

33. Valérie Cantié, 'L'école est plus inégalitaire en France que dans la plupart des pays développés (classement Pisa)', Radio France, 23 October 2018.

34. See Note 3, above on p. 285, on schools in the Netherlands; others did better still. Agence France-Presse, 'Denmark First in Europe To Reopen Schools after Coronavirus Lockdown', The Local, 15 April 2020.

35. See the slide pack accompanying Wilkinson and Pickett, 'The Spirit Level at 15', September 2024.
36. Thomas Piketty, 'De L'Inégalité en France', *Le Monde*, 18 April 2017.
37. These weird notions are dying out because the eugenic theory that underlies them is so obnoxious and easily disproved, but it is still sometimes claimed that particular children have unusual inherent potential waiting to be discovered. See also the section on eugenics in Dorling, *Peak Injustice*, Bristol: Policy Press, 2024.
38. 'Nouveau Gouvernement: "Je suis un pur produit de la méritocratie républicaine", lance le ministre de l'Education nationale, Pap Ndiaye', France Info, 20 March 2022.
39. Mattea Battaglia, 'Aux Sources d'inspiration de "l'école du futur" vantée par Emmanuel Macron', *Le Monde*, 3 June 2022.
40. It has been recommended that the UK end practices including 'academic selection and testing measures, which contribute to the high levels of stress felt by students owing to academic pressure, and ensure that children benefit from a creative learning environment'. UN Committee on the Rights of the Child, 'Concluding Observations on the Combined Sixth and Seventh Reports of the United Kingdom of Great Britain and Northern Ireland', CRC/C/GBR/CO/6-7, 2 June 2023.
41. 'United Nations Committee Says the UK Should Phase Out Grammar Schools', Comprehensive Future, 14 June 2023.
42. John Kenney, 'Eugenics and the School Teacher', *Journal of the National Medical Association*, Vol. 7, No. 4, 1915, pp. 253–9.
43. Fred Skulthorp, 'The Blue Wall Is Crumbling: A Sense of Decline Suffuses the Home Counties', UnHerd, 25 April 2023.
44. Lindsay Judge and Adam Corlett, 'Housing Outlook Q1 2024', Resolution Foundation, London, 25 March 2024.
45. Guillaume Errard, 'Qui sont les héritiers en France et que touchent -ils?', *Le Figaro*, 31 January 2022.
46. Jean-Benoît Eyméoud, 'Patrimoine: "Les inégalités générationnelles pour l'accès à un logement sont un poison lent qui ronge le tissu social"', *Le Monde*, 16 March 2022.

47. Mathias André, Céline Arnold, and Olivier Meslin, 'France, portrait social', Institut national de la statistique et des études économiques, 25 November 2021, insee.fr.
48. 'Housing Conditions and Costs Indicators', OECD, 2020.
49. 'European Index of Housing Exclusion' in Seventh Overview of Housing Exclusion in Europe 2022, Abbé Pierre Foundation and FEANTSA, Brussels, 2022.
50. Taina Hytönen, Juha Kaakinen, and Saija Turunen, 'Homelessness in Europe, Finland: Towards Ending Homelessness instead of Managing It', FEANTSA and European Federation of National Organisations working with the Homeless (AISBL), Brussels, 2017.
51. 'Logement d'abord', Gouvernement de France, 29 March 2018, gouvernement.fr/logement-d-abord.
52. Mike Phipps, 'Learning from Manchester's Housing Catastrophe', Labour Hub, 24 March 2024.
53. Gildas Des Roseaux and Service Infographie, 'L'affaire Fillon résumée en quelques dates clés', *Le Figaro*, 19 June 2020.
54. Connor Ibbetson, 'Where Do People Believe in Conspiracy Theories?', YouGov, London, 18 January 2021.
55. Joel Rogers de Waal, 'Comment from the Academic Director of YouGov on the YouGov-Cambridge Globalism Project', YouGov online, 1 May 2019.
56. Charles Eisenstein, 'Synchronicity, Myth, and the New World Order', Reality Sandwich, December 2013.
57. Anthony Galloway, 'By Calling Out Anti-Semitism on the Left, Albanese Has Created Room for Himself', *Sydney Morning Herald*, 15 July 2021.
58. Wilkinson and Pickett, 'The Spirit Level at 15', September 2024.
59. Will Snell, 'Socially Determined', Fairness Foundation, 20 November 2023.

6. Climate Crisis

1. Headline of the Ipsos Earth Day report: Jamie Stinson and Emilie Rochester, 'Earth Day 2024: Changing Attitudes and Actions Towards Climate Change', Ipsos, 19 April 2024.

2. 'The interesting thing is that humans have a hard time coming to terms with the fact that 2,400 gigatonnes of carbon (our total emissions since pre-industrial times) might make a difference to climate, but very readily get behind the idea of a few hygroscopic flares making 18 months' worth of rain fall in a day.' Richard Washington, 'Don't Blame Dubai's Freak Rain on Cloud Seeding – the Storm Was Far Too Big To Be Human-Made', The Conversation, 19 April 2024.
3. 'Synthesis Report of the IPCC Sixth Assessment Report (AR6)', IPCC, 20 March 2023, para. C.2.3.
4. Bonnie Waring, Mathias Neumann, Ian Prentice, Mark Adams, Pete Smith, and Martin Seigert, 'What Role Can Forests Play in Tackling Climate Change?', Grantham Institute Discussion Paper 6 July 2020.
5. Danny Dorling, *Slowdown: The End of the Great Acceleration*, New Haven: Yale University Press, 2020.
6. Anthony Deutsch, 'Despair Makes Young US Men More Conservative Ahead of US Election, Poll Shows', Reuters, 12 April 2024.
7. Sissi Cao, 'Elon Musk Announces xAI: Who's On the 12-Man Founding Team?', *Observer* newsletter, 12 July 2023. For Musk's impact on Twitter: Shubham Singh, 'Elon Musk Posts Pictures with Engineers Leaving a "Code Review" on Twitter', *Business Today*, 19 November 2022.
8. 'The vast majority of European emissions back then were emitted by the United Kingdom; as the data shows, until 1882 more than half of the world's cumulative emissions came from the UK alone.' Hannah Ritchie, 'Who Has Contributed Most to Global CO_2 Emissions?', Our World in Data, 1 October 2019.
9. Ian Tiseo, 'Estimated Share of Cumulative Carbon Dioxide Emissions Worldwide between 1990 and 2015, by Income Group', Statista, 6 February 2023.
10. Thomas Piketty, *Nature, Culture, and Inequality*, London: Scribe, 2024, p. 79.
11. Helen Keller, 'The Worker's Rights: A Letter Written to the Strikers at Little Falls, N.Y.', November 1912.

12. Connor Ibbetson, 'Where Do People Believe in Conspiracy Theories?', YouGov, London, 18 January 2021.
13. Aliya Uteuova, 'Nearly 15% of Americans Don't Believe Climate Change Is Real', *Guardian*, 14 February 2024.
14. On bias in the Ipsos sample, the surveyors explain that the sample taken at the very start of 2024 included '24,290 online adults under the age of 75, interviewed 26 Jan – 9 Feb 2024. The samples in some countries and regions are more urban, more educated, and/or more affluent than the general population'.
15. Stinson and Rochester, 'Earth Day 2024', p. 49.
16. From the Living Planet index. See Dorling, *Slowdown*, fig. 61 (also available online: dannydorling.org/books/SLOWDOWN/Illustrations.html).
17. It may have slowed slightly during the pandemic, but almost no one argues that it has not now returned to its pre-2019 trend. See ibid., figs 13, 14, 15, 16, 17, 18, and 19.
18. Myles Allen, Vicente Barros, John Broome, et al., 'Climate Change 2014', IPCC Fifth Assessment Report (Ar5), Copenhagen, 2014.
19. Working Group II, 'Climate Change 2022: Impacts, Adaptation and Vulnerability: Summary for Policy Makers', IPPC, 2022, ipcc.ch/report/ar6/wg2/.
20. Had the winter of 2022 been colder, with the mud remaining frozen in late February as it usually did, the Russian tanks may well have reached Kiev, and the war might possibly have ended quickly. That could possibly be attributed to climate change.
21. Christopher Bystroff, 'Footprints to Singularity: A Global Population Model Explains Late 20th Century Slow-Down and Predicts Peak within Ten Years', *PLoS One*, Vol. 16, No.5, 2021, e0247214.
22. Working Group II, 'Climate Change 2022'.
23. Matthew Burgess, Stephen Polasky, and David Tilman, 'Predicting Overfishing and Extinction Threats In Multispecies Fisheries', *Proceedings of the National Academy of Sciences*, Vol. 110, No. 40, 2013, pp. 15943–8.
24. David Bressan, 'Climate Change Could Have Played a Role in the Covid-19 Outbreak', *Forbes*, 8 February 2021.

25. Danny Dorling, 'From the Pandemic to the Cost-of-Living Crisis – What Are We Learning?', in Kalina Arabadjieva, Bianca Luna Fabris, and Wouter Zwysen, *Beyond the Polycrisis: Transformative Ideas for a New Socio-Ecological Contract*, Brussels: European Trade Union Institute, 2023.
26. Yassine Souilmi, Elise Lauterbur, Ray Tobler, et al., 'An Ancient Viral Epidemic Involving Host Coronavirus Interacting Genes more than 20,000 Years Ago in East Asia', *Current Biology*, Vol. 31, No. 16, 23 August 2021, pp. 3504–14.
27. Maria Gonçalves, 'Olive oil prices to finally fall as Spain expects bumper harvest', *The Grocer*, 10 September 2024.
28. 'Summary for Policymakers', IPCC, Cambridge and New York, 2022, p. 3; 'Synthesis Report of the IPCC Sixth Assessment Report (AR6), IPCC, 20 March 2023, Switzerland, ipcc.ch/report/ar6/syr.
29. 'Global Study Determines Economic Value of Shellfish and Seaweed Aquaculture', National Centers for Coastal Ocean Science (NCCOS), 12 February 2022.
30. '5 Facts about Climate Migrants', United Nations University, Bonn, 26 November 2015.
31. '"Intolerable Tide" of People Displaced by Climate Change: UN Expert', United Nations Human Rights, 23 June 2022.
32. 'Refugee Data Finder', UN Refugee Agency, 27 October 2022 (last accessed 29 July 2024).
33. Corey Bradshaw, Paul Ehrlich, Andrew Beattie, et al., 'Underestimating the Challenges of Avoiding a Ghastly Future', *Frontiers in Conservation Science*, Vol. 1, No. 615419, 13 January 2021, pp. 1-10.
34. Ousmane Diagana, 'For Millions of West Africans, Climate Change Is Already Here', World Economic Forum, 27 October 2021.
35. Willem Marx, 'Refugees Flee Conflict Sparked by Climate Change in Central Africa', PBS News, 21 October 2022.
36. Pallak Kashyap, 'Pro-US Chad Has Been Surrounded by Pro-Russia Nations, and Its Surrender Is Inevitable', TFI Global News, 17 October 2022.

37. 'The Human Cost of Disasters: An Overview of the Last 20 Years 2000–2019', Centre for Research on the Epidemiology of Disasters, United Nations Office for Disaster Risk Reduction, Geneva, 2020.
38. Michael Jacobs, 'What Exactly Is the Point of COP27?', Inside Story, Al Jazeera, 4 November 2022.
39. Damian Carrington, 'Devastating Floods in Nigeria Were 80 Times More Likely because of Climate Crisis', *Guardian*, 16 November 2022.
40. Daniel Quiggin, Kris De Meyer, Lucy Hubble-Rose, and Antony Froggatt, 'Climate Change Risk Assessment 2021', Research Paper, Environment and Society Programme, Chatham House, 14 September 2021.
41. Nick Watts, Markus Amann, Nigel Arnell, Sonja Ayeb-Karlsson, et al., 'The 2020 Report of *The Lancet*: Countdown on Health and Climate Change: Responding to Converging Crises', *The Lancet*, Vol. 397, No. 10269, 2021, pp. 129–70.
42. Quiggin, De Meyere, Hubble-Rose, and Froggatt, 'Climate Change Risk Assessment'.
43. Anuradha Mittal, 'The 2008 Food Price Crisis: Rethinking Food Security Policies', G-24 Discussion Paper Series, Paper 56, United Nations Conference on Trade and Development (UNCTAD), New York and Geneva, 2009.
44. Boyd Swinburn, Vivica Kraak, Steven Allender, Vincent Atkins, Phillip Baker, Jessica Bogard, et al., 'The Global Syndemic of Obesity, Undernutrition, and Climate Change: *The Lancet* Commission Report', *The Lancet*, Vol. 393, 23 February 2019, pp. 791–846, at p. 836.

7. Biodiversity

1. Edward Wilson, *The Diversity of Life*, London: Penguin, 2001.
2. Ipsos, 'What Worries the World – April 2024', ipsos.com, 2 May 2024.
3. Clearly the reality has not tracked the dire 1970s predictions, despite what was claimed in 2022 by: Sandrine Dixson-Decleve,

Owen Gaffney, Jayati Ghosh, Jorgen Randers, Johan Rockstrom, and Per Espen Stoknes, *Earth for All: A Survival Guide for Humanity*, Gabriola Island, BC: New Society, 2022, pp. 11 and 53.

4. Christiana Figueres is the daughter of José Figueres Ferrer, who served three terms as president of Costa Rica. Her brother became president in the 1990s. Her mother, Karen Olsen Beck, was Costa Rica's ambassador to Israel in 1982. She herself was executive secretary of the UN Framework Convention on Climate Change between 2010 and 2016.

5. Laura Bonesi and David Macdonald, 'Impact of Released Eurasian Otters on a Population of American Mink: A Test Using an Experimental Approach', *Oikos*, 106, 2004, pp. 9–18 (summary available at conservationevidence.com).

6. Children from the city were not welcome in the countryside where a young Theresa Brasier once naughtily ran through fields of wheat. The 1970s Oxfordshire countryside was a hostile environment for many townies, especially those who were not middle-class or white.

7. Damian Carrington, 'Earth's "Vital Signs" Show Humanity's Future in Balance, Say Climate Experts', *Guardian*, 8 October 2024.

8. Multiple Authors, *Millennium Ecosystem Assessment*, Washington DC: Island Press, 2005.

9. Anthony Janetos, Roger Kasperson, et al., 'Synthesis: Condition and Trends in Systems and Services, Trade-Offs for Human Well-Being, and Implications for the Future', in ibid., available at millenniumassessment.org.

10. The International Panel of Experts on Sustainable Food Systems (IPES-Food).

11. 'Summary of the Ninth Session of the Plenary of the Intergovernmental Science-Policy Platform on Biodiversity and Ecosystem Services: 3-9 July 2022', *IISD Earth Negotiations Bulletin*, Vol. 31, No. 64, 12 July 2022, p. 1.

12. For example, papers warning: 'Every year, at least [one] species goes into extinction.' Imagine if it was only one a year – there would be no mass extinction. See Oladimeji Adebayo, 'Loss of

biodiversity: The Burgeoning Threat to Human Health', *Annals of Ibadan Postgraduate Medicine*, Vol. 17, No. 1, 2019, pp. 1–3.
13. Fang-Zhou Ma, Chen-Bin Wang, Yan-Jing Zhang, Peng Cui, and Hai-Gen Xu, 'Letter: Rapid Loss of China's Pollinator Diversity', *Science*, Vol. 377, No. 6610, 2022, p. 1055.
14. 'Food Security Update: World bank response to rising food insecurity', World Bank, Washington DC, 14 November 2022.
15. Baxter Dimitry, 'UN Food Director Predicts "Hell on Earth" Food Shortages in 2023', NewsPunch, 21 October 2022.
16. Asher McShane, 'Israel "Has the Right" To Withhold Power and Water from Gaza, Says Sir Keir Starmer', LBC, 11 October 2023.
17. See 'Interdependencies', in '*I = PAT*', wikipedia.org.
18. Danny Dorling, 'Don't Panic about the Birth of Baby 8 Billion. Before He's 65 Our Numbers Will Be in Reverse', *Observer*, 20 November 2022.
19. Jasmine Ketibuah-Foley, 'Motherhood in a Climate Crisis: Women Share Their Anger and Fear', BBC News, 19 November 2022.
20. Daniel Immerwahr, 'Are We Really Prisoners of Geography?', *Guardian*, 10 November 2022.
21. Dixson-Decleve, Gaffney, Ghosh, et al., *Earth for All* (see note 3).
22. Elizabeth Allison, 'The Spiritual Significance of Glaciers in an Age of Climate Change', *Wiley Interdisciplinary Reviews: Climate Change*, Vol. 6, No. 5, 10 August 2015.
23. Petra Tschakert, Neville Ellis, Christopher Anderson, A. Kelly, and James Obeng, 'One Thousand Ways to Experience Loss: A Systematic Analysis of Climate-Related Intangible Harm from Around the World', *Global Environmental Change*, Vol. 55, March 2019, pp. 58–72.
24. Daisy Dunne and Aruna Chandrasekhar, 'Loss and Damage: What Happens When Climate Change Destroys Lives and Cultures?', *Carbon Brief*, 28 September 2022.
25. Ibid.
26. Ibid.
27. The word cataclysm has its origins in the biblical flood: from the French *cataclysme*, via Latin, but originally Greek, *kataklusmos*, meaning 'deluge'.

28. Caroline Hickman, Elizabeth Marks, Panu Pihkala, et al., 'Climate Anxiety in Children and Young People and their Beliefs about Government Responses to Climate Change: A Global Survey', *Lancet Planetary Health*, Vol. 5, No. 12, 1 December 2021, pp. 863–73.
29. The full list of countries included was Australia, Brazil, Finland, France, India, Nigeria, Philippines, Portugal, the UK, and the US.
30. Mala Rao and Richard Powell, 'Opinion: The Climate Crisis and the Rise of Eco-Anxiety', *British Medical Journal*, 6 October 2021.
31. Joel Millward-Hopkins, Julia K. Steinberger, Narasimha Rao, and Yannick Oswald, 'Providing Decent Living with Minimum Energy: A Global Scenario', *Global Environmental Change*, Vol. 65, No. 12, November 2020.
32. Robin Maynard and Barbara Williams, 'Letters: Getting Sterilised to Save the Planet Is a Sad but Understandable Choice', *Guardian*, 14 January 2022.
33. Note that in 2015, as the falling birth rate became clearer, the pope said that 'most importantly, no outside institution should impose its views on families'. 'Pope Francis: No Catholic Need to Breed Like "Rabbits"', BBC News, 15 January 2015.
34. Matthew Selinske, Leejiah Dorward, Paul Barnes, and Stephanie Brittain, 'You Are Now One of 8 Billion Humans Alive Today. Let's Talk Overpopulation – and Why Low Income Countries Aren't the Issue', The Conversation, 15 November 2022.
35. John Vidal, 'It Should Not Be Controversial To Say a Population of 8 Billion Will Have a Grave Impact on the Climate', *Guardian*, 15 November 2022.
36. Eduardo Brondizio, Josef Settele, Sandra Díaz, and Hien Ngo (eds), 'Global Assessment Report on Biodiversity and Ecosystem Services of the Intergovernmental Science-Policy Platform on Biodiversity and Ecosystem Services', IPBES, Bonn, 2019 (see esp. p. 11 of the summary for policymakers, available at zenodo.org).
37. Although it appears that more and more species are on the Red List, in the early 2000s, of the roughly 20,000 species that had by then been assessed, a majority were classified as under threat; by 2022, almost 150,000 species had been assessed and a minority

(40,000) were rated as threatened on the Red List. The proportion of species on the list of which it is said they are at greatest danger is dropping over time. A species only gets onto the green list (considered safe) if it is fully recovered, present in all parts of its range (even those that are no longer occupied but were prior to major human impacts/disruption), viable (not threatened with extinction in any way) in all parts of the range, and performing its ecological functions in all parts of the range. As the range in which a species can viably live shifts due to climate change, its geographical location will alter and so it is now very hard for any species to get onto the green list. The major current threat to species is agriculture. Of the 28,000 species noted as threatened with extinction in the IUCN Red List in 2019, agriculture was listed as a threat for 24,000 of them. However, globally, to produce the same amount of crops as in 1961, we need only 30 per cent as much farmland, due to increased yields. This increase in yield was achieved without the genetic modification of crops, but through selective breeding. So, although roughly half of the habitable land of the world is currently being used for agriculture, that could be reduced in future and more people still be well fed, especially if we eat less meat. See Our World in Data; and IUCN Red List (ourworldindata.org/land-use; iucnredlist.org).
38. Christopher Bystroff, 'Footprints to Singularity: A Global Population Model Explains Late 20th Century Slow-Down and Predicts Peak Within Ten Years', *PLoS One*, Vol. 16, No. 5, 2021, pp. 1–20.
39. School of Science, Rensselaer Polytechnic Institute, Chris Bystroff faculty page, archived 10 October 2015: web.archive.org.
40. The closest we have come to this is the current decline in the population of South Korea, halving in the current generation, but even that is a less-steep decline than predicted in Bystroff's Figure 4, worldwide (ibid.).
41. J. Fungi (Basel). 2022 Jun 22;8(7):653. doi: 10.3390/jof8070653.
42. Dina Coole, 'Too Many Bodies? The Return and Disavowal of the Population Question', *Environmental Politics*, Vol. 22, No.2, 2013, pp. 195–215.

43. Caroline Kimeu, 'What Tanzania Tells Us about Africa's Population Explosion as the World Hits 8bn People', *Guardian*, 15 November 2022.
44. Stuart Gietel-Basten, Anna Rotkirch, and Tomáš Sobotka, 'Changing the Perspective on Low Birth Rates: Why Simplistic Solutions Won't Work', *British Medical Journal*, 379, e072670, 15 November 2022.
45. George Getz, 'Dire Famine Forecast By '75', *Salt Lake Tribune*, 17 November 1967, p. 9.
46. 'Dr Ehrlich, Outspoken Ecologist, To Speak', *Redlands Daily Facts*, 6 October 1970, p. 3.
47. Bradshaw, Ehrlich, Beattie et al., 'Underestimating the Challenges of Avoiding a Ghastly Future'.
48. William Rees, 'The Human Eco-Predicament: Overshoot and the Population Conundrum', *Vienna Yearbook of Population Research*, Vol. 21, 2023, pp. 1–19.
49. 'A dynamic speaker, Rees has been invited to lecture on areas of his expertise across Canada and the US, as well as in Australia, Austria, Belgium, China, Finland, France, Germany, Hungary, Japan, Mexico, the Netherlands, Norway, Indonesia, Italy, Korea, the former Soviet Union, Spain, Sri Lanka, Sweden and the UK.' 'William E. Rees', wikipedia.org.
50. Maria Khristine Alvarez and Kenneth Cardenas, 'Evicting Slums, "Building Back Better": Resiliency Revanchism and Disaster Risk Management in Manila', *International Journal of Urban and Regional Research*, Vol. 43, No. 2, March 2019, pp. 207–403, at p. 235.
51. Michalis Vousdoukas, Joanne Clarke, Roshanka Ranasinghe, et al., 'African Heritage Sites Threatened as Sea-Level Rise Accelerates', *Nature Climate Change*, Vol. 12, 2022, pp. 256–62.
52. Oliver Milman, 'New York City is Sinking due to Weight of Its Skyscrapers, New Research Finds', *Guardian*, 19 May 2023.
53. 'Shoreline Management Plans', BBC Programmes, undated, but last accessed 12 August 2024, available at bbc.co.uk.
54. 'UK Climate Projections (UKCP)', The Meteorological Office, Exeter, available at ukclimateprojections.metoffice.gov.uk.

55. 'UKCP18 Factsheet: Sea Level Rise and Storm Surge', Meteorological Office, Exeter, 2018, p. 2, available at metoffice.gov.uk.
56. 'More Sea Defence Work at Friog Corner, Fairbourne', Natural Resources Wales (NRW), 25 January 2021.
57. 'Shoreline Management Plan 2', Cabinet Report, Gwynedd Local District Council, Wales, 22 January 2013.
58. Donella Meadows, Dennis Meadows, Jørgen Randers, and William Behrens, *The Limits to Growth*, Washington DC: Potomac Associates, 1973, p. 23.
59. And as a former 'chair of three Norwegian banks, non-executive member of numerous corporate boards, and member of the sustainability councils of three multi-nationals' on the Club's own website: Club of Rome website, cluboframe.org/member/randers-jorgen.
60. Torsten Bell, James Smith, and Lalitha Try, 'Food for Thought: The Role of Food Prices in the Cost of Living Crisis', Resolution Foundation, London, 19 May 2023.
61. Christian Bogmans, Jeff Kearns, Andrea Pescatori, and Ervin Prift, 'War-Fueled Surge in Food Prices To Hit Poorer Nations Hardest', IMF blog, 16 March 2022.
62. 'Food Prices and Spending', US Dept of Agriculture, Washington DC (last accessed 2 August 2024).
63. Susan Savage, 'Global Food Price Inflation Set To Fall in 2024, Says Rabobank', *Financial Times*, 15 November 2023.
64. David Hall, 'Water and Sewerage Company Finances 2021: Dividends and Investment – and Company Attempts To Hide Dividends', PSIRU University of Greenwich Working Paper, 28 January 2022.
65. Equality Trust, Twitter/X, 3 July 2023.
66. George Dibb, Twitter/X, 28 June 2023.
67. These shifts are enormous, such as the $1.5 billion investment into factories in Aba, Nigeria in 2019 by the Chinese Huajian Group, a shoe-making company. See Hantian Sheng, Xiaomian Dai, and Canfei He, 'Gone with the Epidemic? The Spatial Effects of Covid-19 on Global Greenfield Investment Network', *Applied Geography*, Vol. 156, 2023, pp. 1–11.

68. Concerns vary greatly among individuals. See George Monbiot, 'I Back Saboteurs Who Have Acted with Courage and Coherence, but I Won't Blow Up a Pipeline. Here's Why', *Guardian*, 28 April 2023.
69. 'Global Air Travel Demand Continued Its Bounce Back in 2023', International Air Transport Association (IATA), 31 January 2024.
70. An example, from Dorset: 'Perrodo continued to post photos of racing cars to his Instagram stories on Monday morning while members of the combined emergency response team tackled the oil spill . . . a multibillionaire amateur racing driver who owns 46 sports cars including a £12m McLaren F1 GTR.' Rupert Neate, 'The Billionaire Amateur Racing Driver Who Runs the Poole Oil Leak Pipeline', *Guardian*, 27 March 2023.
71. See Wilkinson and Pickett, 'The Spirit Level at 15', technical appendix, September 2024, p. 10.
72. Ida Kubiszewski, Caroline Ward, Kate Pickett, and Robert Costanza, 'The Complex Relationships between Economic Inequality and Biodiversity: A Scoping Review', *Anthropocene Review*, Vol. 11, No. 1, April 2024, pp. 49–66.
73. Laetitia Pettinotti, Yue Cao, Tony Mwenda Kamninga, and Sarah Colenbrander, 'A Fair Share of Biodiversity Finance: Apportioning Responsibility for the $20 Billion Target by 2025', ODI, London, 20 June 2024.

Conclusion

1. Jane Corbin, 'Doomsday Clock Stays at 90 Seconds to Midnight', BBC News, 23 January 2024.
2. *Bulletin of the Atomic Scientists*, thebulletin.org/about-us/leadership/.
3. If aliens ever do arrive here, they could well be benign peacemakers. Peace-making gentle creatures are far more likely to have survived as a species than ones that are constantly oppressing and fighting each other and destroying the environment that sustains them. Basing so many of our models of alien life on colonising

humans in little green (and humanoid) form does little other than reveal our historic lack of imagination.
4. *Bulletin of the Atomic Scientists.*
5. Turgut Keskintürk, 'Sociology's Inequality Problem', 10 October 2023, tkeskinturk.github.io/blog/inequality.
6. Paul Collier, *Left Behind: A New Economics for Neglected Places*, London: Allen Lane, 2024.
7. Keskintürk, 'Sociology's Inequality Problem'.
8. Dorling, *Seven Children,* figures available here: dannydorling.org.
9. In August 2024, following the release of many statistics that suggested UK economic inequality may be on the turn, it was revealed that the median pay for a chief executive officer of companies in the *FT* Stock Exchange top 100, was 120 times that of the median UK full-time worker in 2023, down from 124:1 in 2022. Andrew Speke and Luke Hildyard, 'Analysis of UK CEO Pay in 2023', High Pay Centre, London, 11 August 2024.
10. See Chapter 2 in this book for the longer argument.
11. Danny Dorling, *Population 10 Billion*, London: Constable, 2013, p. 73.
12. Others proclaim the end is nigh as a joke to help better thinking. See the 1860 Doomsday equation of Heinz von Foerster, at Wikipedia: 'Heinz von Foerster', and 'List of Dates Predicted for Apocalyptic Events', wikipedia.org.
13. William Davies, 'Antimarket', *London Review of Books*, Vol. 46, No. 7, 4 April 2024.
14. Ibid.
15. The phrase has often been attributed to Mark Fisher, although he attributed it to others. See 'Capitalist Realism', wikipedia.org.
16. Dorling, *Peak Injustice.*
17. Dorling, *Seven Children.*
18. More fully, 'characterized by the belief (especially when viewed as irrational) in the goodwill of others or the pervasiveness of serendipity. Opposed to paranoid' – 'Pronoid', *Oxford English Dictionary* online, at oed.com.
19. Some attribute this line to the 1970 film *Catch-22*, rather than the book, with the words spoken by Alan Arkin, who played Capt. John

Yossarian. This could mean that the film's screenwriter, Buck Henry, authored the line. See also David Yaden and Andrew Newberg, 'Synchronicity Experiences: "Everything Happens for a Reason"', in *The Varieties of Spiritual Experience: 21st Century Research and Perspectives*, Oxford: Oxford University Press, 2022, p. 217.
20. Eleanor Peake, 'I'm a Climate Scientist and I Think Society Will Collapse by 2050. Here's How I'm Preparing', Inews, 25 September 2023.
21. Hannah Ritchie, Twitter/X, 3 January 2024, x.com/_Hannah Ritchie/status/1742520385206091837. See also YouGov, Twitter/X, 3 January 2024, x.com/YouGov/status/1742486856745336849.
22. See Alastair Bonnett, 'The New Popular Geography and Pursuit of the Curious', *Scottish Geographical Journal*, 29 March 2023, doi.org/10.1080/14702541.2023.2192704.
23. Maximilian Kotz, Friderike Kuik, Eliza Lis, and Christiane Nickel, 'Global Warming and Heat Extremes to Enhance Inflationary Pressures', *Nature Communications: Earth and Environment*, Vol. 5, Art. 116, 2024.
24. Damian Carrington, 'West Africa Heatwave Was Supercharged by Climate Crisis, Study Finds', *Guardian*, 21 March 2024.
25. Peter Agre, Harvey Alter, Hiroshi Amano, Frances Arnold, et al., 'Nobel Prize Laureates and Other Experts Issue Urgent Call for Action After "Our Planet, Our Future" Summit', National Academies, 29 April 2021.
26. Gareth Bryant and Sophie Weber, *Climate Finance: Taking a Position on Climate Futures*, Newcastle: Agenda, 2024, p. 159.
27. Lucas Chancel, Philipp Bothe, and Tancrède Voituriez, 'Climate Inéquality Report 2023: Fair Taxes for a Sustainable Future in the Global South', World Inequality Lab Study 2023/1, 2023.
28. Chris Lizotte, 'For Ordinary Kindness in Human Geography', *Dialogues in Human Geography*, 1–4, 2023.
29. Peter Buffett, 'The Charitable-Industrial Complex', *New York Times*, 26 July 2013.
30. David Brancaccio and Rose Conlon, 'Why Rich People Tend to Think They Deserve their Money', Marketplace Morning Report, Minnesota Public Radio, 19 January 2021.

31. Anthony Robledo, 'Forbes Billionaires Under 30 All Inherited their Wealth for First Time in 15 Years', *USA Today*, 4 April 2024.
32. Samira Marti, Isabel Martínez, and Florian Scheuer, 'Does a Progressive Wealth Tax Reduce Top Wealth Inequality? Evidence from Switzerland', *Oxford Review of Economic Policy*, Vol. 39, No. 3, 18 August 2023, pp. 513–29.
33. Greg Rosalsky, 'Affirmative Action for Rich Kids: It's More Than Just Legacy Admissions', National Public Radio, 24 July 2023.
34. Lauded as 'the Beyoncé of Economics because of his long list of popular hits in empirical economics'.
35. Geoff Mulgan, *When Science Meets Power*, Cambridge: Polity, 2023, p. 69.
36. Mulgan, *When Science Meets Power*, p. 115.
37. Joseph Stiglitz, 'What Comes After Neoliberalism?', Project Syndicate, 4 June 2024.
38. Ruben Mathisen, 'The Influence Gap: Unequal Policy Responsiveness to Men and Women', *Journal of Politics*, February 2024.
39. My preference would be a ratio of 54:46, but only because that is the number Toots had to wear on his prison uniform at the time I was born ('Toots Hibbert', wikipedia.org). The ratio of 55:45 is suggested at the very end of the first of two books, with the explanation promised in the second (as yet unpublished). Tamás Dávid-Barrett, *Gendered Species*, 2024, p. 257.
40. Dawn Foster, *Lean Out*, London: Repeater Books, 2016.
41. Megan MacKenzie and Nicole Wegner, *Feminist Solutions for Ending War*, London: Pluto, 2021 (available at library.oapen.org). See also 'Jineology', wikipedia.org.
42. Others who like the idea of nation states explain what drives them to this conclusion: 'I too am guided by the anger of the dead and the longings of those unborn'. Maurice Glasman, 'Inside Ukraine's Orthodox Heart: The Holy Monastery of the Caves beneath Kyiv is Threatened by War', *New Statesman*, 10 April 2023.
43. 'Poverty and Shared Prosperity 2020: Reversals of Fortune', World Bank, Washington DC, 2020.

44. 'Poverty and Shared Prosperity 2022: Correcting Course', World Bank, Washington DC, 2022.
45. 'Richest 1% Bag Nearly Twice as Much Wealth as the Rest of the World Put Together over the Past Two Years', Oxfam, 16 January 2023.
46. Carlos Sabatino, Carolina Diaz-Bonilla, Minh Cong Nguyen, and Haoyu Wu, 'April 2023 Update to the Global Database of Shared Prosperity: What's New', World Bank Group, Washington, DC, May 2023, Figure 1.
47. Carlos Sabatino Gonzalez, Carolina Diaz-Bonilla, Danielle Aron, Cameron Haddad, Minh Cong Nguyenm, and Haoyu Wu, 'April 2024 Update to the Global Database of Shared Prosperity: What's New', Global Poverty Monitoring Technical Note No. 37, World Bank Group, Washington, DC, June 2024 (published two months late).
48. Saskia Mostert, Marcel Hoogland, Minke Huibers, and Gertjan Kaspers, 'Excess Mortality Across Countries in the Western World since the COVID-19 Pandemic: "Our World in Data" Estimates of January 2020 to December 2022', *BMJ Public Health*, 2024, 2:e000282, 2024, doi: 10.1136/bmjph-2023-000282.
49. Sam Wollaston, '"I Could Bench-Press 100kg. Now, I Can't Walk": Lucy's Life with Long Covid', *Guardian*, 5 June 2024.
50. I have made it past 56.5 years. Even in quite recent British history, that is an achievement.
51. Thomas Piketty, *Nature, Culture, and Inequality*, London: Scribe, 2024, p. 5.
52. Compare it, for instance, with the final commandment in the Bible: 'Thou dost not desire the house of thy neighbour, thou dost not desire the wife of thy neighbour, or his manservant, or his handmaid, or his ox, or his ass, or anything which [is] thy neighbour's.' (This translation avoids the word 'slave'.)
53. Tim Gill, 'The Socialist 10 Commandments', Rethinking Childhood, 26 July 2011, available at rethinkingchildhood.com.
54. Banner of the East Bradford Socialist Sunday School, Working Class Movement Library, available at wcml.org.uk.
55. Ibid.

56. 'All Things Bright and Beautiful', wikipedia.org.
57. '1848 in the United Kingdom', wikipedia.org.
58. Nancy Lindisfarne and Jonathan Neale, 'All Things Being Equal', *Ecologist*, 17 December 2021.
59. Words typed by the kindest of all *London Review of Books* contributing editors, James Butler, at the start of the August 2024 UK race(ist) riots, Twitter/X, 31 July 2024, x.com/piercepenniless/status/1818930415165431841.

Index

abortion, 34, 221
The Affluence Line (Drewnowski), 51–2
Afghanistan:
   happiness ranking, 125
   US withdrawal from (2021), 106
Africa:
   climate migration from, potential, 182
   impoverishment of, 83
   migrants in Europe, 84
'age of crisis', 3
ageing society, 20, 128, 264
AIDS. *See* HIV/AIDS
air travel, 232–3, 241
Albania, economic collapse, 182
Aliens Act (1905), UK, 58–9
alien contact:
   conspiracy theories, 156–8
   probability, 236, 301n3
All Things Bright and Beautiful (hymn), 268–9
American Economic Review (journal), 31
American Sociological Review (journal), 237–40
Angner, Erik, economist, 121
Ansell, Ben, political scientist, 111–2
anthropologists, 93
antidepressants:
   and happiness, 126–7
anti-immigration rhetoric, 67
antiracism, 67
Antoinette, Marie, Queen of France, 59
anxiety, 6, 13, 15, 101. *See also* eco-anxiety
apathy, 16, 120, 159
   and climate change, 162
Arab Spring, 180

archaeologists, 269
Argentina, 97, 101, 107
arms industry, 116, 119, 173
artificial intelligence (AI), 12–3, 61, 87–8, 236, 277n5
   as potential next crisis, 256–7
asteroid impact, 236–7
asylum seekers:
   in UK, 73, 74, 76, 83, 182
Atlantic (magazine), 108–10, 282n28
atom bomb, 35
austerity:
   and financial crash (2008), 52
   life expectancy, UK, 132, 285n55
Australia:
   concern about climate change, 160, 168
   concern about war, 97
   conspiracy theories, 157, 167, 168
   drought, 194
   inequality, 143
   health and education funding, 142–3
   life expectancy, 132, 133
   pension age, 143
   poverty, 229
Austria:
   heatwave deaths (2003), 190
   housing costs, 149
   poverty, 229
Azmanova, Albena, political scientist, 25, 273n1

baby boom, 19, 139, 148, 214
Backhaus, Andreas, economist, 126
Baggini, Julian, philosopher, 53
Bangladesh:
   uprising (2024), 255
Bank of England, 55, 179
'bank of mum and dad', 118

Index

BBC. *See* British Broadcasting Corporation
bees, 200, 201
Beasley, David, United Nations executive, 203
Belgium, 78, 119, 145, 149
  concern about climate change, 168
  €500 limit on individual donations to political parties, 55
  heatwave deaths (2003), 190
  politicians' views of electorate, 119
Berman, Elizabeth (Beth) Popp, sociologist, 237, 239–40
Besant, Annie, socialist and feminist, 213
The Better Angels of Our Nature: Why Violence Has Declined (Pinker), 105
Big Bang, UK financial deregulation (1986), 73
Bill and Melinda Gates Foundation, 220
billionaires, 44
  ban, proposed, 53
  far-right narcissists, 12
  inherited wealth, 254, 304n31
  tax paid in UK, 55–6
biodiversity, biodiversity loss, 22–3, 169, 195–7, 199–234, 243, 297n37
  geography's focus on, 250
  inequality, 233–4
  Oxfordshire, 199–201
biosecurity:
  Bulletin of the Atomic Scientists reports, 237
birth cohort:
  effects, 62–3
  Sweden, 77–80
  UK, 1919, 122
birth control, 82, 212–3, 215, 221, 257
birth rates:
  decline, 35, 36, 60–2, 77, 213, 22
  during COVID-19 pandemic, 37
  peak years, 33, 34
birth complications:
  and poverty, 135
'Blue Wall', recent Conservative-voting regions of England, 147
bonobos, 93
books:
  by university professors, 13
  consumption as indicator of affluence, 7
  on crises, 3
  with 'love' in their titles, 253
Bradlaugh, Charles, politician and activist, 213
brands:
  impact of crises, 99, 100
Brazil:
  conspiracy theories, 154, 156, 167
  crime and violence, 101
  foreign direct investment, 48
  inflation, 26
  maximum income proposal, 52–3
  poverty and inequality, 26
  war deaths, 107
Brexit, Brexit referendum, 73, 121–2
  economic damage, 78
  followed by rise in immigration, 76
  incitement to hatred, 75
  support for by elderly, 77
  support for by wealthy, 69
Britain. *See* United Kingdom
British Broadcasting Corporation (BBC):
  climate change coverage, 206
  Executive Complaints Unit, 49
  inequality and poverty coverage, 49–50
'British jobs for British workers', political slogan, 67
British Union of Fascists, 74
Brown, Gordon, UK prime minister, 67
Buffett, Peter, philanthropist, 253–4
Bulgaria, 75
Bulletin of the Atomic Scientists, 235, 237
Burn-Murdoch, John, *Financial Times* journalist, 134, 229
Butler, James, journalist, 270
buy-to-let housing, 118
Bystroff, Christopher, biologist, 215–20, 222

Cameron, David, UK prime minister, 72
Canada:
  antidepressant use, 126
  biodiversity spending, 233
  concern about climate change, 168
  concern about crime and violence, 102
  conspiracy theories, 155–6, 167, 168
  health care, 130–1
  life expectancy, 132, 133

politicians' views of electorate, 119
unemployment, 27
war deaths, 107
Le Canard enchaîné (newspaper), 151
Cantril ladder, 125
Capital in the Twenty-First Century (Piketty), 207
capital. *See* wealth
capitalism, 10
   biodiversity loss, 199
   Midas machine for the wealthy, 29
   problem of, 244–5
   war, 260
Carbon Brief report (2022), 208
carbon capture, 160, 212
carbon dioxide, 160, 163
carbon emissions, 160, 162–4, 166, 194, 213, 291n8
care. *See* social care
Cardigan Bay, Wales, 224–5
car washing:
   by hand in rich countries, 87
Catch-22 (Heller), 248, 302n19
censuses, 4, 218
centenarians, 130
Centre for Research on the Epidemiology of Disasters, 188
Chad, 182
   war deaths, 107
Chancel, Lucas, economist, 44, 163
Chandler, Daniel, economist, 55
Chatham House:
   report on climate change, 193–4
Chetty, Raj, economist, 255, 304n34
childcare workers. *See* early-years sector
child labour, 61, 140
child mortality, 129–30, 246
Chile, 97, 101
   uprising (2019), 180, 255
chimpanzees, 93
China, 11, 16, 17, 37, 105
   abortion restrictions, 221
   bat species spread, 176
   COVID-19 pandemic, 132
   economic rise, 33, 82, 258–9
   energy, 232
   family size, 34
   food production, 202–3
   foreign direct investment, 48
   geographers, 203
   Great Famine (1950s), 83, 202
   health care, 19, 128
   home ownership, 110, 282n30
   Institute of Sociology survey, 17, 101, 286n7
   living standards, 37, 164
   migration to UK, 85–6
   natural disasters, 188
   poverty, 82
   seen as threat, 16, 206
   YouGov poll on conspiracy, excluded, 155, 157
   war deaths, 107
Chinese Academy of Social Sciences:
   Institute of Sociology, survey (2006–), 17, 286n7
cholera, 172, 176, 179, 246
Christophers, Brett, geographer, 245
civil unrest, 176, 180–1, 269
climate change, climate crisis, 5, 22–3, 139, 159–95, 198, 242
   Bulletin of the Atomic Scientists, 235
   concern by age and social class, 19, 94, 158, 208–10, 281n9
   concern by gender, 161–2
   conspiracy theories, 155–8, 166, 222
   cost of living, 250–1
   deaths, 139–40, 184–6, 189–95
   droughts, 171, 175–6, 186, 194
   eco-anxiety, 208–10
   elections in 2024, 71
   floods, 171, 172, 175, 186, 194
   food prices, 175, 178
   fatigue, 168, 229
   geography's focus on, 250
   health, 139, 178–9
   'intangible losses', 208, 296n23
   pandemics, 176–7
   'polycrisis', 99
   refugees, 80, 174, 181–2
   reluctance to have children, 209, 297n32
   resource wars, 177–8
   scepticism, 18, 166, 168, 176, 193
   sea levels, 170, 223–7
   social justice emergency, 165
   social media, 162
   tax on wealth, 252–3
   tipping points, 201, 211, 215, 229
   war, 173
   'wicked problem', 251–3
climate reparations, 164, 252
Club of Rome, 199, 228
'coalition of the willing', Iraq invasion (2003), 105
Cold War, 132, 235
Colombia:

concern about corruption, 151
concern about crime and violence, 101
war deaths, 107
communism, collapse of, 131
The Communist Manifesto (Engels and Marx), 269
compassion:
  lower levels among wealthy, 114–5
concentration of wealth, 118, 120, 130, 148
conspiracy theory, conspiracy theories, 152–8, 167
  climate change, 222–3
contraception, contraceptives. *See* birth control
coral reef collapse, 199
coronation, Queen Elizabeth II (1953), 120
coronavirus pandemic. *See* COVID-19 pandemic (2019–22)
corruption, 20–1, 95, 150–3, 198
cost of living, costs of living, 25–9, 35, 38, 58, 92, 100
  concern in Italy and Portugal, 72
  concern in UK, 65
  crisis, 19, 20, 38, 56
COVID-19 pandemic (2019–22), 18, 28, 132, 136–7
  air travel, 232–3
  birth rate, 36, 37
  concern globally, 22, 27, 241, 265
  concern in UK, 73
  deaths in Pakistan, 192
  poverty, 261–3
cricket, county, 67
crime and violence, 20–1, 92–4, 100–3, 128, 198, 247
  geography's focus on, 250
  Latin America, 26
  Sweden, 94–7
  US, 101–2
crisis managers, professional, 10
  See also risk management
cyberattacks, 8–9, 12
Czech Republic:
  heatwave deaths (2003), 190
  housing, 149
  poverty, 229

Davies, William, sociologist, 245
deaths. *See also* mortality
  extreme heat, 139–40, 190
  poverty and inequality, 140
  war, 107

debt, 53–4, 141, 231, 252, 264
deforestation, 169, 249
de-gentrification, 46, 147
de-industrialisation, 66
Democratic Party (US), 122
demography, 4, 19, 31
Denmark:
  conspiracy theories, 154, 157–8, 167
  happiness ranking, 125–7
  poverty, 229
  social mobility, 145
  trust in others, 158
Detroit, 66, 278n12
diseases, 137, 172, 176–7, 179, 246, 262
disruptive technologies, 237
Doomsday Clock, 235–6
Drewnowski, Jan, economist, 51–2
Dutch national election. *See* Netherlands, national election (2023)

early-years education:
  wages in UK, 54
Earth for All: A Survival Guide for Humanity (Dixson-Declève, Gaffney, Ghosh, Rockström, Stoknes, Randers), 199, 206–7
earthquakes, 183, 186
East Germany, former, 131
Easter eggs, chocolate, 179, 251
Easterlin, Richard, economist, 62
  Effect, 62, 63
  Hypothesis, 62
  Paradox, 62
Eastern Europe:
  migrants from further east, 85
  foreign direct investment, 48
East India Company College, 60
eco-anxiety, 208–10
economic growth:
  proposed as solution for poverty, 44
economic violence, 92
economics, 33
  as aid to exploitation, 37
  disciplinary claims to be a science, 120–1
  inequalities research, 239
  teaching, 28–9, 244
economists:
  claims about Australian data, 143
  claims about economics as moral science, 120–1
  claims about poverty reduction, 29–30
  doubts on severity of inequality, 48

Index

economy:
  as shorthand for concerns about unemployment, 72, 73
education, 86, 128, 139–41
  corruption, 142
  cost, 25, 140–2
  geography's focus on, 250
  private schools, 70, 141–2
  state schools, 7, 68, 140–2, 242
  to create compliant workforce, 141
East Bradford Socialist Sunday School, 267–8
'eating or heating', political slogan, 42
egalitarian societies in prehistory, 269
Egypt:
  debt, 54
  food crisis protests (2007–8), 194
  YouGov poll on conspiracies, 154–5, 157, 167
  war deaths, 107
Ehrlich, Anne and Paul, researchers, 36, 181, 220, 222
Einstein, Albert, 235
the Elders, 206
elections:
  around world in 2024, 71
  France (2024), 38–9
  UK (2024), 21, 47, 94
electricity, 245–6
elite projection, 12–3
elites:
  concerns of, 7, 12, 13, 15, 48, 197
  French Revolution, 59
  partisan perspectives, 19, 153
  rise in interest in inequality, 237
EM-DAT International Disaster database, 184–5, 187, 189
empathy:
  lower levels among wealthy, 114–5, 254
employment. *See* jobs; unemployment; work
Encyclopaedia Britannica, 81
energy prices, 9, 20, 42, 169, 178, 230
Engels, Friedrich, philosopher, 269
England:
  food bank use, 89
  life expectancy compared to US, 132–3, 134
England and Wales:
  deaths in police custody, 103
English Channel, 69
English language:
  factor in immigration to UK, 78

English-language publications:
  frequency of references to 'crisis' in, 1, 2, 3
environment, 23, 197–8
environmental collapse, 203, 207, 210
environmental crisis:
  'intangible losses', 207–8
epidemics, 2, 177. *See also* COVID-19 pandemic
equality, 38, 110, 113–4, 117, 127
  Australia, 143
  and biodiversity, 233
  Finland, 150
  France, 145
  gender, 93
  John Maynard Keynes on, 89
  Sweden, 94
Equality Trust, 231
equitable societies, 127, 251
An Essay on the Principles of Population (Malthus), 81
Estonia, housing, 149
Ethiopia, conflict in, 9, 173
eugenics, 146, 212, 240–1
Europe, 91
  climate-related deaths, 188–91
  heatwave (2003), 190–1
  unemployment, 26
European Community:
  UK crisis over membership, 67
  UK workplace rights, 69
European Conservatives (EPP), European Parliament grouping, 38
European Union:
  children per class, 143
  definition of deprivation, 41
  documents used to train AI, 256
  housing, 149
  immigration to UK, 76
  UK membership, 72
  UK vote to leave, 77, 121–2
eurozone, 72, 78
extinction, 169, 197, 198, 211–2, 242, 297n37
extreme weather events, 166, 180, 186, 191, 204, 224
  E. O. Wilson on, 201–2
  food insecurity, 172
  IPCC report, 174, 178
  UNDRR report, 183
extremism, 10, 13, 151, 198, 273

Fairbourne, Wales, 223–7
famines, 2, 36, 83, 202, 222, 228

farming:
  biodiversity, 200–1
  monoculture, 169
far-right:
  France, 38, 43
  global rise, 236
  UK riots (2024), 69, 76, 89, 95
fascism:
  in UK, 74–5
fear(s), 5–9, 16
  about the future, 9, 15, 27, 36
  impact of economic and social status, 6, 7
  of strangers, 57–60
Federal Institute for Population Research, Germany, 126
feminism:
  as means to end war, 260–1
Figueres, Christiana, diplomat, 199, 295n4
Filion, François, French prime minister, convicted of fraud, 151
Filion, Penelope, convicted of fraud, 151–2
financial crash (2008), 72
  UK, 73
  US, 132
Financial Times (newspaper), 119, 122, 134, 139, 229
Finland:
  conspiracy theories, 155
  Far Right Finns Party (Perussuomalaiset), 120
  happiness ranking, 125–7
  Housing First homelessness policy, 149–50
  Left Alliance political party, 261, 266
  poverty, 229
  social mobility, 145
  trust in others, 158
  wealthy Finns and public life, 51, 276n32
  working-class university students, 142
fire deaths, 110
First World War, 98, 241, 267
floods:
  Nigeria (2022), 193
  Pakistan (2022), 192–3
Floyd, George, racist murder of, 104
food:
  crisis, 2007–8, 194
  crop yields, 174
  prices, 9, 25, 175, 229–30
  poor quality, 91
  production, 214
  security, 160, 171, 178
  speculation and profiteering, 194, 204, 230
  UK, cost-of-living crisis, 46
food banks:
  Scotland and rest of UK, 89
foreign direct investments, 48
fossil fuels, 7, 159, 160, 169, 246
France, 41, 78
  alcohol and tobacco consumption, 137
  biodiversity spending, 233
  concern about climate change, 72, 168
  concern about corruption, 151
  concern about inequality, 45
  concern about unemployment, 64
  concern about war, 97
  conspiracy theories, 154, 156, 167
  education, 143–6, 288n30, 288n31
  far-right, support for, 38, 43, 138
  gender inequality, 39
  happiness ranking, 127
  health care, 136–8, 286n14, 286n15
  housing, 147–50, 289n46
  inequality, 39, 42–3, 113, 148
  inheritance tax, 148
  labour shortage, 138
  law on ethics in public life, 152
  left, support for, 138, 274n15
  life expectancy, 132, 133
  national elections (2024), 38, 42, 43, 48, 138
  Office of the Prime Minister, 40
  Oxfam report on poverty, 40
  pension age, 39, 42, 143
  Petits Frères des Pauvres, 138
  poverty, 40–2, 229
  PPL bien vielllir parliamentary bill, 138
  public spending, 39, 43, 136
  'school of the future', Marseille, 146
  Senate Committee of Inquiry into the State of Hospitals, 137
  social mobility, 145
  Social Position Index (SPI), 144
  wealth, 43, 112, 113
fraternity, 38, 51, 54
Free and Equal: What Would a Fair Society Look Like? (Chandler), 55
French Revolution:
  overpopulation proposed as cause, 59

Index

furlough:
  benefit payments during COVID-19 pandemic, UK, 28, 84

gas and electricity prices. *See* energy prices
Gaza:
  killing and starvation of population (2023–), 9, 22, 100–1
  not surveyed by Ipsos, 27
gender gap:
  in public life in Norway, 259–60
  Sir Keir Starmer on international law, 296n16
  war on (2023–), 9, 18, 97, 98, 108, 173
genocide, 100
gentrification, 118
geographers, 4, 250
  and I = PAT equation, 204–5
geography:
  as study of crises, 250
geopolitics:
  reactionary authors, 206
  geography's focus on, 250
German Central Bank, 250–1
Germany, 131–3, 143
  biodiversity spending, 233
  concern about climate change, 168
  concern about corruption, 151
  conspiracy theories, 156, 167
  immigration, 72
  health care, 132
  housing costs, 149
  politicians' views of electorate, 119
  poverty, 229
  taxation, 70
  war, 97–8
  work, 64, 143
Gietel-Basten, Stuart, sociologist, 202
Gini coefficient (measure of inequality), 37
global warming. *See* climate change
Great Britain. *See* United Kingdom
Great Depression (1930s), 59
Greece:
  conspiracy theories, 154, 156, 167
  lack of opportunities, 104, 145
  police violence, 104
greenhouse gases, 190
Grenfell Tower fire (2017):
  social murder, 111
gross domestic product (GDP), 33, 77–8, 119

'guest workers':
  exploitation in UK, 84
  in Middle East, 84

The Hague, 51
Haileybury school, 60
Haldane, Andy, chief economist of Bank of England, 55
Half-Earth: Our Planet's Fight for Life (E. O. Wilson), 218
happiness, 62, 125–7, 251, 285n1, 286n6
Harford, Tim, journalist, 49–50
health, 14, 128, 264. *See also* health care
health care, 128
  concerns in China, 19
  concerns in UK, 72, 74
  cost, 25
  crisis in France, 137
  equitable societies, 127
  Europe, failing system, 91
  geography's focus on, 250
  private, 66, 132, 142, 242
  state, 7, 68, 76, 122, 242
  US, 129–36
heat-related mortality, 172, 188–91
heatwaves, 165, 188–91
Hiroshima, 36
HIV/AIDS:
  conspiracy theories, 155–8
  pandemic, 176–7
Home Counties, England:
  de-gentrification, 46, 147
home ownership:
  in China, 110
  in France, 138, 148–9
homelessness, 149–50
hospitals, private, corruption, 151
Hothouse Earth: An Inhabitant's Guide (McGuire), 248
housing, 25, 110–2, 117–9, 122, 140, 147–9
  anti-apartment exceptionalism, 119, 284n47
  Atlantic magazine on US home-building, 108–110
  buy-to-let market, 118
  corruption, 150
  crisis in China, 110
  France, 147–9
  inequality, 111
  market in unequal affluent countries, 118–9
  rent controls, 150

rent crisis, post-pandemic, 108
social (state), 147, 150, 152, 168
UK, 147
US supply throttled, 109
wealth 111
housing associations, 152
Hsieh, Chang-Tai, economist, 109–10
The Human Cost of Disasters: An Overview of the Last 20 Years 2000–2019 (United Nations Office for Disaster Risk Reduction), 183, 187, 188
human geographers. *See* geographers
Human Mortality Database, 79
Hungary:
  concern about corruption, 151
  concern about crime and violence, 102
  conspiracy theories, 157
hunger, 15, 229–30
Hunt, Jeremy, former chancellor, UK, 115, 283n41
hydrogen bomb, test, 235
hyperinflation, 20

Ibbetson, Connor, YouGov data journalist, 154, 167
Ice Age:
  predictions in 1980s, 205
Iceland:
  happiness ranking, 125–6
  poverty, 229
I = PAT equation, 204–5
  using gerbils, 205
ignorance, 43, 166
  among the wealthy, 115
immigrants, immigration, 14–5, 57–9, 76–7, 84–6, 90
  accused of driving down wages, 60
  Brexit, 69
  concerns in Germany, 72
  concerns in UK, 67, 72, 73, 74, 75
  factor in 2024 elections, 71
  fear of, 80, 247
  geography's focus on, 250
  Sweden, 78–80
  US attempts to ban, 58
India, 34, 45, 104, 262
  climate change, 193–4
  concern about climate change among the young, 209
  concern about poverty and inequality, 45
  COVID-19 impact, 193–4

famines, 83
foreign direct investment, 48
inequality, 44
life expectancy, 194
Indonesia:
  concern about crime and violence, 102
  concern about inflation, 26
  concern about poverty and inequality, 26
  food crisis protests (2007–8), 194
  war deaths, 107
inequality, inequalities, 25–7, 35–8, 44–51, 110–4, 198, 207
  geography's focus on, 250
  housing, 111, 118
  moral problem, 121
  population rise/fall, 218–9
  research on, 237–40
  UK, 71, 73, 75, 117
  World Bank on post-pandemic rise, 261–3
infant mortality, 15
  Pakistan, 192–3
inflation, 21, 25, 27, 72, 100
  global concern, 20, 197
  impact on poor, 28
  impact on wealthy, 28
  2024 elections, 71
influenza, 176
inheritance taxes:
  Daniel Chandler on, 55
  France, 148
  Injustice: Why Social Inequality Still Persists (Dorling), 4
  Norway and Sweden, 111
INSEE, National Institute of Statistics and Economic Studies, France, 40, 148
Intergovernmental Panel on Climate Change (IPCC), 159–60, 170–80
Intergovernmental Science-Policy Platform on Biodiversity and Ecosystem Services (IPBES), 214
International Monetary Fund (IMF), 39, 106
Ipsos, polling company, 16–7. *See* What Worries the World global survey (2011–)
Iran:
  abortion restrictions, 221
  fears of war, 98
  war deaths, 107
Iraq:
  US and 'coalition of the willing' invasion (2003), 105

Ireland:
  food bank use in Northern Ireland, 89
Israel:
  concern about terrorism, 26, 97
  concern about violence, 26–7
  concern about war, 97–8
  COVID-19 pandemic, 125
  happiness ranking, 125, 127
  inflation, 26–7
  invasion of Lebanon, 97–8, 99, 235
  October 2023 attack, 127
  US weapons, 106
  war on Gaza (2023–), 18, 26, 97–8, 108, 127, 173
Italy:
  biodiversity spending, 233
  birth rates, 64
  concern about climate change, 168
  concern about economic turmoil, 72
  concern about unemployment, 41, 64
  conspiracy theories, 154, 156, 167
  housing, 149
  life expectancy, 131, 132, 133
  poverty, 229
Japan:
  car use, 84
  concern about corruption, 151
  concern about crime and violence, 102
  concern about war, 97
  conspiracy theories, 154, 156–7, 167
  poverty, 229
  pro-natalist policies, 221
  return on investments, 47
  stock markets, 48
Jewish migrants to UK:
  and 1905 Aliens Act, 58
job security. *See* unemployment
jobs, 64, 66–9, 86–7
  precarity and fear, 66–7
  opportunity hoarding, 142
Johnson, Boris, UK prime minister and journalist, 70
Journal of Fungi, 217
Journal of Happiness Studies, 62

Keller, Helen, activist and author, 165
Keskintürk, Turgut, sociologist, 237–9
Keynes, John Maynard, economist, 88–9, 280n35
Ki-Moon, Ban, United Nations secretary-general, 206
kindness, 58, 253

Korea. *See* South Korea
Kristersson, Ulf, Swedish prime minister, 95
K-selected species, 217

Lancet (journal), 194
landlordism, 52, 118
Latin America:
  concern about crime and violence, 26
  migrants to the US, 84
Lebanon:
  happiness ranking, 125
  invasion by Israel (2024), 9, 97, 98, 99, 235
  war deaths, 107
Le Pen, Marine, French far-right politician, 42
'levelling down', 46
liberty, 38, 41
life expectancy, 15, 35
  England, 132, 134
  higher for wealthy than poor, 33
  impact of austerity in UK, 132
  US, 132, 133, 134
Liles, Fred, politician and socialist, 267–8
The Limits to Growth (Meadows, Meadows, Randers, Behrens III), 199, 207, 228
literacy, 15, 45, 141
Lizotte, Chris, geographer, 253
love:
  in academic book titles, 253
Luxembourg:
  happiness ranking, 125
  income study, 229

MacKenzie, Megan, legal scholar, 260
Macron, Emmanuel, French prime minister, 146
Major, John, UK prime minister, 67
Malaysia:
  concern about corruption, 151
Mali:
  CO_2 emissions, 81
  war deaths, 107
Malta, 135
Malthus, Thomas, economist and eugenicist, 60, 81–2, 243, 279n32
Marx, Karl, philosopher, 88, 269
maternal mortality. *See* mortality, maternal
maternal suicide, 136

maximum income, maximum wage:
    Brazil proposal, 52–3
    Ingrid Robeyns proposal, 52–3, 283n33
    Maureen Ramsay proposal, 52
McGuire, Bill, geophysicist, 248
media:
    bias, 9
    public opinion, 9, 28, 120
    views on immigration, UK, 73
Medicaid and Medicare, US healthcare provision, 131
medically assisted reproduction: COVID-19 pandemic, 37
Met Office (UK), 225–6
Mexico:
    concern about crime and violence, 94, 101
    irregular migrants to US, 174
Midas machine. See capitalism
middle classes, financial insecurity, 58
migrants, migration, 57–9, 61, 77, 78, 86
    detention centres, 180
    from places the West bombs, 108
    search for security, 62
migration controls:
    in affluent countries, 76
Milanović, Branko, economist, 126–7
Miliband, David, former UK minister, 55
Millennium Ecosystem Assessment (2005), 201, 214
military conflict, 22, 71–2, 94, 95
    See also war
military-industrial complex, 116
money, concerns about, 27, 46
    See also inequality, inflation, poverty, wages
mortality:
    global rate, 184
    maternal, 135, 136
    poverty as leading cause worldwide, 44
    US, 129, 286n12
Montgomerie, Tim, Conservative activist, 46, 147
moon landings, conspiracy theories, 155–8
moral decline, 119–22, 151, 198
Moretti, Enrico, economist, 109–10
mortgages, 46, 110, 147
Mosley, Oswald, fascist, 74–5

Mulgan, Geoff, UK government adviser, 257–8
murder:
    fear of, 76, 93–4
    Oxford in fourteenth century, 103
    social, 103, 110
Murdoch, Rupert, billionaire, 157
Musk, Elon, billionaire, 29, 162

Najam, Adil, international relations scholar, 213
Nakate, Vanessa, climate activist, 207
National Health Service (NHS):
    part-privatisation, 132
    priority for government spending, 64–5
    waiting lists, 122
natural disasters, 175, 183–93
    deadliest (2000–19), 188
Nature Sustainability (journal), 163
Ndiaye, Pap, French politician, 146, 289n38
neoliberalism:
    alleged wonders of, 32
    softer, kinder version, 258
Netherlands:
    concern about climate change, 26, 160, 168
    concern about crime and violence, 102
    concern about inflation, 26–7
    happiness ranking, 125
    heatwave deaths (2003), 190
    housing, 108
    national election (2023), 26
    social mobility, 145
    taxation, 70
    views on maximum wealth, 53
New York City:
    sea-level rise, 224
New Yorker (magazine), 244–5
New Zealand:
    biodiversity spending, 233
    COVID-19 quarantine, 126
    happiness ranking, 125
    mothers aged under 20, 145
Nigeria:
    floods, 193
    pandemic, 193
night-watchman state, 74
9/11 terrorist attacks, conspiracy theories, 155–8
'the 99 per cent', 7

Nobel laureates:
  on more equal societies, 251
non-dom (tax avoidance) status, UK, 56, 277n46
Nordic model, 127
Northern Ireland, 89
Norway:
  biodiversity spending, 233
  concern about inequality, 45
  gender gap, 259–60
  happiness ranking, 125
  inheritance tax, abolition, 111
  trust in others, 158
nuclear test, 235
nuclear war, 98, 265
nuclear weapons, 98

Obama, Barack, US president, 106
obesity:
  Malta, 134
  UK as world leader, 134
O'Connor, Kelsey, 62
oligarchs, in UK, 55–6
'the one per cent', 7
Oppenheimer, Robert, physicist, 235
opportunity hoarding, 142
Oracle Global Report (2022), 125
Organisation for Economic Co-operation and Development (OECD), 39, 136, 147, 252–3
otters, 200
Our World in Data (OWID) website, University of Oxford, 28, 30–2
overfishing, 174–5, 179, 199, 222
overpopulation:
  The Population Bomb, 36
  rise of idea in eighteenth century, 59
  Thomas Malthus on, 81
Oxfam:
  advocacy on inequality, 44
  poverty in France, 2022 report, 40
  World Bank inequality estimates, 262
Oxford:
  city, 5, 103, 295n6
  prosperity, 5
  University, 5
Oxfordshire:
  biodiversity and farming, 199–201

Pakistan:
  debt servicing, 54
  floods (2022), 192–3
Palestine, Palestinians:

intifada, 180
  killing of in Lebanon (2024–), 9
  not included in Ipsos' *What Worries the World* survey, 22
  See also Gaza; genocide; Israel
pandemics. *See* COVID-19 pandemic, HIV/AIDS
paranoia:
  and conspiracy theories, 153
patriarchy, 117, 260
Peak Injustice: Solving Britain's Inequality Crisis (Dorling), 268
Peru:
  concern about corruption, 151
  concern about inflation, 26
  concern about poverty and social inequality, 26
  crime and violence, 101
  war deaths, 107
Perussuomalaiset (Far Right Finns Party), 120
Petits Frères des Pauvres, 138
Philippines:
  fear of climate change among the young, 209
  Manila floods (2009), 224
Phoenix, Arizona, US:
  heat-related deaths, 139
phone:
  lack of as indicator of lack of freedom, 38
physical geographers. *See* geographers
Piff, Paul, psychologist, 114
Piketty, Thomas, economist, 145, 207
Pinker, Stephen, psychologist, 105
Poland:
  abortion restrictions, 221
  concern about crime and violence, 102
  concern about war, 97–8
  conspiracy theories, 154, 157, 167
political apathy. *See* apathy
political correctness, 16
political extremism. *See* extremism
political scientists, 48
politicians, 141
  corruption, 21
  landlords, 150
  perpetrators of harm, 92
  overestimation of electorate's right-wing views, 119, 284n48, 284n49
politics:
  as method to aid exploitation, 37
polling companies, polling firms, pollsters, 3, 13, 17; *see also* Ipsos, YouGov

'polycrisis', 1, 7, 8, 99–100, 271n1
The Population Bomb (Ehrlich and Ehrlich), 36, 220
population growth, 61, 184, 215, 218
    calls to curb, 212
    decline and climate change, 170–1
    fears of overpopulation, 36, 212
    slowdown, 15, 19, 214
    Thomas Malthus on, 81
populism:
    fears of, 236
    views on immigration, UK, 73
Portugal:
    concern about cost of living, 72
poverty, 20–1, 25–9, 33–5, 38, 44, 66, 92
    caused by inequality, 241, 244
    child, in UK, 147
    China, 82
    conservative economists on, 29–33
    COVID-19 pandemic, 261–3
    difficult births, 135
    $1.90 a day threshold, 31, 261
    geography's focus on, 250
    immigration, 59
    in 1820, 31–3
    population growth, 36
    weather event mortality, 192–4
Poverty and Shared Prosperity 2020: Reversals of Fortune (World Bank), 263
Poverty and Shared Prosperity 2022: Correcting Course (World Bank), 263
pregnancy, deaths during or shortly after, 135
price rises. *See* inflation
Private Eye (magazine), 231
pronoia, 247–8, 302n18
public opinion:
    right-wing tendencies overestimated, 119
purchasing power parity (PPP), 78

Queen Victoria, 269

racism:
    and UK views on immigration, 73, 83
Ramsay, Maureen, political theorist, 52
Randers, Jørgen, climate academic, 228, 300n59
Reagan, Ronald, US president, 32
recession, 1980s, 59, 71

redistribution, 39–40, 114
Rees, William, ecologist, 222–3
refugees:
    Germany, 132, 149
    homelessness, 108
    Sweden, 96
    UK Conservative Party supporter views on, 83
    war, 181–2
religious teachings, 202
    against killing, 241
    on environment, 242
    on strangers, 58
Republican Party (US), 122
    supporters' views on poverty, 65
Resolution Foundation, think tank, 117, 147
resource wars, 176–7
return on investments:
    fall in 1970s and 1980s, 47
risk management industry, 8, 10, 12, 272n7
Rise Up Movement, 207
Ritchie, Hannah, data scientist, 248–9
road safety, 91
Robeyns, Ingrid, philosopher, 52
robbery, 93, 117
Russia:
    climate-related deaths, 188–9
    collapse of communism, 131
    collusion in Donald Trump election victory (2016), 156, 157
    foreign direct investment, 48
    pro-natalist policies, 221
    violence, 104
    war deaths, 106, 107
    war with Ukraine, 9, 97–8, 173, 175, 177, 235
Russian Empire:
    Jewish people fleeing pogroms, 59
Rwanda:
    Conservative government deportation scheme, UK, 69
    war deaths, 107

Sahel, region in Africa, 9, 173
salaries. *See* wages
safety:
    our need for, 92, 108
salt contamination, 195
San Francisco, California, US:
    housing, 109
Sarkozy, Nicolas, French president, convicted of corruption, 151

Index

Saudi Arabia:
    concern about poverty and inequality, 45
    war deaths, 107
    YouGov poll on conspiracies, 155, 157, 167
Science (journal), 202
Scotland:
    child poverty, 147
    food bank use, 89, 280n38
    Scottish Child Payment, 89
sea-level rise, 166, 169, 170–1, 223–7
Second World War, 89, 98, 137, 139, 235, 241
selfishness, genetic, 114
shelter. *See* housing
Singapore:
    concern about climate change, 160
    concern about crime and violence, 102
singularity, global model of population, 215–20
slavery, cross-Atlantic, 83
Slovenia, housing, 149
'small boats':
    refugees crossing English Channel, 74, 182
'smuggling gangs', 75
social care, 65, 68, 121, 128
social housing. *See* housing
social inequality. *See* inequality
social media:
    polarisation, 13, 155, 161–2
social murder, 103, 110
social programmes, 10, 128, 129, 151, 265
socialism, 55, 238, 248
    Thomas Piketty on, 266
Socialist Sunday Schools, 245, 266–8, 305n53
sociologists, 48, 120, 237–9
sociology:
    inequalities research, 237–40
    role in exploitation, 37
South Africa:
    anti-apartheid struggle, 180
    concern about corruption, 151
    concern about crime and violence, 101
    concern about war, 97
    conspiracy theories, 154, 157, 167
    war deaths, 107
South Asia:
    fall in conceptions in 1960s–1970s, 34

South-East Asia:
    foreign direct investment, 48
South Korea:
    birth rate, 222
    concern about crime and violence, 102
    pro-natalist policies, 221
Southern Europe:
    lack of in-migration, 86
Soviet Union (USSR), 131, 180
    nuclear test (1949), 235
space race:
    as preoccupation of elites, 16
Spain, 41, 264
    biodiversity spending, 233
    birth rates, 37, 64
    concern about crime and violence, 102
    concern about unemployment, 41, 64
    conspiracy theories, 154, 156, 157
    heatwave deaths, 190
    life expectancy, 131–3
    war deaths, 107
Starmer, Sir Keir, UK prime minister, 75, 296n16
starvation, 9, 203, 204
state violence, 102–5
Steiner, Achim, United Nations Development Programme, 13
Stiglitz, Joseph, economist, 257–8
student debt, 141
success, as defined by wealth, 35
Sudan, conflict in, 9, 173
'sunlit uplands', 115
'surplus people', 59–60
Surrey, England, UK:
    de-gentrification, 46, 147
surveys, public opinion, 3, 18, 93, 243
    China, division by sex, 232
    exclusion of Palestine, 27
    framing of, 11, 71–2
    over-representation of middle class, 168, 209
Sweden, 77–80, 94–6, 145
    biodiversity spending, 233
    concern about corruption, 151
    concern about inequality, 45
    concern about war, 97
    conspiracy theories, 154, 157, 167
    COVID-19 policies, 125
    crime and violence, 94–6, 101
    far-right political parties, 96
    happiness ranking, 125
    inequality, 95–6

poverty, 96, 229
taxation, 50, 111–2
trust in others, 158
unemployment, 96
Switzerland:
COVID-19 policies, 125
happiness ranking, 125
heatwave deaths (2003), 190
politicians' views of electorate, 119
poverty, 229
social mobility, 145
taxes on wealth, 255
Syria, civil war, 105, 173

'take back control', political slogan, 69
Tanzania, 220–1
Tawney, R. H., Christian socialist, 56
tax, taxation, 68, 113
  Brexit, UK, 69
  indirect, in UK, 70
  inheritance tax, 44, 111, 148
  Germany and the Netherlands, 70
  Sweden, public records, 50
terrorism, 10, 22, 26, 91, 93–4, 100
Thames Water, 231
Thatcher, Margaret, UK prime minister, 32
'there is no alternative', political slogan, 115
The Times (newspaper), 135
Tooze, Adam, historian, 80–3
trade unions. *See* unions
trickle-down myth, 29, 34
Trump, Donald, US president, 91
  conspiracy theories, 156–7
  elected president (2016, 2024), 38
  6 January 2021 attack on Washington, 180
Truss, Liz, UK prime minister, 75
  2022 budget, 46
Trussell Trust, 89
trust, 101, 156–8, 251
tsunamis, 183, 186, 188, 224, 236, 250
TUC, Trades Union Council (UK), 75
Turkey:
  concern about crime and violence, 102
  concern about war, 97
  conspiracy theories, 154, 157, 167
  pro-natalist policies, 221
  war deaths, 107
Twitter. *See* X

Ukraine:
  nuclear war risk, 235
  refugees, 182
  war deaths, 106, 107
  war with Russia, 9, 22, 97–8, 100, 173–8
  US weapons, 106
Understanding the Challenges of Avoiding a Ghastly Future (Ehrlich and Ehrlich), 181
unemployment, 20–1, 25–7, 57–8, 64–5, 68, 71
  anti-immigrant sentiment, 86
  artificial intelligence, 241
  'the economy', 72–3
  France, 136
  poorest countries, 274n4
  UK, 67, 70, 75, 90
  US, 66, 70
UnHerd (magazine), 147
'unicorn fluff', 121
unions:
  restrictions on, 47, 69
  Trades Union Council (TUC), 75
United Kingdom (UK), 46, 54, 115, 147
  antidepressant use, 126
  asylum seekers, 73
  austerity, 132
  biodiversity spending, 233
  Brexit, 69, 73, 75–7, 78, 121–2
  British Broadcasting Corporation (BBC), 49–50, 206
  children's heights, decline, 247
  concern about climate change, 168–9
  concern about health care, 130
  concern about unemployment, 64, 71
  Conservative governments, 76, 121–2
  Conservative voters, 47, 77, 83
  conspiracy theories, 154, 167
  COVID-19 pandemic, 73
  deaths in police custody and prisons, 104
  de-gentrification, 46
  economics teaching, 28–9
  farmland, 199–201
  far-right riots (2024), 69, 76, 95
  furlough payments, COVID-19, 84
  general election (2024), 21, 94
  housing, 108, 111, 147, 149
  immigration, 73, 75, 76, 78, 84, 90
  inequality, 50, 67, 71, 75, 83–4, 117, 302n9
  life expectancy, 132, 133, 134
  maternal mortality, 136

Index

military size, 258
National Health Service (NHS), 64–5, 122, 132
obesity, 135
Oxfordshire, 199–201
poverty, 78
refugees, 83, 108
Sheffield, Chinese immigrants to, 85–6
Socialist Sunday Schools, 245
students, foreign, 85–6
tax, 50, 55, 67–8, 70, 113, 275n27
Thames Water, privatised utility, 231
unemployment, 64, 71, 73, 90
wealthy, 47, 112, 115, 121, 278n17
United Nations:
  Department of Economic and Social Affairs (DESA-EN), 133
  Development Programme (UNDP), 13
  Human Development Report, 13
  Office for Disaster Risk Reduction (UNDRR), 183–4, 188
  population projections, 34–5, 60, 170–2, 215, 219–20
  Special rapporteur on the right to housing, 108
  World Food Programme (UN WFP), 203
  World Population Prospects, 185, 187
United Nations University World Inequality Database, 44
United States (US):
  'active shooter incidents', 102
  Afghanistan war, 106
  antidepressant use, 126
  concern about climate change, 167
  concern about unemployment, 71
  concern about war, 97
  conspiracy theories, 154, 157, 167
  crime and violence, 102–3
  deaths in custody, 104
  economics teaching, 28–9
  education, 146
  fears about collusion with China, 16
  firearms mortality, 102, 281n12
  gun laws, 102
  health care, 129–36
  housing, 109–10
  inequality, 45, 117
  Iraq invasion (2003), 105
  life expectancy, 132, 133, 134
  maternal mortality, 135
  military funding, 65, 258
  mortality rates, 129, 130, 135–6
  mothers aged under twenty, 145
  police violence, 102, 104
  politicians' views on electorate, 119
  poverty, 45, 65, 229
  unemployment, 64
  university admissions, preferential for wealthy, 255, 304n33
  US Centers for Disease Control and Prevention, 102
  Texas, 102
  wealth, 112, 130
universal basic income, 55
university, universities, 63, 84, 152,
  admissions, preferential, US, 255, 304n33
  benefiting the already advantaged, 142
  France, 143–4
  inequalities research in, 237–40
  targets of far-right pundits, 16
  tuition fees, Europe, 143, 287n22
University of Oxford, 5, 103
  Our World in Data (OWID) website, 28, 30–1
university professors:
  authors of books on crises, 13
  job losses, 57
university students:
  use of artificial intelligence (AI), 61
US Center for Disease Control and Prevention, 102
utilities, privatised, 230–2

vaccination, vaccines:
  conspiracy theories, 156–8
  COVID-19, 265
  India during lockdown, 194
Vidal, John, journalist, 213
Vienna Yearbook of Population Research, 223
violence, 117; *see also* crime and violence; war
  and housing, 110, 119
  gang, 101
  likelihood of effecting change, 123
  state monopoly on, 103
  voting, 4, 93

Walker, Jarrett, public-transit consultant, 12
wages, 20, 28, 40, 134
Wales:
  food bank use, 89
  sea-level rise, 223–7

321

Wall Street Journal (newspaper), 135
war, wars, 9, 91–4, 97, 98, 116–7, 122
  climate change, 173
  deaths, 107
  future crisis, 265
  Gaza, 18, 97, 98, 100, 108, 173
  geography's focus on, 250
  patriarchal capitalism, 260–61
  refugees, 57, 78
  rich on poor, US, 131
  Ukraine/Russia, 9, 22, 97–8, 100, 173–8
water utilities, UK, 230–2
wealth, 117
  concentration, 118, 120, 130, 148
  inheritance by women, 116
  perceived influence on politics, UK, 47
  pooling among families, 117–8
  reduced by inflation, 28, 44
  westward flow, 258–9
wealth inequality, wealth inequalities. *See* inequality, inequalities
wealth taxes, UK, 111, 113, 150
wealthy people:
  belief in their own specialness, 114
  seen as more powerful than governments in UK, 121
  unaffordability of, 118
  underestimation of own wealth, 115
weapons industry. *See* arms industry
Wegner, Nicole, peace studies scholar, 260
Welsh Shoreline Management Plan, 225
Western Europe:
  fall in return on investments, 47
What Is ChatGPT Doing . . . and Why Does It Work? (Wolfram), 87
What Worries the World survey (2011–), 19–20, 25–7, 41, 45, 136, 197, 232
  climate change findings, 159–61, 168
  Palestine not included, 22, 27
  'polycrisis' update (2023), 99–101
  respondents' class composition, 168, 209, 292n14
'wicked problems', 251–3, 257
William, Prince of Wales, 213

Wilson, Edward O., biologist, 197, 201–2, 218
The Wizard of Oz (film), 5
Wolfram, Stephen, computer scientist and entrepreneur, 87
work, 45, 57, 58, 62, 92
  ability to exercise choice, 38
  geography's focus on, 250
World Bank, 31, 104, 106, 182, 203
  'nowcast', i.e., guessing, 261, 263
World Economic Forum, 1, 8, 9
  Global Risks Perception Survey, 8, 9, 10
World Inequality Database, United Nations University, 44
World Population Living in Extreme Poverty, Our World in Data, 30–1
World Population Prospects, United Nations, 133
World Weather Attribution group:
  and chocolate Easter eggs, 251
worries, worrying; *see also* Ipsos
  about the future, 6, 11
  about one's own country, 14
X (formerly Twitter):
  and climate change, 162
  Elon Musk purchase, 162

Yemen:
  conflict in, 9, 173
  food crisis protests (2007–8), 194
young people:
  climate change, 19, 159, 161–2, 208–10
  literacy, 45, 141
  poverty, 33
  right-wing views, 120, 159, 160–1
  search for meaningful employment, 63
YouGov, polling company, 72, 74
  climate change, 167
  conspiracy theories survey, 153–8

zero-hour contracts:
  prevalence in UK, 66
Zoological Society, 169